Praise for *Fast Future*

"In *Fast Future*, David Burstein provides a personal and compelling picture of his generation. Millennials are pragmatic idealists and the first digitals, able to handle the fast pace of today's world while they remake our economic and democratic political systems. Read this book not only to understand the future but also how the Millennials are poised to shape it."

—MICHAEL D. HAIS and MORLEY WINOGRAD, authors of *Millennial Momentum*

"We are leaving the young with an unacceptable future—ballooning debts, unthinkable tax increases, historically slow growth, an economy vulnerable to crises, and a paralyzed politics. Until now, the involvement of the young has been viewed as a combination of ignorance and apathy. I was delighted to read *Fast Future*, a book with such a hopeful outlook."

—PETE PETERSON, former secretary of commerce, cofounder, The Blackstone Group

"*Fast Future* is an incisive look at the generation that elected Barack Obama and is changing the way we do everything. David Burstein has written a must-read book about the most individually empowered generation in history—his own."

—HOWARD DEAN, former governor of Vermont

"The Millennial Generation is the biggest and most diverse in American history; soon they will run the country. In the great tradition of writers who help define their own generations, David Burstein offers a moving and insightful portrait of Millennial America."

—PETER LEVINE, director, CIRCLE (Center for Information & Research on Civic Learning & Engagement)

"The Millennials are a unique generation with a strong entrepreneurial streak that has seen them create some of the most impactful businesses of this century. As a Millennial entrepreneur, I found *Fast Future* to be an inspiring and powerful account of the world we live and work in every day."

—BEN LERER, founder and CEO, Thrillist

"Burstein's generation . . . has already changed the face of politics from Washington to Cairo and beyond. Millennials are distinct and powerful, though scholarship about them has been slapdash and haphazard. Enter David Burstein. With *Fast Future*, Burstein cements his reputation as the Millennial Generation's most thoughtful and insightful public intellectual."

—DAVID C. KING, senior lecturer in public
policy, Harvard Kennedy School

"Today's young people really are unique. Technology has made them the best-informed generation of young people that the world has ever seen. Their understanding of the problems facing the world has made them the most socially responsible generation ever. And finally their knowledge and understanding of how to use the tools of the digital and social revolution has made them the most powerful generation ever. David Burstein's excellent book tells the story of his own generation: read it and you'll know why we should all be listening to them."

—DAVID JONES, CEO, Havas Worldwide,
cofounder, One Young World

"David's reflections are a fast, fun, informative read."

—NANCY LUBLIN, CEO, DoSomething.org

"*Fast Future* speaks to young, social entrepreneurs by telling the story of an exciting turning point that will change the course of history. David Burstein takes a deep and nuanced look at the potential that young people have and the terrible missed opportunity if we don't capitalize on the innovation of the Millennial Generation."

—JESSICA POSNER ODEDE and KENNEDY
ODEDE, cofounders, Shining Hope for
Communities

"An inspiring look at what the millennial generation is doing in America . . . Burstein's interviews and firsthand accounts bring to light these young people, and readers will gain a deeper appreciation and awareness of the rapid progress and changes that have occurred worldwide since the advent of the Internet. Stimulating accounts of what is being accomplished by an ambitious generation."

—*KIRKUS REVIEWS*

Fast Future

Fast Future

How the Millennial Generation
Is Shaping Our World

David D. Burstein

BEACON PRESS
BOSTON

Beacon Press
25 Beacon Street
Boston, Massachusetts 02108-2892
www.beacon.org

Beacon Press books
are published under the auspices of
the Unitarian Universalist Association of Congregations.

16 15 14 13   8 7 6 5 4 3 2 1

This book is printed on acid-free paper that meets the uncoated paper
ANSI/NISO specifications for permanence as revised in 1992.

Text design and composition by Wilsted & Taylor Publishing Services

Library of Congress Cataloging-in-Publication Data

Burstein, David D.
Fast future : how the millennial generation is shaping our world /
David D. Burstein.
     p. cm.
Includes bibliographical references.
ISBN 978-0-8070-4469-8 (hardcover : alk. paper)
ISBN 978-0-8070-4470-4 (electronic)
1. Generation Y. 2. Generation Y—Social conditions. 3. Generation Y—
Political activity. 4. Technology and youth. 5. Generation Y—Attitudes.
I. Title.
HQ799.5.B87 2013
305.2—dc23   2012034457

*To my mother and father, the greatest Boomers I know:
you raised me with the deepest care and strongest love to be all that
I am, instilling in me the best parts of your generation's legacy.*

*To my grandparents Leon, Dorothy, and Joan, members of the
Greatest Generation: you came through the hardest of times and
helped build our country. It's a joy to have your love in my life.*

*And to my generation: you never cease to inspire and excite me.
It's a privilege to have the chance to tell our story.*

CONTENTS

In the fall of my sophomore year in high school, two friends approached me with an idea. Many of our peers in film class had produced great work, but there was nowhere beyond the classroom where these films could be shown. We had a solution: create a first-of-its-kind film festival exclusively for high school students. It sounded like a fantastic idea, and we couldn't wait to get started. During the next seven months we built a team, raised thousands of dollars, gathered submissions from around the world, secured corporate sponsors, and convinced a local movie theater to donate their venue to us. In May 2004, the first Westport Youth Film Festival took place. We screened sixty films, and hundreds of people flocked to see the work of young filmmakers they did not know. It was a success. And it has lived on: I'm happy to say that the festival will celebrate its tenth anniversary this year.

This story illustrates two things that I think are unique about my generation. First, looking back on it, I find it remarkable that not one of my collaborators ever stopped to ask, "Can we do this?" We never thought, "We're just high school kids, we can't put on a film festival." We had no earthly idea how to go about it. But we learned how to do it quite well by "bootstrapping," a term from today's entrepreneurial language that we would have used then if we had known it. Just two decades ago, it was unusual for high school students to start their own organizations, businesses, and initiatives. But, as you'll see throughout this book, today it has become far more common. The fact that a group of fifteen- and sixteen-year-olds believed we could create a film festival without any prior experience is a true testament to our generation's potential.

The second thing that strikes me was the sophistication, quality, and content of the films we screened. Most of the films were thoughtful and dealt with important, relevant themes. We screened films that dealt with gang violence in students' neighborhoods, teen suicide, drugs, and education. One student made a documentary about her parents' interracial marriage. Even the comedies were smart and original rather than sophomoric. Devoted young filmmakers have been able to create their own work for several decades, but the new affordability and accessibility of film technology and tools have allowed virtually everyone to be a creator, and many are creating meaningful content.

The following November, I invited two dozen friends (many of whom were part of the festival team) over for an election-night party. There was pizza, popcorn, soda, and the self-caricaturing madness that is cable news election coverage. We watched as each set of polls closed and results were projected state by state. All the safe states for Kerry and Bush were called first, putting Kerry at a mathematical Electoral College advantage. It was a school night, so my friends peeled off and left by midnight, even though the outcome was still unclear and the biggest states were yet to be decided. We were all expecting that young people would turn out at the levels so many youth activists had hoped and worked for. But the anchors and pundits declared it another disappointing turnout by young voters.

While I couldn't yet vote, the 2004 election was the first in which I could understand the details of the election and the candidates. I understood the importance of the youth vote. I also knew that young people did not have an impressive record of participation. When the final numbers came in for the 2004 presidential election, youth turnout was actually up 11 percent from 2000. Even so, that meant that just 48 percent of young voters had voted in 2004. Beyond my frustration with turnout levels, and with the media calling a substantial 11 percent increase in turnout "another failure of the youth," I was most concerned with the implications: a few hundred thousand more young voters could have changed the course of history. My high school peers and I were active and engaged. We cared about politics and policy. While I knew the same was not universally true of my generation—indeed, it wasn't even true for everyone in my school—I also knew that if we didn't step up, our generation's voice would get shut out of the political process. If the crucial connection between our future and our vote could be made clearer, our generation could become a political powerhouse. It was then that I decided to throw myself into what would become a massive effort to turn out young voters in the next presidential election in 2008.

Setting out in 2005 armed with nothing but a camera and a big idea, I began work on a documentary film called *18 in '08*, designed to encourage my peers to vote. In retrospect, I realize I never paused to ask how to make a film, I just started doing it. I traveled all over the country, interviewing a cast of over one hundred political leaders and thinkers, including senators Barbara Boxer, Robert Byrd, Chris Dodd, John Kerry, Joe Lieberman, and John McCain, Representative John Lewis, Governor Jeb Bush, Newark mayor Cory Booker, strategist James Carville, General Wesley Clark, and Academy Award–winning actor Richard Dreyfuss, as well as many young people from communities all over America.

The thirty-five-minute film that resulted premiered in 2007. Soon afterward, I created a nonpartisan, not-for-profit organization, now called Generation18, that used the film to register, engage, and mobilize young voters. We held over 1,000 screenings, each followed by discussions and voter registration. Ultimately, we registered some 25,000 new voters, developed a celebrity get-out-the-vote public service announcement series, and *18 in '08* was adopted in educational curriculums across the country. I was asked to explain young Americans' political attitudes to visiting foreign correspondents writing about the United States election. I met with government officials from Botswana to help them figure out how to bolster youth involvement in their country. As I traveled our country, I was continually inspired and reminded of the power, promise, and potency of my generation. Much of what I was doing then and continue to do today was not possible for a young person to do just a few decades ago. The technological, media, and social networking tools we have available to us, and the recognition and respect now afforded to young people, have combined to provide my generation with incredible new opportunities.

As the campaign drew to a close, something else started to come into focus. I saw that my generation was reshaping areas outside of politics. I met members of my generation who were starting new kinds of businesses, organizations, and initiatives in record numbers. Their experiences turned out to be neither aberrational, nor occasional like the election cycle. While the national media had been focused on the role of young people in the election, a much bigger and largely unreported story had been unfolding. In these pages, I'm eager to share this story with you. Removing all of my own bias is impossible, but there is no better way to understand a generation than to hear about its experiences and worldview straight from the people who are in it.

Introduction

"You are the future." It seems like the right message. I've heard politicians give this speech to groups of high school students. I've heard it from distinguished men and women speaking to graduating college seniors. I've heard it from parents speaking to their teenagers. But my generation is not the future. We are the present, and we're already making a major impact. Think about the twenty-eight year old who created and runs the largest social network in the world, or the thirty-one year old who directs the White House office of speechwriting, or the high school students in Danbury, Connecticut, organizing their peers in an effort to end the genocidal crisis in Darfur, half a world away. From the streets of the Bronx to the streets of Tehran, from inside the West Wing to the tech labs of Palo Alto, from rural Ohio to the mountains of Nepal, the Millennials have seized hold of the world around them, decided to make a difference, and are doing it right now. What's more, they've been doing it for the last decade.

It took us a long time to get here. At the beginning of the twentieth century, the industrial revolution was accelerating. The prior century had given us the steam engine, railroads, powerful looms, interchangeable parts, and the cotton gin. These innovations paved the way for a political and cultural infrastructure that resembled the hierarchical factory system. But now the industrial revolution was moving into a new phase that would see quantum breakthroughs in technology—automobiles, airplanes, and the harnessing of electricity and light—and that would also bring about a radical set of democratizing political and cultural paradigm shifts. To a society accustomed to railroads and horses, the world seemed to be in a state of chaos. Government-sponsored compulsory education, women having the right to vote, and the progressive reforms that curbed abuses of monopoly power and child labor and allowed workers to organize labor unions all seemed radical. Some businessmen didn't see how different the new era would be. Some refused to adapt. Some tried, and failed. When the winds began to shift, the business titans of an earlier era missed the flight to the new industries of the future. Younger upstart competitors emerged, confident in their ability to harness new discoveries as well as comfortable with the shifting social and political realities. When the dust of this new industrial revolution had settled, the visionaries of the early twentieth century emerged—people like Thomas Edison, who imagined a new world of electric power without worrying about its effect on railroads or carriage and buggy manufacturers, and Franklin Delano Roosevelt, who saw the opportunity to enact a century-defining New Deal. Their visions were so powerful that they still play a major role in shaping our world today.

The new breed of leaders was comfortable with change. They saw and embraced the new world that was fast approaching. They let go of their preconceptions and not only adapted, but succeeded. The accepted truths of the Anglo-American gilded Victorian age—about race, religion, and the limited role of government in the economy, among many other questions—eroded amid a new world order of technology, immigration, urbanization, consumerization, reform of capitalism's most outrageous disparities, and the first stages of demographic diversity.

Once every few generations, there is a revolution that shifts the fundamentals of our economy, society, culture, communications, and social relations in this kind of top-to-bottom way. We are living through a period like that today. The modern world has always been in a state of flux. Indeed, some significant frequency of change is definitional to modernity. But the impact of change has arguably never been as sweeping or disruptive as it is today. This is in part because the rate of change itself is exponentially greater than it has ever been. As a result, more transformation takes place in a single year than in some previous decades. New technologies are being adopted at an exponentially faster rate. Consider this: When the Palm Pilot was introduced in 1997, it took eighteen months to sell one million units—and was considered a stunningly transformational product as a result. Yet it took just twenty-four hours for the iPad to sell the same amount immediately after it debuted in 2010.

Political change is also happening more rapidly. Though many politicians of the nineteenth and twentieth centuries spent years building their resumes and relationships so that they might one day be able to run for president, in 2004, a little-known state senator keynoted the Democratic National Convention and was sworn in as president five years later. In 2010, the Tea Party wiped out much of the Democrats' congressional power. Yet the Tea Party itself, seen as a sweeping game changer, crumbled only two years later. Similarly, the Occupy Wall Street movement gathered and reached massive visibility in late 2011, only to be swept away and virtually disappear in the first few months of 2012.

This is part of the new world order. This is the fast future. Change is fast and constant. In the fast future our culture, institutions, government, and citizens don't always have time to catch up with these tsunamis of reinvention, so they are often left dizzy, surprised, or angry. As these institutions and their leaders are trying to figure out the new world, one generation hasn't had much trouble adjusting: my generation, the Millennials.

Millennials are people born in the 1980s and 1990s (that is, people who came of age in some way around the turn of the millennium). There is considerable debate over how to count the Millennials. Some demographers and generational experts have measured as many as eighty million members of my generation, which would make Millennials the largest generation in American history, slightly larger than the boomers, who originally numbered seventy-six million. The eighty million figure for Millennials is derived by counting all those born between 1980 and 1999. This particular two-decade period of generally rising birth rates and a mini–baby boom (sometimes called the "echo boom" because Millennials were being born to Baby Boomer parents) provides a fair comparison to the two decades of the original Baby Boom, which many demographers cite as spanning the years 1946–1964. But if you leave the bulges in birth rates aside, there are more relevant social, economic, and cultural characteristics that define these generations more narrowly.

This book is focused on the Millennials who were born between 1980 and 1994, who are today between nineteen and thirty-three. In addition to sharing the demographic characteristics of being the "echo boom," this group shares certain important generational experiences that shaped our childhood and young adult years. The Millennials born between 1980 and 1994 are old enough to have consciously experienced the terrorist attacks of September 11, 2001, a major defining event of our generation. In addition, those born in this fifteen-year period share the characteristic of having had one foot in the pre-Internet, pre–cell phone, pre-Facebook world, while the other foot is in the new world, as changed and redefined by the proliferation of web, mobile, and social technologies. Even using my narrower definition, there are more American Millennials than Boomers living today, since the Boomer headcount has started to shrink, owing to the adverse impact of death rates, while the ranks of Millennials have increased in number, not to mention in diversity, with the growing population of Millennial immigrants. But no matter how you define us, we are one of the largest generations in history. What's more, as we settle into full-bodied adulthood, we are fast becoming the most influential demographic slice of the American pie, disproportionately driving economic indicators and social, cultural, and political trends. In many countries in Africa, the Middle East, and Asia Millennials make up over a third or even half the population. Worldwide, there are 1.7 billion Millennials—almost one-third of the people on earth.

So it is no surprise that in reality, and in our own perception, we are the most global generation. We can be in touch with our peers almost anywhere in the world with just one click. We are the most connected generation. We are also the most aware of our connectedness and global reach. Our formative years have taught us that resilience and adaptability are essential for survival. We saw the 9/11 attacks. Two wars have raged on for more than half of our lives. We saw the impeachment of a president and the escalation of the politics of personal destruction. We saw our peers kill each other in Columbine. We witnessed the devastating effects on our families, jobs, and homes of a dysfunctional financial system and mega-collapses of companies and national economies from Enron, Lehman Brothers, and Greece to our own American debt downgrade. All of these events took place at key moments in our psychological and intellectual development. They shaped our view of the world, making us more focused on trying to solve the big challenges that lie at the core of our future.

In the 2008 financial crisis, while older Americans often reacted with frustration, embitterment, and despair, Millennials were learning about the uncertainty in our world and how to combat it. As the economic crisis got worse, Millennials actually became more optimistic about their own economic future, while every other demographic group became steadily more pessimistic. This is an interesting indicator, suggesting that our future economic and social success may mirror that of the Greatest Generation. Our grandparents, who were children and teenagers during the Great Depression of the 1930s, when despair ruled the land, ultimately leveraged their youthful energy and resourcefulness to become a highly civic-minded, self-sacrificing, and prosperous generation.

Our society runs on an unseen and usually undiscussed "operating system" that reflects the set of cultural knowledge and assumptions and other rules of the road that will lead to positive outcomes, successful lives, rising living standards, and general progress. Like a computer operating system, it gets regular updates. Some are small and routine. But some are bigger, requiring an upgrade to a new version. Today there is a brand new operating system running, and the Millennials are the primary authors of that system. Some authors of this code are visible and successful Millennial leaders. Others are ordinary young people whose social attitudes, user power, and influence even in small communities of friends and peers are helping to fill in millions of lines of necessary code, making it stronger and more able to withstand future attacks.

Unlike Boomers, members of Generation X, and others who have preceded us, we understand this new operating system intuitively. Unlike Generation Z and others who will succeed us, we have context. We understand the world before the fast future. We weren't born with iPhones in our hands. Many of us didn't have computers until our teenage years. We did our first research projects in physical libraries. These experiences allow us to understand how the old world worked and how to effectively solve problems in the new one. Because we are the ones writing the code, we are also the ones who can most effectively tweak it. We're open source, so other developers may participate, but ultimately we're the ones best suited to make the biggest changes.

Millennials are far from the first generation to want to change the world. Under the specter of the Vietnam War and intense racism, the Boomers wanted to end war and achieve equality for all. They saw the political system as the enemy—an impossible partner. Some advocated for the overthrow of the entire system. Their goals were specific: enact civil rights legislation and end the war in Vietnam. When those incredible goals were accomplished, many of them moved on to other pursuits and professions.

But because Millennials have grown up in the fast future, we think of the world practically and pragmatically. We know it as constantly changing and changeable. The problems we face seem bigger and more global, and the solutions we envision are both longer-term and more structural—and yet at the same time, more urgent than ever. We know we'll be working on solutions to these problems for our whole lives— and we also know we need to start now.

Every group of people is influenced by and, in some sense, a product of their times. But the Millennials have come of age on the cusp of a once-in-a-century revolution. We have the potential to be the greatest agents of change for the next sixty years. Already, we've had an important impact on the world and done some impressive things. We've toppled dictators, helped elect a president, created social networks that have connected the world, forced businesses to adopt a social agenda broader than profit—and all before most of us have turned thirty.

Millennials may not be as radical as their Boomer forebears, and may never fight such clear-cut moral battles as those who lived through the civil rights movement, for example. But in the range of issues Millennials choose to tackle, in the huge power of our numbers augmented by technology and other tools, and in the unique combination of our passion and our pragmatism, we may actually prove to be as effective or even more effective change agents.

Some skeptics will say that the youth demographic is congenitally excited, easily engaged and mobilized, but that we ultimately fizzle out. Others think of us in the same way gen Xers came to be stereotyped—apathetic, bitter, and nihilistic. As an insider to the Millennial Generation, I've seen a tremendous amount of optimism and idealism, tempered by an appropriate if sometimes surprising amount of realism and pragmatism. Millennials have a passion for making a difference. But we also have a genuine interest in policy, process, and institution-building. The mix of these ingredients will help make our long-term optimism sustainable.

Millennials are not strangers to criticism—or, for that matter, to having our power and influence overlooked, ignored, or doubted. Pundits, prognosticators, and politicians dismissed the importance of young people before the 2008 election. The youth vote was all "talk," they said. But, defying these predictions, the 2008 election saw one of the highest turnouts of young voters in history, and almost all studies show that it was the youth vote in key states that created the margin of victory for Obama over McCain.

History is full of the achievements of amazing young people. Thomas Jefferson was thirty-three when he wrote the Declaration of Independence. Mozart composed his first concerto at age five. Bill Gates founded Microsoft at nineteen, Steve Jobs built his first Apple computer prototype at twenty-one. From rock music to sports, young, talented stars have defined those cultural worlds for the last half-century. Today, however, there is a new level of ease with which even "ordinary" young people—who are "merely" smart, passionate, and engaged with the world around them, not necessarily prodigies—can become standouts in our society doing amazing things.

In previous eras, young people haven't had the resources or tools to bring their ideas and vision into the world instantaneously. But as inhabitants of an increasingly digital world, we need very few physical tools or resources to make an impact. With just a few clicks or key-strokes, even the least powerful among us can instantly reach at least thousands of people all over the world.

Nowhere is this more evident than in the not-for-profit field, where Millennials have become key players. More young people than ever are starting their own not-for-profits and organizations, in fields from chronic disease research to climate change. I saw this firsthand in June of 2009, when I was given an award by DoSomething.org, the country's largest organization dedicated to supporting young people taking social action. My first introduction to DoSomething.org came a year earlier when I attended one of their not-for-profit "boot camps," which they host across the country. When I arrived early on a Sunday morning, I found myself in a room with about a hundred of my peers, all under twenty-five. Each person ran their own organizations focused on a wide range of issues, from promoting understanding of autism to aiding homeless youth and everything in between. I looked around and thought: we're not geniuses; we're just young people with an idea and a passion to make it happen. We worked hard and had to be good at recruiting others from outside our generation to help us. Many of us had strong leadership and organizational skills. But we were all regular people who used the tools and resources at our disposal to build extraordinary organizations and social movements. Today, Millennials are so frequently active in forming new organizations and initiatives to address causes and issues that the fast-growing sector known as social entrepreneurship has become synonymous with the Millennial Generation.

Generations are tricky to write about, perhaps especially when you're young and writing about your own. In 1972, a young Joyce Maynard (who would later gain a measure of fame as the lover of J. D. Salinger, and still later as a novelist) observed, "Every generation thinks it's special—my grandparents because they remember horses and buggies, my parents because of the Depression. The over-thirties are special because they knew the Red Scare of Korea, Chuck Berry and beatniks. My older sister is special because she belonged to the first generation of teen-agers (before that, people in their teens were adolescents), when being a teen-ager was still fun. And I—I am 18, caught in the middle. Mine is the generation of unfulfilled expectations."[1]

Indeed, every generation does think it is special. As a Millennial, I undoubtedly see special characteristics in my generation that others don't recognize—or at least don't recognize yet. The long-term impact and view of generational experiences changes with time. The Boomers, seen as so focused on social and political change in the 1960s, are now viewed through the prism of the "Me Generation" label that was affixed to them in the mid-1970s by Tom Wolfe. And don't forget: the same people we know and respect today as the Greatest Generation were seen in the 1970s as the Silent Generation, who survived the Great Depression and World War II and fought the Korean War, but drank and smoked their way through the postwar world, doing little to oppose racism, sexism, and injustice at home.

This book is by no means an account of every single Millennial. Nor do I intend to paint a picture of my generation as perfect. Some of us are excessively materialistic, some of us are part of the "everyone-gets-a-trophy" mentality, some of us feel entitled, some are overly focused on celebrity culture, and some of us are apathetic and angry. These flaws have been pointed out by a number of critics and have become part of the popular understanding of the Millennial Generation. In this book I have identified a number of the transformative ideas and trends that are not just nascent, but quite prevalent among the Millennials—and what those ideas and trends may mean as they play out over the next several decades. There are exciting and promising movements afoot in this generation, and there are others that may generate cause for concern. It is important to understand both the positive and the negative in the proper context of their power and reach.

I've spent the past six years criss-crossing the country, having conversations with hundreds of Millennials doing amazing things but also with intellectual leaders, politicians, actors, journalists, business leaders, and everyday people at all ages and stages of life, all of whom are trying to make sense of living in the fast future. If you want to get one of the best glimpses possible into what the future has in store for us, follow me on this tour of what the Millennials are already accomplishing. I think you will be inspired to see that the future is bright and that we are uniquely qualified to rise to the challenges it poses.

Historically, young people have been pioneers of "The Next Big Thing." They've led movements and developed attitudes that anticipated where the rest of society would go before the general population caught up. Young people are often the first to see big changes in our world and often the first to figure out how to respond. So there's good reason to pay close attention to how this generation is thinking.

But don't take it only from me. In 1813, as America was coming into its own, Thomas Jefferson wrote, "The new circumstances under which we are placed call for new words, new phrases, and for the transfer of old words to new objects."[2] Quoting Jefferson in a 1962 commencement speech at Yale University, President John F. Kennedy said, "New words, new phrases, the transfer of old words to new objects—that is truer today than it was in the time of Jefferson, because the role of this country is so vastly more significant. . . . You are part of the world and you must participate in these days of our years in the solution of the problems that pour upon us, requiring the most sophisticated and technical judgment; and as we work in consonance to meet the authentic problems of our times, we will generate a vision and an energy which will demonstrate anew to the world the superior vitality and strength of the free society."[3] What was true in Jefferson's time, and truer in Kennedy's time, is even truer today. We always have and always will need to adapt, create new words, and solve new problems. In the fast future world, the Millennials will need to do much of this work.

ONE

Pragmatic Idealists

> There's a realism and a pragmatism that just hasn't been there
> before. But it's taken a while for older people to see that this
> isn't just a hobby. . . . We're working hard to make change
> happen, and on very pragmatic and realistic fronts.
> —Kelsey Swindler, twenty-two, Wilmington, Ohio

It's November 2004, in the nation's election battleground: swing-state
Ohio. It's raining hard as voters, many fed up with the Bush administration and looking for a chance to express themselves, have come out
across the state to vote. Lines are particularly long in Gambier, Ohio, a
small town of about two thousand people. Gambier's major industry is
Kenyon College, which sprawls through the heart of town. Like many
small liberal arts colleges, Kenyon was a bastion of youth activism in the
1960s and '70s. But in 2004, while the Kenyon campus is a beehive of
intellectual activity, political and social activism are no longer the hall-
marks of the college experience they had once been.

Many freshmen and sophomores are thrilled to be voting for the
first time, especially in such a hotly contested election. One in particular, then-nineteen-year-old freshman Matt Segal, heads to the polling
place at 6 a.m. and votes quickly. He stays to volunteer at the polls.
But he soon sees long lines forming, forcing people to wait for hours
for their turn in the booth. Many of those waiting in line are young;
many of them are Kenyon students, and many are Matt's friends. Those
who stick it out will, in some cases, end up waiting upwards of twelve
hours. The last person that Election Day will finally cast their ballot at
4 a.m.[1] "It was injustice," Matt tells me years later; I can still hear his
outrage. "I was frustrated, but I was also energized. I said, we've got to
do something about this. This isn't the way democracy was sold to me;

my peers disenfranchised, waiting in line all day simply to exercise their right to vote."

And Matt did something. He called Congresswoman Stephanie Tubbs Jones, who represented nearby Cleveland and was closely monitoring turnout in the state. That call launched an unusual partnership: Matt, a young, newfound political activist and Tubbs Jones, a seasoned politician with a grandmotherly vibe. After the 2004 election, Tubbs Jones became a leading proponent of election reform and a champion for young voters. She was so concerned about the disenfranchisement that Matt and other Ohioans (young and old, black and white) had experienced that she objected on the floor of Congress to the necessary certification of the 2004 presidential election results, forcing the House of Representatives to debate election reform for hours. For Matt, the simple act of walking in to cast his ballot in November 2004 would alter the course of his life. A month later, he would be called to testify before Congress on his experiences. His interest in election reform and student voter access grew as he became involved with a series of political organizations, including the Roosevelt Institute, a campus think tank network. In 2007, he founded the Student Association for Voter Empowerment, also known as SAVE. Today the organization is called Our Time, and it advocates for young Americans on all issues from voter empowerment to economic opportunity.

Matt certainly didn't go to his polling place on that Election Day in 2004 to start SAVE, or to become a leading advocate for young voters. He just wanted to vote. By most standards, Matt was a pretty regular guy. He grew up outside Chicago in an ordinary middle-class family, hung out with his friends, went to school, and did all the usual things high schoolers do. Matt had been to rock concerts in support of various causes and considered himself "politically informed," but he was not, by his own definition, any sort of "activist" in November 2004. And that's what's so interesting about Matt's experience—and many similar Millennial stories. Matt didn't have a history of activism, but what Matt saw in those twelve-hour voting lines was so powerful, he just *had* to take action. The organizing structure would emerge organically over time. Matt just had a simple instinct to try to do something authentically and effectively to help his peers. His first reaction was not to organize a march to the Gambier town hall or lead a giant rally on the Kenyon quad. Rather, his first action was a highly pragmatic one: he called his congresswoman.

While it seemed perfectly natural to Matt to work "within the system," he also knew intuitively that to be powerful inside it, you have to work with people outside. He developed a hybrid approach, which he sums up this way: "I don't have a very ideological theory of change. I don't believe you have to be confrontational or agitating all the time. On the other hand, I also don't believe that you have to put on a suit and tie and dress like a middle-aged lobbyist. To get things done, I have to be able to demonstrate that SAVE represents lots of young people who want to make the voting booth and political power more accessible."

Through this approach to effecting change, Matt has become one of the most powerful young advocates in Washington. Years later, Matt's approach can be seen throughout this generation. The pattern has played out in countless stories of young people across the country: ordinary people, concerned by a problem, an issue, or an injustice, have been empowered to become extraordinary and effective champions of change. This is the Millennial approach to activism, as well as to business, personal attitudes, and sometimes even overall life choices.

This approach comes from a mindset that I call *pragmatic idealism*.[2] Millennials definitely have high ideals—and a strong commitment to those ideals, values, and beliefs. But they also know their ideals must be actionable and realizable. They therefore tend to be comfortable and confident taking small, steady, incremental, practical steps to accomplish their goals—even when their goals are ultimately big, ambitious, idealistic visions.

Pragmatism and idealism are often viewed as lying at opposite ends of the continuum of political, economic, social, and cultural change. Throughout much of the 1950s, in post–World War II America, the pendulum swung very far in the direction of pragmatism: society was led by a deep focus on careers, families, automobiles, homes, and a general mentality of personal success, "getting ahead," and sharing in the abundant and growing economic pie. This was an approach to life leavened by comparatively little idealism about the possibilities for progress in the outside world.

Just a decade later, by the late 1960s, many young people were advocating total revolution and frontal assault on capitalism and every manifestation of "the system" and its values. Extreme action, some believed, was the best way to change society. The pendulum had now swung very far toward idealism, with pragmatic concerns frequently thrown overboard into a sea of angry marchers and demonstrators who believed that only hyperbolic rhetoric and action in the streets could bring about change. The cultural energies today are quite different, and the national agenda has been significantly transformed. Today's Millennials generally view change in society as a project to work on, not something to demand.

This is not to say there are no protests and demonstrations anymore, or that no one in the Millennial Generation believes in revolution. But while there are many Millennial activists who are passionate about their causes and about achieving large-scale social change over time, there is only a small minority who would identify themselves as radicals or revolutionaries, or who believe in putting every issue on the table now and fighting to overturn the entire system. The Occupy Wall Street movement was one instance of a handful of radicalized Millennials, but even that movement had its pragmatic side (organizing daily life in New York's Zuccotti Park, for example). In any event, even the Occupy protests of late 2011 all but disappeared by the spring of 2012.

In the Arab Spring, Millennials were actively protesting with the idealistic goal of removing the dictators in charge of their countries. However, these Millennials were also pragmatic in that they intentionally limited their goals to the removal of dictators and did not attempt to articulate or gain support for a full program of social change that would inevitably need to follow. Pragmatic idealism was also on display in the blending of online and offline tactics that were used in organizing the Arab uprisings of 2011–2012. Pragmatic idealists are at the center of many of today's youth-led movements, and their thinking and life experiences are very different from those of the radicals who dominated the movements for social change in the 1960s.

While many complex and conflicting trends were at work in the '80s and '90s, it is fair to say that the Generation Xers who emerged from those decades had a different mindset than either the Boomers who came before them or the Millennials who would come after. The worldview of the Xers mixed nihilism, anger, cynicism, and irony in ways not seen before, as well as a new ultra-pragmatism bred by the new avenues toward extreme wealth open to young people who went into careers in business and finance. As Julie Barko Germany, a member of Generation X, says, "I wish I had been born a Millennial. It would have been so much easier to accomplish the goals I believe in if my generation had benefited from both the idealism and the practical thinking of the Millennials."

While there were moments in the '60s and in other eras when pragmatism and idealism were combined and balanced, they have not been fused together in the prevailing mindset within a rising generation until now. In our modern world, the most complex questions require a meaningful mix of an idealistic vision with a pragmatic approach. The possibilities for success in solving long-intractable problems will be vastly expanded if Millennials can break down the wall between idealism and pragmatism to allow the ideas and energy from both sides of the equation to flow freely. We know that, in order to effect change on issues we care about, we have to master the workings of our society's existing institutions. As Marci Baranski, twenty-five, observes, "Our generation is beginning to internalize the ideals of social justice and environmental conservation. Though we may not be acting out the way past generations have, we now have the option of having a career based on sustainability—whether it is in business, politics, engineering, or science. . . . We are not passive on these pressing issues; we are simply learning to work within the system. A few years of college activism just isn't going to cut it. We are aiming for change on a larger scale. We also understand that these changes may take the rest of our lives to accomplish. And that's why we want to go into careers where we could be contributing to those changes on a lifelong basis."[3]

Millennials have a high degree of trust in their society's institutions. A Pew Research Center study found that Millennials are "more supportive of business than their elders. A higher percentage of Millennials than other cohorts agrees that 'business corporations generally strike a

fair balance between making profits and serving the public interest.'"
This feeling is shared by 44 percent of Millennials, compared with 35
percent of gen Xers and boomers and 32 percent of the Greatest Generation.[4] We don't blindly trust these institutions; we understand their
limitations and know that greed and corruption are inevitable, and thus
we are not shocked by scandals and crises.

But we also know that these institutions can be compelled to per-
form better and to make fairer, more just decisions. We can and are
creating our own institutions and organizations, and at the same time,
we're working alongside and inside established ones. Our generation,
just like any demographic group, has extremists on the Right and the
Left, young ideologues as well as young pragmatists. An effort to re-
establish Students for a Democratic Society (SDS), the legendary student organization that was the most visible organization on the campus
Left in the 1960s, has produced about forty campus chapters around the
country. On the Right, a small number of Millennials have been active
in the Tea Party movement. But SDS is barely on the radar screen even
on the campuses where it is active, and when asked in 2012 survey conducted by CIRCLE, only 10.8 percent of Millennials identified themselves as members of the Tea Party.[5] But in a period of unprecedented
polarization, the youth demographic is less polarized, less focused on
what divides us, and more open to intelligent compromise.

A 2010 Pew Research Center study concluded that the Millennial
demographic is "confident, self-expressive, liberal, upbeat and open to
change."[6] In opinion polling, Millennials exhibited a striking openness
and even consensus on issues that have been at the center of the polarization of American politics. Not only have they declined en masse to
engage with divisive movements like the Tea Party, but they also are
less divided on the social issues that have played a key role in our polarization. For example, 69 percent of Millennials support same-sex marriage, compared to 38 percent of seniors and 59 percent of the American
public overall.[7]

The same spirit of pragmatic idealism is responsible for the Millennials' optimistic attitude about their economic prospects, even in
the depths of a lingering recession that has hit our generation hard and

diminished our prospects of finding our first jobs. The same Pew study found that although Millennials' "entry into careers and first jobs has been badly set back by the Great Recession . . . they are more upbeat than their elders about their own economic futures as well as about the overall state of the nation."[8]

Millennials are part of the quiet progression toward significant, scalable, and lasting change, and they are learning that they can do extraordinary things when they mobilize their peers. One example is Nashville native Marvelyn Brown. At nineteen, she was flattered when her "Prince Charming," as she calls him, wanted to have sex with her without using a condom. Soon thereafter, the unthinkable happened: Marvelyn was diagnosed with AIDS. She became an outcast, shunned by her parents (who told her to tell people she had cancer), shunned by her friends (who thought they could "catch it" from her), and faced such torment and ridicule from her fellow students that she was forced to drop out of school. Confronted with these obstacles, Marvelyn decided that she would devote her life to preventing, educating, and raising awareness about HIV/AIDS. Today, she travels the country and the world telling her story, educating people about safe sex and asking people to get tested for HIV on the spot. On average, two-thirds of her audiences get tested after hearing her speak. Her unique appeal is built on putting herself out there to talk about a big and troubling issue in a very personal way. As Marvelyn told me, "After being told I had contracted HIV, I felt like not enough was being done to prevent it from happening to others. . . . I wanted to make a difference." She adds that today, through her activism, "Life feels so much more rewarding. I know I am doing what I am destined to do." She is doing something each and every day, and that something is both idealistic (educating people and working toward the goal of a world someday free from the scourge of AIDS) and yet still pragmatic (educational, evolutionary, one person and one audience at a time).

Marvelyn isn't a scientist working on AIDS research, but she has helped raise money for the cause. She's not a Hollywood celebrity, and her regular speaking engagements at high schools and colleges don't draw national headlines, but she's having a meaningful impact. Marvelyn is taking pragmatic action speech by speech and school by school, getting people tested. Her actions are quietly building toward progress in the fight against AIDS.

Today, as a result of both the Millennial mindset and the new power of technology, it's relatively easy to become a leader. Matt Segal and Marvelyn are ordinary people who responded to injustice and hardship by launching movements for change, becoming extraordinary leaders and champions for their causes. When we speak about activists, we're almost by definition talking about people who are out of the ordinary. But in the fast future, ordinary people can seamlessly begin doing extraordinary things. The tools we have at our disposal, from social media to text messaging, give us a much bigger and faster platform than those available to prior generations. It's easier for people to become engaged, and to become leaders. Even ordinary Millennials can use their available time, skills, and passions to make an immediate impact. In other words, being a pragmatic idealist doesn't mean you have to commit every waking hour to an issue to be effective. Many of us ask, What can I do to help with the time and resources I have? Millennials across the country have found their own answers to this question, like Eleanor Mulshine, twenty-three, who regularly volunteers and went on two trips to the Gulf to assist with Hurricane Katrina recovery efforts. She thinks about engaging with the world very pragmatically and almost instinctively. "I'm trying to give back," she told *USA Today*. "What else would I do with my spare time?"[9]

During the 2008 election, I caught up with Kate Lupo. Kate, twenty-four, had wanted to work in the art world in high school, but in college she had become very active in environmental issues. It started with a class she took simply to fill a requirement: "I took this environmental justice class the winter of my sophomore year, and I can honestly say it changed my life. I realized that I had been totally caught up in my romantic notions of the New York City art world and that there was so much more to be done, so many issues that needed to be solved."

Soon after that class she went to Washington to participate in Powershift, a large rally of young environmental activists. She described the experience to me in vivid detail: "I felt, this is the movement I want to be involved in. This encompasses so much. I was there with my other friends, and I felt like we had gotten off our butts and we were doing something. We were out there in the cold screaming for something that we cared about."

But for Kate, rallies are not the chief way to bring about the environmental consciousness and change she seeks. In her last year of college, Kate developed an organization called Murals for America that combines her passion for the arts with environmental justice. The project gives high school students the opportunity to paint environmentally themed murals in their school hallways. Students create art and raise fellow students' awareness of environmental issues at the same time. "Organizing the mural project, I felt the incredible energy and potential of youth and schoolkids working on these projects," Kate said. We should observe that she isn't storming Congress for action on cap and trade; nor is she abandoning environmental activism for expediency's sake. Instead, she has found a way to bring her passions, resources, and capabilities together to play a small role as a change agent on a huge issue. Kate demonstrates one of the approaches that pragmatic idealism encourages: taking small but significant—and sustainable—actions. Criticisms that "big small actions" like Kate's are nothing more than laziness or "activism lite" abound. Naysayers deem actions like wearing a cause-oriented bracelet, or simply clicking to join a socially minded Facebook group, "slacktivism." These critics might also question the seriousness of someone like Kate's involvement, feeling that what she is doing isn't "enough."

"They can't e-mail it in,"[10] wrote *New York Times* columnist Tom Friedman in a now-seminal column exploring what he believes is wrong with the activism of Millennials—or, in Friedman's chosen term for us, "Generation Q" (with "Q" standing for Quiet). Although Friedman admits that he's impressed with the strength of Millennial "optimism and idealism," he is "baffled" by our pragmatism. He wants us to be radicals, as many in his generation were at our age. He wants us to express moral outrage in ways that might have made sense in the 1960s, but which are less appropriate or effective today. He wants us to "demand" answers from every candidate arriving on a college campus about what he believes are the pivotal youth issues of our times—mitigating the effects of global climate change, reforming social security, and dealing with the U.S. budget deficit. Friedman opined, "America needs a jolt of the idealism, activism and outrage (it must be in there) of Generation Q. That's what twenty-somethings are for—to light a fire under the country . . . an online petition or a mouse click for carbon neutrality won't cut it." He went on to state the obvious about the past, with rhetorical flourish: "Martin Luther King and Bobby Kennedy didn't change the world by asking people to join their Facebook crusades." He seems to believe Millennials think social media is synonymous with political action, and therefore thinks we don't see the limitations of "virtual politics." The opposite is true. Most Millennials who are politically active understand the need to create linkage between online and offline political action. We also understand that while social media campaigns are valuable new tools, they are not the be-all and end-all of activism.

The Friedman piece about our so-called Quiet Generation sparked responses from many Millennials. Cara Downs, a student at Denison University, invited Tom Friedman to come visit her school, asserting, "My generation is not the quiet generation. Yes, Denison University in Granville, Ohio, is a picturesque campus about as far away from the Iraq quagmire, Darfur, and American poverty as one could get. But despite the unrealistic setting, we're involved in tangible and significant ways with social activism."[11]

Friedman made several incorrect assessments. First, he has an old-world view of "what twenty-somethings are for." He thinks young people are supposed to be the shock troops who can afford to stage attention-getting protests to catalyze the rest of the country into acting on important issues. But what if today's Millennials want deeper success for their causes? While rallies have occasionally proven to be useful tools for Millennials on issues like Darfur and climate change, and while they can have a powerful effect on participants, as Kate's experience at Powershift demonstrates, most Millennials are engaged in more pragmatic efforts to effect change that are more in tune with our times. Furthermore, Friedman's dismissal of "virtual" politics is outmoded. Although technology-based activism may still be more prevalent among Millennials than those in other generations, the use of social media has been growing for a decade. No political, economic, or organizational campaign led by people of any generation would today be without an important social media component.

Will Bates, a Millennial from New Hampshire, wrote to Friedman after the Generation Q piece appeared. "We're not just blogging and harnessing the power of online networks; we're trying to inspire on-the-ground activism and political engagement," he said. "We're using every tool we have, the Web included."[12] Any of us who have organized successfully recognize that online and offline actions need to be connected and integrated. What's more, just thirteen months after Friedman's Generation Q piece was published, young people played a decisive role in the outcome of the 2008 election, contributing to Barack Obama's victory. And in the 2012 fight against the Stop Online Piracy Act (SOPA) and the Protect IP Act (PIPA), which would have placed severe restrictions on online sharing and downloading, an online community—led by Millennials—succeeded in stopping the legislation in its tracks.

One of the main messages that came out of the Live Earth concerts organized by Al Gore in 2007 was the role that young people could play in addressing global climate change, by taking actions as minimal as turning off lights or turning thermostats down. Some experts laughed off the value of asking young people to turn off their lights. But many Millennials did, in fact, become more conscious about conserving energy. Is turning off the lights an important political or moral action? Maybe not. But we live in a world—and face problems like global climate change—where the impact of millions of people taking small, even trivial actions, can actually add up to something quite large. Bill Drayton, founder of the social entrepreneurship center Ashoka, put it well when he said, "More and more local change-makers are emerging. Some of these learn and later expand the pool of leading social entrepreneurs. To the degree they succeed locally, they give wings to the entrepreneur whose idea they have taken up, they encourage neighbors also to become change-makers, and they cumulatively build the institutions and attitudes that make local change-making progressively easier and more respected."[13]

It's certainly fair to distinguish between "helping out" and "being an activist." But in aggregate, actions can be valuable even if they are "lite" and easy. In the aftermath of the 2010 Haiti earthquake, the State Department organized a campaign encouraging donations of $10 to the relief effort via text message. This campaign illustrated the power of "easy" instant actions to make a material difference in people's lives. Reporting on a March 2010 study of Millennial habits when it comes to charitable giving, the *Chronicle of Philanthropy* found that "seventy-seven percent of people in the survey said they had heard about the opportunity to make a donation via their cell phones after the Haiti earthquake, and 36 percent said they would be willing to contribute via text after an emergency occurs." The same study found that Millennials "have a strong desire to help others and to raise money and attention for their favorite causes from friends and acquaintances."[14] The bottom line: over $100 million was raised for Haiti relief through texting and similar cell phone campaigns. In the first few days after the quake, the American Red Cross was absolutely stunned by the power of thousands upon thousands of people contributing to Haiti relief efforts in this way. "We honestly have no clue how much more to expect, but have been really surprised and overwhelmed by the amount of donations via texting," said Red Cross spokeswoman Carrie Housman. The $8 million total raised less than three days after the earthquake ravaged Haiti was "unheard of," she said. "We never raised this much money with a mobile campaign, especially $10 at a time."

Housman noted that smaller domestic mobile campaigns have been tried since 2008. The Haiti mobile fund-raising campaign, she said, "blows [those] results out of the water." She attributed the response to the dire emergency, the closeness of Haiti to the United States, and the simplicity of donating via text. "It's something that an average person can do—and the $10 amount has been key. It's doable," she said. "A 10-year-old girl texted her donation and called to tell us and said she was planning to spread the word through her classmates. It was very emotional for her."[15]

Substantial political, intellectual, and romanticized baggage from other eras attaches itself to the concept of activism, and much of this baggage is rooted in the impressions of youth activism from the 1960s and early '70s. Past images of young people "in the streets" have become the standard against which today's youth action is judged. So it's tempting to assume that if we don't rise to that level of precedent-setting outrage, volume, and visibility, we aren't doing much. But as pragmatic idealists we realize activism can take many forms. Political scientist Natalie Davis noted that Millennials, in comparison to Generation Xers, are "neither cynical nor alienated, and you seem to like your parents. You're not like the boomers who are ideologues and tend to listen only to those who share their ideology. You are seen as being inclusive when it comes to race, ethnicity, and sexual orientation. . . . You want to build coalitions. . . . You are networked, and you tweet. And most importantly for our time, you are problem-solvers."[16]

But some, like conservative writer and Emory College professor Mark Bauerlein, would have us believe that not only are Millennials not activists, but we aren't even remotely engaged in the world. In his book *The Dumbest Generation: How the Digital Age Stupefies Young Americans and Jeopardizes Our Future (Or, Don't Trust Anyone under 30)*, Bauerlein proclaims, "It isn't enough to say these young people are uninterested in world realities. They are actively cut off from them. Or a better way to put it is to say that they are encased in more immediate realities that shut out conditions beyond—friends, work, clothes, cars, pop music, sitcoms, Facebook. Each day the information they receive and the interaction they have must be so local or so superficial that the facts of government, foreign and domestic affairs . . . never slip through."[17] I won't pretend that there aren't members of my generation who fit this description. But it's hard to claim that disengagement with politics is a major epidemic among American youth when the 2008 election saw 51.1 percent of eligible Millennials vote, one of the largest young voter turnouts in history.[18] And as for Bauerlein's complaints that we're idling away on Facebook, how would he explain the Facebook group "1 Million Strong for Barack" started by a passionate Millennial, which managed to attract nearly five hundred thousand members, or the fact that more than twenty-six million people "like" Barack Obama on Facebook? While we know not all of these people are deeply engaged with politics, it would be hard to say they are, as Bauerlein puts it, "actively cut off" from politics.

Objectively speaking, there has never been a time in American history when so many people have had so much access to opportunity, wealth, and advanced technology. For just one example, consider the paradigm-shifting opportunity that the Internet allows people to increase their own social upward mobility, and then consider the fact that as of March 2012, 78.3 percent of Americans have Internet access (the figure is higher among Millennials).[19] Quantitatively, we have more assets as a country than in any other era, but undoubtedly immense issues of inequality remain unaddressed, as do many other challenges in our society. Millennials respond to this by asking: how can we improve what's here? From a pragmatic point of view, it wouldn't make sense to tear it down, because the system that exists has produced strong, if not always equal and not always unblemished, results. But we know and believe we can solve—or at least improve on—many of those outstanding problems.

Millennials have a strong belief that government is an important part of the solutions to major problems in society. According to Ruy Teixeira from the Center for American Progress, "When asked in the 2008 National Election Study whether we need a strong government to handle today's complex economic problems or whether the free market can handle these problems without government being involved, Millennials, by a margin of 78 to 22 percent, demonstrated an overwhelming preference for strong government."[20] Those numbers illustrate a fairly striking faith in government to deal with the economy. This sentiment is echoed by Millennials like twenty-five-year-old Amelia West, who says, "On a scale of 1–10, my level of faith in government is a 7. I say this because I grew up with the support of several government-run programs like food stamps, S-CHIP, the school lunch program, etc., so while I don't necessarily love the direction of our country right now, there is a deep-rooted appreciation for what government *can* do for its citizens."

Some of our current politicians are entrenched in debating the legacy of Ronald Reagan and whether the deregulation of business, the shift to small government, and the strong free market he ushered in were beneficial. While Millennials understand and recognize this history, we find it less productive to focus on that debate. Instead, we're more engaged with thinking about what we as individuals can do to change things and how we can use government, business, and NGOs to make that change.

A LOOK BACK AT THE TUMULTUOUS DECADE: 1960–1969

We Millennials do not think total change is practical, possible, or even desirable. We are much more evolutionary than revolutionary. In this spirit, we actually have more in common with the activism of the *early* '60s, which showed us that pragmatic idealism can work.

The '60s was full of significant accomplishments, many made possible by the work of youth activists. Whether or not they agreed with the war in Vietnam at the beginning, by its later stages most Americans had turned against it. Youth activists played a key role in catalyzing that change, ultimately bringing an end to one of the deadliest military campaigns in American history. Young people were also major forces pushing for comprehensive civil rights legislation, which was passed, leading to the greatest progress on equality, justice, and empowerment for African Americans and other minorities in a century. These and other accomplishments of the '60s, propelled initially by youth, put in motion reforms and waves of change that have continued for the past five decades. There is little doubt that without the movement of the '60s, young people would not have had the opportunity to support Barack Obama's candidacy in 2008. Surely Millennials are standing on the shoulders of a generation of giants who kicked off significant cultural and political shifts, but ours is a different path.

The world is fundamentally different today. The twenty-first-century agenda, with pressing issues ranging from health care reform to the role of government in restructuring the U.S. economy, responding to global climate change, and learning how to live in a world where terrorists and rogue states are a fact of life, is more complex and nuanced. The Millennial mindset is particularly appropriate and sustainable when it comes to addressing these kinds of intricate, generation-long challenges, where the solutions are not always obvious, where extensive experimentation and creative policy thinking are needed to develop models that can actually work, and where each citizen has a role to play and a contribution to make.

In the early '60s, a kind of pragmatic idealism was present—briefly. One place it was on display was the Free Speech Movement at the University of California, Berkeley in 1964. The popular impression of all things Berkeley is of ultra-radicalism. But, in fact, the leader of the Free

Speech Movement, Mario Savio, had an initial approach that contained many elements of pragmatic idealism. The original goal of the movement was to give students the freedoms of speech that adults off-campus enjoyed. Although the movement started with civil disobedience— blockading a police car in the middle of campus for days—Savio and other movement leaders soon entered into negotiations with the university administration. Savio and his activist colleagues didn't particularly like or agree philosophically with the administrators. But they knew the only way to achieve their goal would be to work with them. Through practiced pragmatic idealism, Savio ultimately secured major concessions and won the right of freedom of speech for students on campus.

After this initial success, the Free Speech Movement broadened its scope to encompass sweeping change throughout the entire system of higher education. Some of the reforms the students proposed included getting rid of grading, establishing student control of the curriculum, and student approval on professor tenure. This next iteration of the movement failed. The new effort lacked the focus of the original, which had a compelling logic to it—why shouldn't young adults at one of our freest institutions, the university, have the same first amendment rights as others? The faculty and the public were generally supportive of free speech. But educational reforms, perceived as turning control of the institution over to the students, defied practical common sense for most non-students and could not win the same level of support from the public, or even from the student population. The students' pragmatic idealism was lost along with their cause.

Martin Luther King Jr.'s approach of nonviolent civil disobedience was also a case study in a kind of pragmatic idealism. But as the '60s wore on, and as the Vietnam War escalated, the ideas that gained momentum seemed to be revolution, overturning the system, and destroying capitalism. These ideas ultimately led to limited but very significant pockets of militant and aggressive action, such as the Weather Underground bombings and the students who took over buildings at Columbia University in 1968.

That same year at New York University, members of the campus chapter of SDS disrupted two speeches on the same evening. One was by the South Vietnamese ambassador to the United States, and another was by *New York Times* executive editor James Reston. The students were protesting the ambassador because they didn't recognize his government's legitimacy and didn't think he should be allowed to speak. (The anti–Vietnam War movement thought—with good reason—of the South Vietnamese government as a "puppet" of Washington.) On the other hand, the students were protesting James Reston because the *New York Times* was considered "part of the media" and anyone in media was part of capitalism and therefore part of the problem. In a statement following the protest, the SDS members decried the terrible conditions of America's cities and the world, saying, "We live in a state of chaos, and capitalism is its name. Under such conditions, the desire to do away with the present forms of social life, to overcome the chaos that already exists in capitalism, is a creative force."[21] The students' urge to rid society of oppression and war was no doubt idealistic. But there was no serious step-by-step plan for how capitalism would be destroyed and how the government would be overthrown—although many of the passionate activists in this era truly believed these actions would come to pass. Without a realistic plan, it's not difficult to see why their ambitions went unfulfilled. Today, these kinds of statements read as rants, not as practical plans for solutions to problems. Demanding urgent action in response to a particular injustice or problem is not synonymous in the Millennial mind with taking on the system as a whole.

The Millennial mindset of pragmatic idealism—and the progressive initiatives undertaken by so many Millennials—may be just as relevant to the early twenty-first century as protest activism was to the 1960s generation. Even many '60s activists are optimistic about the potential for the Millennial Generation. Bettina Aptheker, who worked with Mario Savio during the Berkeley Free Speech Movement and is now a professor of feminist studies at the University of California, Santa Cruz, describes Millennial activists as "the most brilliant that I've seen. Just brilliant. Brilliant organizing, brilliant ideas." Bettina is excited and optimistic about new technology as a tool for activism, although not without reasonable caveats and a call for balance in offline and online activity. "The Internet is a fantastic resource. You can put things up. People can get educated and have access to it. But people have to be motivated to do it, and to motivate people to do it, you have to talk to them. You can have all the websites in the world, but if people don't go to them, it's meaningless. On the other hand, you can get one hundred thousand signatures on a petition in two hours on the Internet. It would have taken us weeks to get that number of signatures. Technology holds enormous potential for organizing today, but it doesn't substitute for face-to-face organizing. You have to do both together."

Many other '60s activists share Bettina's views, and are trying to help and support today's youth movements. Late Boomer and hip-hop mogul Russell Simmons may have expressed the happy medium between these positions when he remarked, "Social media is the rock and roll of the sixties, the hip-hop of the '80s, the radical new equalizer, giving parity to new voices and levelling the access to culture, politics, and social justice."[22]

Millennials are trying to incorporate issues, causes, and beliefs they are passionate about into busy, complex, multifaceted lives. Even many of the most passionate Millennials are not devoting every minute to the causes they are most passionate about. It isn't pragmatic to do so. Millennials are looking for sustainable commitments that can engage them and allow them to contribute to society, but not take over their lives. At Berkeley, Savio, Aptheker, and their fellow organizers famously had marathon strategy sessions that went on for upwards of eight hours. Savio himself was known to forgo sleep during some of the most intense periods of the movement. But today, just as sustainable agriculture and sustainable energy have become twenty-first-century pursuits, so has sustainable activism. This doesn't mean we aren't deeply committed to our causes. But our pragmatism leads us to conclude that overworking ourselves will not generate the support and attention that we want, let alone sustain our own commitments. Unlike the '60s, when arrests for protesting were considered par for the course, if a Millennial were arrested today while protesting, it would likely stop them from getting a job, including a job working for a green energy company, an opportunity that a Millennial would recognize as an avenue for affecting change. However, we're not avoiding protesting because we are afraid; rather, it's because we don't think that protesting in our modern world is the most effective tool for change. As Matt Segal told me, "Given the direction we're moving as a country sociologically, marches and protests are becoming less effective. They'll get some press attention, but there's no other real impact. It's preaching to the choir rather than affecting change within government and institutions. People should channel their enthusiasm and energy with a less antagonistic and more collaborative approach, and they'll achieve quicker and more effective results than shouting with a megaphone."

While Millennials are idealistic, we understand that simply having the best ideas or the strongest arguments isn't enough to accomplish our goals or advance our causes. We understand that we have to work with a diverse group of institutions and organizations, including those we don't see eye to eye with, in order to effect change. If you're a Millennial who wants to bring about environmental justice, you don't simply dismiss corporations like McDonald's or Walmart, which are major parts of the American economy and therefore major players in any solution to our environmental challenges. This view of business is not as naive as it may sound. Our willingness to partner with business has to be based on mutual benefit and gain. The kind of environmental change that Millennials seek will not come about in our lifetimes without the cooperation of major corporations, and Millennials have been pushing companies to become more socially responsible. Consumer power— and an increasing trend of Millennials and others expressing their brand preferences for socially responsible companies and products—is working. An analysis by the Haas School of Business at the University of California, Berkeley, concluded that over 80 percent of Millennials will "switch brands if they have no CSR [corporate social responsibility] initiatives."[23] A study by the cause marketing agency Cone Inc. found that 69 percent of Millennials "consider a company's social and environmental commitment when deciding where to shop."[24] These numbers are not lost on major corporations, who have taken major steps in the past few years to strengthen their social and environmental responsibility to appeal to Millennial consumers.

The pragmatic idealist mindset of the Millennials is already changing politics, life choices, and social attitudes. But business is also being disrupted by this new approach. Indeed, the unique rise and dominance of the world's largest social network presents us with an example of how pragmatic idealism and the Millennial mindset may revolutionize the future of business.

Mark Zuckerberg grew up in Dobbs Ferry, New York, a self-admitted geek. He spent most of his teenage years obsessed with software development. He was so gifted technologically that, while still in high school, he developed a music recommendation program called Synapse, which Microsoft and AOL offered to buy for a reported $1 million. But Zuckerberg, more interested in the power of technology to impact communities and the world, turned down Microsoft's million and put the application online for free.

In 2004, while a sophomore at Harvard, Zuckerberg developed a social network, a place where friends could connect online. As the site grew from a dorm-room project to a major company, Zuckerberg became the youngest self-made billionaire in the world. Facebook passed landmark after landmark, quickly becoming one of the most popular sites on the Internet, now with an unprecedented one billion users.

Facebook has faced major ethical tests as it has grown. One key moment occurred in February 2009, when the company had to manage a controversy after it changed the privacy afforded to users in its terms-of-service (TOS) agreement. Like most online services, Facebook can change its terms of service without getting users to re-agree to those terms. The new changes implemented that February would have made all content that users uploaded to Facebook the property of Facebook in perpetuity. There was an immediate uproar, particularly from Millennials. As *BusinessWeek*'s Bruce Nussbaum observed, "The Facebook Flap over privacy shows that the Gen Y cohort may be just as worried about controlling their own data as their Boomer parents."[25] Millennial backlash was strong, with a group called "People Against the New Terms of Service" (TOS) gaining tens of thousands of members in the days following the initial TOS change (the group since grew to over one hundred thousand members). This group served as a forum for users venting their frustration, anger, and concerns. A perusal of the group's "wall" shows phrases from Millennials that include "betrayed our trust," "I'll sue," "BS," and "I'm quitting Facebook."[26]

The controversy led Facebook to revert quickly back to the old terms. But then, through a series of posts on the official Facebook blog, Zuckerberg began to work out these issues in a very public way. The posts show him admitting mistakes, apologizing, explaining reasoning, discussing new actions going forward, and finally opening the issue up to the entire Facebook user community for discussion. Ultimately, in April 2009, Facebook adopted a system in which any modifications to its terms would be put up to a vote. After a comment period, if 30 percent of all Facebook's active users voted, the results would be binding, but if less than 30 percent of active users voted, the vote would merely be advisory.[27] (In the first test of this system, the 30 percent threshold was not met, and those who voted were overwhelmingly supportive of the change.) One can question the value of this type of user democracy, but Zuckerberg deserves credit for giving the user community a formal role in the governance of a huge company that they do not own or control. In a post on February 18, 2009, announcing this new system, Zuckerberg wrote:

> More than 175 million people use Facebook. If it were a country, it would be the sixth most populated country in the world. Our terms aren't just a document that protects our rights; it's the governing document for how the service is used by everyone across the world. Given its importance, we need to make sure the terms reflect the principles and values of the people using the service. . . . Since this will be the governing document that we'll all live by, Facebook users will have a lot of input in crafting these terms.[28]

This kind of open and transparent process for changing key aspects of a business of Facebook's size was quite radical at the time. With a good portion of Facebook's users being Millennials, and Zuckerberg a Millennial himself, he is on the same page as his users when he says that he wants to build a company and community that reflect its users' "values and principles." He also knew that this level of transparency was smart business. After seeing the initial angry response to the changed terms of service, Zuckerberg realized that Facebook's brand and cachet with young people could be irreparably harmed if he didn't manage this issue with respect for the Millennial-dominated user community, so making amends in an on-brand way was necessary. The Facebook brand is in tune with Mark Zuckerberg's Millennial vision: to build a place for people to connect and share things online. That approach was also in tune with the values of Facebook's users. Pragmatic idealism is not always easy to achieve. All companies change with time, and Millennial companies are no exception to that rule. But wouldn't we rather have more companies that are more pragmatically idealistic, even if they are not totally idealistic?

Early on, before Facebook exploded—and before the world was watching its every move—Mark Zuckerberg said his initial interest in developing the site was motivated more by the intellectual and technological challenge than by the desire to make money. Profitability became a factor later in the game. In 2004, Zuckerberg told the *Harvard Crimson*, "I'm just like a little kid. I get bored easily and computers excite me. . . . I just like making it and knowing that it works and having it be wildly successful is cool, I guess, but I mean, I dunno, that's not the goal." Six years later, Zuckerberg expressed a similar spirit with a new perspective in light of the responses to privacy changes, remarking, "We view it as our role in the system to constantly be innovating and be updating what our system is to reflect what the current social norms are . . . a lot of companies would be trapped by the conventions and their legacies of what they've built."[29] Facebook's future, he promised, wouldn't be so constrained. By 2010, he had developed a deeper philosophy, explaining that "the biggest difference between Facebook and other companies is how focused we are on our mission. . . . Different companies care about different things. There are companies that care about, just really care about having the biggest market cap. Or there are companies that are really into process or the way they do things. For us, it is the mission."[30] Staying true to this vision, in Facebook's pre-IPO regulatory filing, Zuckerberg wrote, "Facebook was not originally created to be a company." Instead, it is a company with a "social mission— to make the world more open and connected."[31]

Let me be clear: Facebook is a highly successful for-profit company, and Mark Zuckerberg, as well as many others who work for Facebook or invested in Facebook, has become very rich. But it is a different kind of company than most of those served up by the history of American business. It is infused with a unique Millennial ethos that may last even after Zuckerberg and other executives get older. And it is not alone.

There is an interesting comparison to be drawn with one of Zuckerberg's heroes and his counterpart from the Boomer Generation, fellow Harvard dropout Bill Gates. Back in the 1980s, when Gates was only a little bit older than Zuckerberg is today and Microsoft was rising to dominance in the software marketplace, Gates was pressured to open up his company's process and technology. Advisers inside and outside of Microsoft told Gates that failure to open up would lead to future problems. But Gates wouldn't budge. He never listened; he never changed until government anti-trust decisions in the United States and Europe forced him to. There's no question that Gates is brilliant and that he built one of the most successful companies and one of the biggest personal fortunes of all time. There is also no question that he is today doing important things for the benefit of the world through the charitable work of the Gates Foundation. But his intransigence in the 1980s and '90s on numerous key issues, even when advisors, customers, and eventually government agencies were calling out for a more open Microsoft, led the company to develop a negative brand image and to get hit with years of anti-trust lawsuits. In broadly similar circumstances, Zuckerberg took a different stance. He acknowledged his mistakes and said, in effect, "Yes, the users are right. Let's listen to the critics and take at least some responsive action. It's the right thing to do, and it's good business."

The Facebook story is illustrative of what may happen with other Millennial-run companies as a result of pragmatic idealistic thinking. We will adapt, open up the process, increase transparency, and listen to a broader circle of people inside and outside of our companies. But we will also adapt to the realities of running a business, without changing the fact that our companies are inherently Millennially influenced. Our pragmatic idealism may persist long after we're gone. Like Facebook, many Millennial-founded companies will be new and innovative. They'll often have a social value, and they'll often be driven to create a sense of community where community is declining in the "real" world. We'll also bring the spirit of pragmatic idealism to more traditional companies, when the first Millennials will start to become CEOs and senior executives of established companies in the next few years. As these Millennial entrepreneurs and intraprenuers grow stronger ranks, the influence of pragmatic idealism will grow, ultimately transcending generations to have a universal impact.

TWO

Fast Future, Present Shock

We're a generation that has seen so much change
so fast. We saw big old clunky Macintosh computers
in our first-grade classroom turn into iPhones. . . .
That kind of growth breeds optimism.

—Katharine Knight, twenty-four, in a
May 19, 2012, op-ed for the *Seattle Times*

Towers on fire, crumbling and falling as people run and scream. A finger-wagging president parsing the definition of sex on national TV. A student opens fire at a high school in Colorado. CEOs in shackles, hauled off to jail. A dictator's statue smashing to pieces as it hits the ground. Stock charts soaring to the skies—and then back down again. A newly minted president in a jubilant Chicago park and a moment of hope. Logging on and logging in from everywhere. Profound world-historic events mixed up and mashed up with celebrity gossip as news. War reports from somewhere in the Middle East. Families facing foreclosures, belt tightening, and hard times. These are some of the moments, images, and experiences that have defined the Millennial Generation's formative years. Many of us have experienced them in just this way, as a rapid-fire jumble. Sound bites, words, icons, images, videos, clips . . . short, interrupted, and out of context, but somehow coming together like puzzle pieces to create our own context and consciousness.

While this diverse blend of visual imagery, fragmentary ideas, sounds, and clicks continues to come at us, we scarcely notice the overall dissolution of authority in society, the collapse of institutions, the increasing level of complexity and the inability of existing systems to manage through it and solve problems. Rapid change is the only constant. And the chief survival skill for Millennials is keeping our

25

balance in this sometimes mad, sometimes surreal, always changing, topsy-turvy world.

Not only is there more constant change, but the rate at which America and all countries undergo change has been increasing exponentially. Consider the accelerating curve of change in technology and media: daily newspapers were the dominant form of mass communication for more than a century before they were challenged by radio; radio had about sixty years before TV eclipsed it; TV about forty years before the rise of the Internet; now, in just the last decade, the Internet itself has fragmented into thousands of new directions, from websites and blogs and Facebook pages to Twitter, cell phones, apps, and much more. It took about thirty years for the majority of American homes to have cable television, but only about ten years for the majority of American homes to have broadband connections. It took ten years for mobile phones to reach a million subscribers, but it took only a few weeks after the introduction of the iPad in 2010 for that device to have a million users. Even a "prophetic" speech by Microsoft CEO Steve Ballmer in 2005 now sounds like ancient history: "I believe we're going to see more change in technology over the course of the next five years than we have in the past decade," he said. "Just remember, a decade ago most people didn't have a cell phone, a PC, and didn't know what the Internet was."[1]

On top of this amazingly rapid technological change, the social context of our lives is changing at a similarly rapid rate. The informal rules that govern everything from how we talk to how we date, from how and where we make a living to how we carry out political campaigns, are in constant flux as well. In 1991, John Brockman, upon founding the website Edge.org, which is dedicated to promoting a "third culture" that weaves together the best from science and from the humanities, proclaimed: "We now live in a world in which the rate of change is the biggest change."[2] Around that time, when this level of mega-change in our society became most observable to big picture thinkers and trendspotters like Brockman, the majority of the people who are now Millennials were in their early childhood years.

Even the very notions of authority and power are undergoing rapid change, as is the infrastructure for decision making in every aspect of our society. In fact, the authority and dominance of centralized power have been crumbling for more than a century. We might date this fundamental change to Nietzsche's famous pronouncement that "God is dead" in the late nineteenth century, to Einstein's publication of his theory of relativity in the early twentieth century, to the collapse of the old order that followed World War I, or to all the new ideas and innovations that followed World War II.

In 1970, futurists Alvin and Heidi Toffler observed that our society had entered a period of such rapid change that we were beginning to experience "future shock"—so much change, in such a short period of time, that people and social institutions could not keep up.[3] The acceleration of change has been so rapid over the last forty years that we might well call the world of today's Millennials a time of "present shock." We've moved so far into the future, so fast, that our culture, its institutions, its government, and its people haven't always had time to catch up. But for Millennials born into this fast future, there is comparatively little "shock" at all. This is one of the defining aspects of the Millennial experience. For us, time is always in "fast forward" mode. Indeed, the line between the future and the present is sometimes blurred to the point where it's unclear if we're living in the present or the future.

Young people today have come to see the future as very close at hand. Very few predictions about new technology seem unrealistic or distant to us. In 1968, *2001: A Space Odyssey* imagined what the world might be like in the then far-off year of 2001. In 1968, thirty years in the future seemed like a long time away, but it seemed like it could be a reasonable amount of time for a massive change to a space-world to take place. But today the future is approaching so fast that we can't even dream of what the world might look like thirty years from now. In the fast future, the future has become a seamless part of the contemporary reality of the Millennial world.

One year no one has heard of YouTube, the next year it's the most common way that people watch videos. Twitter goes from being an odd-sounding word to having two hundred million users in two years. One problematic news story about a powerful governor or congressperson on track for the White House, and days later they are pushed out of office in disgrace. The rate of change has gone from rapid to quantum. Through this, Millennials are trying to embrace change, adapt, and remain optimistic while keeping our core values, beliefs, and spirit of pragmatic idealism intact. Brendan Stack, twenty-three, epitomizes the Millennial response to this fast future when he remarks, "I just see the world as continuously changing and I'm OK with that. . . . I'm OK with just dropping the equation and seeing the changes as a continuous factor. . . . I think a lot of us are like that."[4]

The Boomers have lived through a remarkable era of social change. They can remember when milkmen delivered milk to their homes, when doctors made house calls, and when the president of the United States and the Congress commanded enormous respect. The Millennials, on the other hand, have grown up against a backdrop of change and tumult, in which the presumption of respect for authority and institutions doesn't exist in the first place.

The big battles of the 1960s and '70s were generally fought over major political issues for which opposing sides had different political and ideological views. Where these battles came to a head, they usually reached conclusions and passed definitive legislation. This was the trajectory of the Civil Rights Act of 1964 and the decision to end the Vietnam War in the 1970s. The Civil Rights Act, long opposed by many, was passed and became a transformational force in the lives of millions of people. The draft ended, American troops withdrew from Vietnam, and the war itself came to an end.

Today, we see a whole new dimension in the fragmentation of our society. Major healthcare reform legislation is passed after a huge battle, and it immediately moves into a new battle in the courts with opponents refusing to accept it. We elected a president who was vocally opposed to the original deployment of American troops to Iraq, and he chose to continue and in some cases widen the scope of American military commitments in the Middle East.

Boomers and their parents grew up in a world where there were two great stock market crashes—1929 and 1987. We are growing up in a world of much more numerous and frequent market crashes and volatility—even "flash crashes," in which 10 percent of the market's wealth evaporates in minutes and no one can explain why, even after stock exchange and congressional investigations.

The fundamental nature of what is fact and what is fiction is also being called into question, marking another major shift that Millennials have adapted to. Although many have dubbed this era the "information age," it could just as easily be called the "misinformation age." This is a time when a large number of people persist in believing "facts" that are pure fiction, "truths" that are falsehoods, and in finding just enough "truthiness" (to use Stephen Colbert's clever coinage) in certain ideas to adopt them. The discussion about Barack Obama's birthplace has continued to swirl through the web and through American politics like a crazy leitmotif of our times. When the Republican governor of Hawaii, Linda Lingle, produced Obama's "certificate of live birth" in an effort to call an end to the discussion, the questions persisted: skeptics claimed that a certificate of live birth was not the same as a birth certificate and demanded more. Even after Obama released his actual birth certificate, a poll found that 10 percent of all Americans continued to believe the president was born outside of the United States.[5]

Despite all the well-publicized facts that have been presented, and despite all the public officials who have called on the mythmakers and the myth-believers to look at the facts, the myth of Obama as "foreign born" and not legally eligible to be president persists. More than two years after Obama's inauguration, perennial potential presidential candidate Mike Huckabee referred to Obama as having "grown up in Kenya," when in fact Obama was never there in his youth. In parallel, rumors about Obama's alleged Muslim faith maintain a substantial hold on a surprisingly large number of otherwise seemingly rational minds, once again in spite of the facts, and in spite of Obama's own oft-cited record of Christian faith. How can authority be effective and meaningful in a society where a significant group of that society's citizens don't even believe the most fundamental things, like the fact that the president has been legitimately elected? In the *Atlantic*, Michael Hirschorn observed of this trend toward fundamental disruption in factuality: "How does society function (as it has since the Enlightenment gave primacy to the link between reason and provable fact) when there is no commonly accepted set of facts and assumptions to drive discourse?"[6]

In the American past, there have been a number of close elections (Kennedy vs. Nixon, Hayes vs. Tilden, Bush vs. Gore) where quirks of the system, from the strange nature of the Electoral College to the propensity of dead people to vote in Cook County, Illinois, have come into play. But for more than a century after the Civil War, U.S. presidential elections, even when marred by mudslinging and allegations of scandal, always resulted in an acceptance, grudging or otherwise, of the legitimacy of the president. Even in the case of the 1860 election of Abraham Lincoln, the southern states that refused to vote for him did not question his legitimacy to serve as president. Instead they questioned their own allegiance to the United States, and ended up seceding, sparking the Civil War. Secession from the facts—and the declaration of a new reality independent of the facts—has become a viable option in an America that is so abstracted and fragmented.

The social software and the institutional infrastructure we rely on to undergird the organization of society is groaning under the shifting weight of this complex and diverse America. While we can find instances in modern history where backlash movements have risen up quickly, never have they gone from nonexistence to winning dozens of seats in government in two years time, as the Tea Party did from 2008 to 2010. And while we can find precedents for bitter partisanship in our history, we can find little precedent for the kind of political gamesmanship that has come to dominate the Congress today. Much of our debate is based on misinformation, political posturing, ignorance, and cynicism. Unlike previous eras, no one is really forced to take a side. Citizens can hold any view they like about Obama's legitimacy and go about their daily lives, while the political process grows more complex and entangled as a result. This new reality makes the inner workings of our political system congested and unable to produce the kind of change we desperately need.

There is no longer consensus about basic definitions, either. What is a war? It used to be obvious—national armies engaged in combat, declared, in America's case, by an act of Congress. But now war has been redefined by IEDs, counterinsurgencies, and terrorism, conditions under which all rules of engagement have been rewritten and the enemy is hard to define, let alone locate. Not surprisingly, Congress did not declare the last five wars our country has fought. Despite the constitutional provision that refers to the need for Congress to declare war, our country hasn't been in a formally declared war since World War II, seven decades ago. The wars in Afghanistan and Iraq could never even find a name. Everything from the "war on terror" to the "war against Islamo-Fascism" was tried, but in the end, no name stuck, leaving the longest, most expensive war in American history nameless and without a consensus regarding against whom or why we were fighting in the first place.

In short, things aren't as neat, clear, and categorized as they used to be. More players are involved, and the world has become so complex that it simply no longer works the way it once did. Yet because this fast-moving, ever-changing, increasingly complex world is the only reality Millennials have known, we enjoy a precious asset. We are not surprised or shocked or troubled that this is the way of the world. We don't spend much time worrying about this state of things nor wishing it were otherwise. Rather, we are focused on how to cut a path through the complexity and focus on getting things done in a pragmatic fashion. Millennials aren't necessarily "happy" about this new world, but we understand that this is the world as it is. We know that we need to live within this framework. We are pioneering the strategy for coping and making life decisions amid this incredibly perplexing and always-changing array of factors and complexities. Not everyone living through the same whirlwind of change is able to adjust. Social trends researcher Hugh Mackay has observed, "The older generation is not coping with the rapid rate of change, whereas Generation Y are not just coping, but are thriving on it. They have learned how to adapt, learned how to be flexible, how to incorporate all of this uncertainty and unpredictability in their approach to life. . . . Having grown up in a turbulent, unstable, and unpredictable world, the pace of change has taught them to anticipate change and, indeed, to embrace change."[7]

In the fast future, the 24/7 news cycle has been thriving. Although a comparatively small number of Millennials actually watch cable news shows, social media has allowed their inflammatory content to spread virally within Millennial circles. As a result, we are all living in the cycle. After the introduction of the scrolling headline ticker on news networks (known as "the crawl") in the days following 9/11 and the redefinition of what constituted a "news alert," we've become accustomed to "news" occurring all around us, and to being encouraged to have an immediate reaction to each development.

As the tone of 24/7 media creeps into other spheres of life, the lines between perception and reality have become even more blurry. In May 2012, for example, after months of hype and laudatory commentary by media across the spectrum about the impending IPO of Facebook, the company actually held its public offering. Within minutes of the commencement of stock trading, the company that just moments earlier everyone had wanted to have in their portfolio was suddenly being described as an abject failure. Half an hour after trading began, Facebook's falling stock price led one CNBC anchor to ask a guest the patently absurd question, "Is this the end of technology companies?" In the weeks that followed, the stock continued to fall, and news media outlets and individual citizens began to jump on the "end of technology" bandwagon. There was little effort to pause and reflect on the fact that the company had only been trading for a short time. The company's shortcomings in revenue generation, which were well known and rarely the focus of much objection in the run-up to the IPO, suddenly became cause for righteous outrage by investors. One digital analyst, Eric Jackson, went so far as to predict, only weeks after the IPO, that Facebook would be "gone" by the end of the decade.[8] Facebook's stock will continue to rise and fall, but its true value cannot be judged by its first few minutes, days, or weeks.

The Facebook IPO reflected another challenge in our society. The underwriters as well as the NASDAQ were blamed for numerous technical errors and trading glitches that caused the stock to start off on a rocky footing. Even after weeks of investigation, no one could say for sure what exactly happened to cause the problems. The technology and the trading patterns were apparently so complex and so fast that even those who were in charge of setting the rules could not determine how the events played out.

Millennials did not ask for, nor create, this dizzying fast future world. It's a world that prior generations propelled into existence. But we are the ones who have to live in it and who have to make this world work better for our generation and all who live in it.

THE 9/11 GENERATION?

An analysis of Millennial thinking by the political consulting firm Greenberg Quinlan Rosner concluded, "Formative moments in the lives of each American generation shape how they will view the world around them. . . . These collective experiences, along with more personal life events, sculpt a distinct world-view in this generation. The result: a generation that loudly asserts its individualism, yet shares common views of tolerance and community."[9]

Much has been made of the impact of 9/11 on Millennials. *Newsweek* labeled us the "9/11 Generation" just two months after the attack. The actual experience of the attacks may prove to be one of the first seminal generational moments that was simultaneously unifying and fragmenting. Despite frequent comparisons between the assassination of President Kennedy and 9/11, the two events are quite dissimilar. Many of our parents first saw the Kennedy news through the eyes of Walter Cronkite, who famously took off his glasses, revealing his normally stoic face to be wet with tears as he looked up at the clock to report the exact time and the death of the American president. In 1963, with only a handful of media outlets and the infrequency of truly breaking news, there was a greater uniformity in the way people experienced the tragedy, or at the very least how they initially learned about it. The Kennedy assassination truly marked the first time that the vast majority of Americans shared a profound national experience via television, watching almost the exact same content. At one point during Kennedy's funeral, over 60 percent of American households tuned into the same live feed. According to *TV Guide*, the day of John F. Kennedy's funeral represented the highest number of Americans ever to watch the same scenes on television simultaneously.[10] Almost all of our parents can remember the details of their own experience of the Kennedy assassination in vivid detail, nearly half a century later. That kind of coverage no longer occupies the same command over the American experience.

When Millennials heard that a plane had crashed into the World Trade Center on September 11, 2001, the news arrived in fragments. There was no single moment of impact, as there had been with the Kennedy assassination. Shortly after the first plane hit, we heard about the second plane; then we learned about the attacks in Shanksville, Pennsylvania, and at the Pentagon. Then we started hearing about Osama bin Laden, Al Qaeda, and the forces behind the attack. Next came the commentary, analysis, interpretations, proclamations, and declarations from every angle, a product of the then-bourgeoning 24/7 news media environment. No matter where Millennials were receiving the news, we all saw similar visuals and heard similar sounds—and on TV we saw those images and graphics over and over and over. This actually took away from the deep and unifying kind of impact felt during the Kennedy assassination coverage in a prior era. Unlike the image of Walter Cronkite taking off his glasses, the image of the sailor kissing the nurse in Times Square celebrating the end of World War II, the man standing in front of the tank in Tiananmen Square, or the girl crying over the body of the dying student at Kent State, there is no such single overarching identifiable image for 9/11. Instead, there are many images, many sounds, and many videos. What we've come to call "9/11" was really a series of events and a vast amount of news, not to mention multiple paradigm shifts in our understanding of America and the world. All this unfolded over a period of months, beginning on that day in 2001. Although it was a seminal event, the event was hardly experienced in the same way by each individual Millennial.

Is it possible for the impact of 9/11 on the Millennial Generation to be overstated? "Absolutely," says Mary Yonkman, twenty-nine, who works at The Mission Continues, an organization that helps wounded and disabled veterans engage with new forms of public service. "I don't think about 9/11 on a daily basis; it's not a reason why I'm involved in service. That isn't what defines me, or this generation. Some Millennials have entered service because of 9/11, but just as many, or more, got involved for many other reasons." Speaking of her husband, who is a Navy pilot, Mary added, "His service isn't defined by 9/11." He signed up for the Navy right after the attacks, she says, because "he never wanted other children to feel what he felt that day. That wasn't just about 9/11; it was about helping to shape a different world."

There is no doubt that 9/11 is a critical part of this generation's experience. It set off an important series of activities and attitudes, particularly in encouraging Millennials to engage in military service as well as civilian civic action. In the wake of the attacks, young people began to volunteer for the armed forces in numbers that hadn't been seen since World War II. Vietnam had turned many young people off to military service; three decades later, 9/11 encouraged them to consider it. Thousands of young men and women instilled with a sense of civic duty dropped everything in order to serve their country. But 9/11 also brought people like Christopher Nulty, twenty-six, from Fairport Glen, New York, into civilian service and volunteerism. Nulty recalls "walking into the principal's office with one of my friends and deciding to organize a Red Cross drive. I knew that students in other schools were doing something similar, and I knew that my efforts combined with theirs and with the efforts of millions of other people across the country were part of something larger. For many Americans, it gave them a concrete reason to get involved with service. This desire for public service reached even beyond our local communities. You could say 9/11 nationalized the importance of service in the minds of a lot of young people."

Millennials were not the only demographic who became more engaged with traditional acts of service and citizenship after 9/11. But for us, it took place at a key time in our lives, just when we were in transition and trying to establish our identities. These were the impressionable and self-defining days when most of us were leaving or entering middle or high school. More specifically, it was just a week or two after most of us had returned from summer to our new routines. We were already in an intense process reorienting our lives, reconnecting with friends, focusing on the next new stage of life in our academic and social communities, when the twin towers were hit.

As a result of the attacks, many Millennials became more aware of foreign policy in some form or another. Many developed at least a temporary working knowledge of the key issues of the then-emerging war on terror. An American University study assessing the impact of September 11 on Millennials hinted at the deep impact on our worldview that those events had. The study found that in a post-9/11 world, Millennials were 67 percent more likely to follow news, and nearly half of the respondents said that 9/11 had made them "more likely to study international affairs." The same study found that in the five years immediately following 9/11, language courses in Arabic and Persian became more popular on college campuses, as did religion and international affairs courses.[11]

Slowly, over the next five or six years, the themes of a new world, with new dangers, new complexities, new fears—but also new needs for cooperation, problem-solving, and public service—would start to weave their way into our thinking. Scott Merrick, twenty-seven, told me that the events of 9/11 woke him up "to the complexities, terror, and unlimited bounds to which extremists would go to cause pain to their enemies. Responsibility to teach tolerance and freedom of religion became vitally important, even amongst the harshest of times where it was easy to hate an entire religion."

The emotional impact of 9/11 dovetailed with the intellectual impact. We saw people drop everything and rush to help at Ground Zero. We saw neighbors helping neighbors and random acts of kindness. We heard the stories of good deeds, people risking their own lives to save someone they didn't even know, individual citizens pitching in to help their friends, their town, their state, their country, and their world. These acts and stories of heroism were inspiring to Millennials, especially at a moment when we were developing our values and our worldview. These experiences helped create a great reservoir of personal commitment among Millennials to be willing to get involved, to contribute, and to "do the right thing." Of course, in these moments we experienced fear, anxiety, and stress about our own physical safety and that of our families and communities. But overriding the fear and the trauma, we experienced a brief shining moment when communities came together and showed us America at its best.

Knowing from the very beginning of our lives that there are people in the world who wish us ill and despise our values, we grew up fast, without illusions about the world and America's place in it. We could have become a generation traumatized, cowed, and afraid, but we became the exact opposite. Shedding the idyllic illusions of childhood, knowing we live in a complex world with many dangers, has made us more prepared to adapt and evolve, more balanced in our thinking, and more able to cope. It has helped to emphasize the *pragmatic* in our pragmatic idealism. In his book *The Way We'll Be*, pollster John Zogby observed that, as a result of this generation's experiences with 9/11 and the wars in Iraq and Afghanistan, Millennials "want a foreign policy as inclusive and embracive as they are."[12] Ben Cole, twenty-four, who grew up near Manhattan, explained the impact 9/11 had on him this way: "For the first time, I was forced to look outside the small sphere I had inhabited in my childhood. It was around this time that I took up a keen interest in international affairs. 9/11 and the understanding that came from it planted the seeds of the international work I'm doing now."

While some rightly bemoan the absence of "civics education" in schools, there was, for at least a little while after 9/11, a surge in civic-mindedness that proved very important to the identity of our generation. Millennials began to realize what a group of people with a powerful message for positive change could do. We learned not only that we should try to do good in the world, but that if we tried, we could make a meaningful change. That commitment has lasted. According to one analysis, Millennials overwhelmingly believed that the attack on 9/11 meant that America should be more connected with the rest of the world.[13] Leah Adinolfi, who works with Millennial volunteers at the United Way, has seen firsthand that events like 9/11 have caused Millennials to "believe in the power of the community coming together" and that "together they could make a difference."[14]

The attacks of 9/11 played a major role in instilling a sense of service and civic duty in the members of the Millennial Generation. When the first class of college students who had experienced 9/11 graduated, applications for Teach for America were up 40 percent and Peace Corps applications were up 80 percent. Many more graduates were choosing not-for-profit careers, and fewer were taking jobs on Wall Street (and this was in the boom years of 2005–2007, before the crash of 2008).[15] A 2005 study by the Corporation for National and Community Service found a 20 percent increase in volunteerism of Millennials in the three years following 9/11.[16]

These statistics led to an important update for Robert Putnam, author of the book *Bowling Alone*, which had been published in 2000. In the book Putnam argued that America's civic institutions were in decline and that Americans had become cut off and atomized from each other. But in the wake of 9/11, he was pleasantly surprised to see the changes in the American sense of community, especially among Millennials. He observed that 9/11 "reinforced a sense of obligation to a cause greater than oneself. In terms of civic engagement, it could be a really new day."[17]

Unfortunately, the spirit of unity and confidence in our country that followed 9/11 was broken apart in 2003 with the onset of the Iraq War. Opposition to that war was one of the first overtly political causes that some Millennials took up. The support Americans enjoyed from the global community on 9/11 turned in short order into angry international opposition to America's policies. These realities eroded the pristine new spirit of civic engagement that had briefly swept America. While much of the country remains quite polarized today, the unified civic spirit felt by Millennials remains powerful and enduring. Millennials remain willing in both mindset and action to pitch in for change, to recognize a responsibility, to serve, and to give something back to the community.

The Millennials' civic-mindedness is the product of multiple influences. Our Boomer parents are famous for their history of activism, particularly during the 1960s. So as parents a few decades later, Boomers introduced that activist sensibility to their children. Scott Merrick told me that those regular conversations he had with his parents "always meant that I had a view of what was going on in the world. They challenged me to ask questions, and if I didn't agree with something, to ask why. . . . This helped shape my ability to reason and take into consideration ideas and philosophies that may not be aligned with my own."

During the 1960s, when our parents were in their youth, they participated in the breaking down of the traditional family hierarchy, rebelling against their parents' and their family's values. This led many Boomers to envision a different type of relationship with their own children and a different type of family dynamic. Millennials tend to enjoy more open relationships with their family members, including participating in a wide-ranging set of conversations about civic and world affairs. Many Millennials grew up in homes where key ideas of the 1960s—favoring tolerance, fighting against injustice, doing something about problems, and a good citizen's responsibility to try to change things for

the better—were as much a part of their formative years as more traditional life lessons. This was especially true for girls and for African
Americans, Latinos, and other minorities, since Boomers were the first
generation of parents to deliberately instill in their Millennial children
the possibility of "being anyone you want to be," and the necessity of
fighting back against discrimination and those who would deny their
children opportunity. As Brittney Boyd, an African American Millennial, then a senior at Friendly High School in Fort Washington, Maryland, remarked after Obama's election, "It's a pivotal moment, because
forty years ago, Martin Luther King Jr. was marching for desegregation,
and now we have a person of color who I believe was well qualified to be
president. Everybody has hope now."[18]

While the fighting in Iraq and Afghanistan has wound down, the reality is that these wars have raged for the majority of the Millennials'
conscious lives. But as the wars dragged on the embedded reporters
who had provided wall-to-wall coverage came home, and Afghanistan
and Iraq came to occupy a place further and further to the margins of
American life. These wars haven't required a great deal of sacrifice from
today's eighteen to twenty-four year olds, the age cohort that typically
fights and dies in wars. Although many Millennial men and women did
and do serve, the volunteer nature of today's military has meant that
most of us were not forced or even particularly encouraged to do so.
Most of us have remained unmobilized and largely uninvolved at home.
Unlike our grandparents' generation, whose members were almost all
deeply engaged in the war effort for World War II, either at home or
overseas, and also unlike our parents' generation, who were consumed
by the divisive nature of the Vietnam War, we have had to sacrifice little,
and most of us have had the luxury of remaining very distant. Nearly 50
percent of young men served in the armed forces during World War II
(women served, too, but at that time it was still relatively rare). Yet less
than 5 percent of the men and women in the Millennial Generation
have served in the armed forces during Iraq and Afghanistan.[19]

   While Millennials might not all have a personal connection to the
war, we have been aware of the issues involved and the trajectory of
the war's progress. In fact, these experiences seem to have strengthened

our generation's commitment to tolerance and human rights. According to a 2004 National Election Survey, 57 percent of Millennials classified human rights as a "very important" emphasis of American foreign policy, significantly higher than any other age cohort. This strong consensus was attributed in large part to the aftereffects of 9/11 and the war in Iraq, from concern about Guantanamo and Abu Ghraib, to the plight of Kurds in Iraq and women in Afghanistan.[20]

Have the stay-at-home Millennials lost an appreciation for sacrifice? Have we been acculturated to assume that some "other" people will always step up to fight our battles? I put this question to Seth Moulton, a Millennial who, much to his parents' dismay, enlisted in the Marines shortly before 9/11. Seth fought in Afghanistan and then in Iraq, where he served as a top aide to General David Petraeus, then the overall commander of U.S. forces in the field. When I spoke with Seth, he told me he was concerned about the divide between those who have served and those who have not. "Today it's a much smaller slice of America that serves in the military. Only those who choose to serve have to worry about their safety, their friends, their family back home. Everybody else knows they're not going to get drafted . . . there's this divide and there are all these people who are eighteen-, nineteen-year-olds who never even considered going and never even think about the fact that it's their peers who are fighting this war." It's not a lack of caring or a lack of patriotism, and certainly not a lack of desire to serve. For most Millennials, though, service has acquired a different meaning than fighting in the armed *services*, which was once the traditional way to "serve" one's country.

Many in this generation followed the war from the outside, discussing and debating it, while remaining more removed from it than any prior generational experience with war. On August 18, 2010, when the final combat brigade left Iraq, one of those in that brigade was a lieutenant, Steven DeWitt, from San Jose, California. Lt. DeWitt recounted to embedded reporter Richard Engel how he watched the war start on TV when he was just a seventeen-year-old high school student. Now—leading a quiet convoy across the Iraqi border into Kuwait with hardly any fanfare—he spoke with mixed emotions. He called Iraq "a war that has defined this generation of military men and women."

America has been suffering from war fatigue for some time now.

These wars entered our lives with "shock and awe" and then—more quietly—seeped into our consciousness, where they've stayed—albeit quietly—and where they may never fully leave. In the process, it seems that we've come to accept, although not necessarily embrace, foreign conflict and war as part of our world. Indeed, 84 percent of Millennials now believe that terrorism will always be with us.[21] Given the U.S. involvement in the Middle East for much of our lives, Millennials watched the events in Iran in 2009–2010 and the Arab Spring in 2011–2012 with great interest. These were movements of our generational brothers and sisters. The people of these Arab nations were demonstrating that Millennials all over the world were pragmatic idealists, eager to remake their societies in new and positive ways, and that the force of the prior trend toward radical jihadists was losing its hold among the Millennial population in those countries.

The precision U.S. Navy Seal mission that killed Osama bin Laden on May 1, 2011, was as important for its symbolism as for its practical significance. But it was seen as a special victory for Millennials. We embraced and celebrated a sense of closure to a decade-long war on terror and the hunt for Osama bin Laden that had dominated our lives. We placed a bookend on an era of American history we had grown up with. Upon the death of bin Laden, Iraq veteran Paul Rieckhoff, founder of the advocacy organization Iraq and Afghanistan Veterans of America, commented, "When I was young, I worried my generation would never experience historic events like my grandfather's did. I don't anymore. Every generation has their defining moments. This is one of ours."[22] Young people who were anti-war and never thought the United States should have gone into Iraq in the first place celebrated along with veterans who had not only gone to Iraq but fought and been wounded there. Rallies and spontaneous celebrations broke out in parks, bars, college campuses, and homes around the country. Millennials grabbed their cell phones, cameras, and blackberries and took the celebrations viral instantly. On that night and into the next day, we engaged in a dialogue online and offline in a way we couldn't have on September 11, 2001. The events of the night Bin Laden was killed generated three thousand tweets per second, the longest sustained tweet rate ever seen on Twitter.[23]

■   ■   ■

On April 20, 1999, at Columbine High School in Colorado, two students opened fire, killing thirteen people and wounding twenty-one more. For most Millennials, the Columbine massacre took place while we were in elementary, middle, or high school, although some of us were just toddlers. We saw the images of our peers and knew intuitively that, while this was a rare event, it could just as easily have happened to us in our school. If 9/11 was our defining moment for political and global engagement, Columbine was perhaps our most defining psychological and emotional moment. Mary Yonkman, a teenager at the time, recalled her Indiana high school principal's announcement after the shootings that the school planned to bring in metal detectors. But more important than the metal detectors was the need for students to take notice and say something if they saw something troubling in classmates' behavior. Eleven years later, she vividly remembered the feeling she had at that moment: "That was so empowering for me . . . the idea the principal would say: we'll put in metal detectors and systems, but ultimately, me and my peers are the ones who have the best chance of helping someone in trouble." While every school put in place different specific measures in response to Columbine, Mary's feeling that she could and should reach out to her peers was common across the generation. Writing on the eleventh anniversary of the Columbine shootings, the Millennial editors of the Arizona State University paper put it well: "We have been shaped by tragedy—advancements and successes too, but tragedy without a doubt. Our growing-up years were marred by violent events . . . we have heightened sensitivity, and our [awareness of our own] mortality shows us how much we can do with our lives. The events that marked our childhood and adolescence have made us a socially conscious generation."[24]

Millennials have come to understand that we're not going to eliminate violence, much as we might like to, just like we're not going to eliminate war or terrorism. But we can be aware. We can try to help those in psychological trouble and we can try to protect ourselves and be responsible to each other. Regarding the Millennials' experiences of shared tragedy, Frank Harrison, twenty-seven, opined that an experience like Columbine "shocks us into a sense of community. It's not a sense of fear—'Are we next?' 'Could it happen here?' It's more a sense of urgency that we have to stay together."[25]

Columbine also led to an increased focus on child protection and safety by schools, parents, and government at all levels. As Neil Howe, the author of the first major book about Millennials, *Millennials Rising*, observed in a 2009 report, as a result of post-Columbine discussion and concerns, "Millennials have been the objects of one of the great child protection movements in American history . . . from the surge in child-safety rules and devices . . . to the lockdown of public schools to the heightened security of college dorm rooms and workplaces. Like a castle under construction, new bricks keep getting added—V-chips and 'smart lockers' last month, campus underage drinking monitors this month, wellness seminars and life counseling in workplaces next month."[26]

Even as our parents and administrators try to take the risk out of childhood, Millennials have increasingly faced up to those risks in a generally well-balanced manner. Neither Columbine nor 9/11 made us paranoid or excessively fearful. We live knowing the reality of our world as a fundamentally dangerous place. But we still have to live our lives, and we can't allow fear to dominate us. Columbine was preceded by horrific events like Waco and the Oklahoma City bombing and followed by other tragedies, including more school shootings at Virginia Tech and 9/11. Silas Pugatch, a Millennial who lived in the Washington area during the DC sniper attacks in 2002, said that these rogue tragic incidents helped our generation, allowing us to "just kind of realize you're at a great time in life and you should just enjoy it while you can, because you never know."[27] Andrew Siddons, twenty-six, echoes that opinion: "I didn't see what good it would do to just live in fear."[28]

While some, like psychologist Robin Gurwitch, who works with the National Child Traumatic Stress Network in Oklahoma City, were concerned that "so many tragic events in a short time" would produce a "cumulative traumatic impact on the generation," Millennials seem to have proven that we are more resilient.

Just as Columbine shaped our thinking about our relationships with each other, the national headlines of the 1990s shaped our thinking about politics and our political leaders. In the mid-1990s we saw the beginning of a series of scandals, led by the Bill Clinton–Monica Lewinsky affair and President Clinton's subsequent impeachment. The Lewinsky scandal happened as Millennials were just becoming old enough to un-

derstand political events—and sex. With all its historic political narrative, as well as the personal and steamy sexual story, for most Millennials
Bill Clinton's affair with Monica Lewinsky and impeachment was our
introduction to national politics. Our parents or grandparents may have
learned of the personal character flaws of FDR or JFK, but not until
long after they were dead. Millennials, on the other hand, never had
the opportunity to know Clinton without the context of the scandal; instead, we knew about his problems almost from the first moment we understood he was president. Despite the scandal, Clinton was a president
whom most Millennials at the time liked, respected, and trusted—and
someone Millennials still consider an important and respected figure
today. As a result, we developed a built-in assumption that politicians—
even the best of them—carry baggage.

The imperfection and humanity of politicians became our political
reality. From the Clinton years on, little in politics—personal or policy-
oriented—would surprise us. Millennials internalized this notion fairly
quickly, and we were able to separate that understanding from our feelings about the politicians themselves. According to a 1998 CBS/*New
York Times* poll of Millennials who were then between the ages of thirteen and seventeen, "A majority of the teen-agers approve of the way
President Clinton is doing his job, and consider the Lewinsky episode
a 'private matter' for the president." After Clinton, political scandals,
especially those involving sex, would become much more central to the
media's depiction of politics. Political operatives would devote more
time to trying to create, expose, and defend against these controversies,
and the 24/7 media environment would become obsessed with cover-
ing them. The narratives would become even more lurid and explicit.
While malfeasance and nefarious acts ranging from financial corruption
to sexual escapades have always been a part of American politics, until
the later part of the twentieth century they frequently went unreported
and thus were unknown to the general public. But in the last twenty
years, acts of illegal and inappropriate behavior have received unprecedented media coverage. In the wake of Clinton's impeachment, even the
most personal and formerly private details became much, much more
widely discussed in the fishbowl of the media and public opinion.

The partisan rancor and "Washington gridlock" that reached new

heights (or lower depths) during the Clinton years became the new normal for politics in America at the turn of the millennium. As Timothy
Egan wrote in the *New York Times*, the Clinton years "ushered in the
modern era of hyper-partisanship. Right-wing talk radio hosts were just
entering their steroid phase, threatening any Republican who voted for
a bill that ultimately led to budget surpluses. From then on, nobody
could 'respectfully disagree.' Moderates were called wussies, traitors
and socialists." Today, he continues, things are "coarser still with the
'Tea Party' extremists, who taught Republicans in Congress how to
shout 'You lie!' to the president and cast aspersions on something so
innocuous as a pep talk to school children."[29]

We saw government fail in another stark way in the aftermath of
Hurricane Katrina in the summer of 2005. Throughout America, and
indeed all over the world, people could not believe the images they saw
on television of an American government standing by idly while American citizens were subjected to horrifying conditions and treatment in
the wake of the hurricane that destroyed large parts of their city.

When I interviewed then Congressman Adam Putnam—one of
the youngest members of Congress at the time he was first elected—
he observed that after 9/11, Millennials "believed the government has
more of a role in their life and that faith was restored and strengthened after 9/11." However, he added, "that same faith was shaken
in the response to Hurricane Katrina, where you saw local, state,
and federal government entities that were not as responsive as they
could have been or should have been." In a case where most people
of varying political ideologies agreed that government needed to play
a significant role, government failed. The imagery of Washington
abandoning mostly poor African Americans in a majority black city
made Katrina one of the most striking racially tinged events of our
formative years.

However, the Millennial perspective on race is very different from
the perspective of Boomers when they were our age. We've grown up
in a world that is very much the product of the civil rights movement
that many in our parents' generation championed, and our peers and
public figures have been of all ethnicities. As a result, Millennials have a
"default" position of openness when it comes to racial issues. But Hur-

ricane Katrina reminded Millennials that racism, and the impoverish-ment, discrimination, and marginalization of whole populations that it produces, is not just the product of attitudes and ideas, but of sys-temic problems with our governmental, economic, and even physical infrastructure. While we were never ignorant of the existence of ra-cial problems as we were growing up, Katrina put a spotlight on the fact that continuing to combat racism would be a responsibility of our generation—not just in terms of basic rights or "integration," but in terms of addressing the real causes of economic and institutionalized racial disparity.

As with other challenges in the last decade, Millennials saw Ka-trina as a time to engage in volunteerism and philanthropy. Millenni-als around the country—many far from New Orleans—raised money through bake sales and organized packages to send down to their dis-placed peers. Millennials of all ages came to New Orleans with school and church groups to try and help rebuild the city. Brian Bordainick, a Millennial from New York State who was among those who came to New Orleans to help, reflected on his experiences: "Many of us look abroad for chances to get knee-deep in recovery work, and I think for the first time in our generation there was work to be done, and a large group of young people rose up to take the challenge."

From Monica to Katrina, with the important exceptions of the period of time immediately after 9/11 and the excitement of the 2008 Obama campaign, Millennials have rarely seen our political system or our political leaders in an overwhelmingly positive light. This stands in stark contrast to the way that many of our parents and especially our grandparents saw the New Deal of FDR or the Camelot of JFK or the Great Society of LBJ. Without idealizing the politics of a previous era, it is safe to say that for our parents and grandparents, it was a common occurrence to see comprehensive legislation pushed through as a re-sult of bipartisan efforts by members of Congress and the White House working together. Having never seen politics in any other form than today's rancor and gridlock, Millennials are the least likely to be sur-prised that Obama is facing challenges in bringing about the sweeping changes he campaigned for. Perhaps this is one of the reasons youth support for Obama, although it has dropped since its 2009 inauguration zenith, is still the highest of any age demographic.[30] This same mentality gives us hope to keep pushing pragmatically and patiently for solutions to problems.

It is said that the Boomers, reared in an era of the invention of "instant" products, wanted "instant" solutions. Some experts mistook this as a permanent trend for young people. But the Millennials, reared in an even faster future than the Boomers, like to sip their carefully brewed and mixed coffee beverages slowly at Starbucks. We really don't expect instant solutions. We assume real solutions to real problems will take time, and that we have to keep at it.

In addition to political scandals, Millennials were witnesses in our formative years to major corporate malfeasance during the early 2000s. Although those situations are now largely forgotten (or dwarfed by the financial crisis of 2008), the Enron crisis in 2001 and the WorldCom collapse in 2002 played a significant role in shaping the Millennial outlook on the role of business and power in our society. We saw multibillion-dollar corporations crumble to dust and several of their corporate leaders locked up in jail. This happened just as many Millennials were first beginning to think about their future and careers. As a result of witnessing these scandals, Leah Reynolds, a specialist in generational issues for Deloitte Consulting, concluded that for Millennials, "Wall Street has lost its luster."[31]

Enron and WorldCom showed us the worst of business, so that, just as we are not shocked when politicians fall short, we are not shocked when we learn that a corporation like BP willfully defied safety protocols and chose to cut costs rather than take the measures that could have prevented the 2010 oil spill off the Louisiana coast.

In speaking of our formative experiences, Neil Howe observed, "Boomers came of age worrying that institutions may be too strong . . . in all these instances, the real danger seems to come not from out-of-control institutions, but from out-of-control individuals, teams of conspirators, or failed states, who have become a menace to humanity because national or global institutions are not strong enough to even monitor them. Hence the hugely positive shift in the youth perception of government power."[32] Understanding the rogue actors and out-of-control individuals that Howe describes, our generation seems able to

separate out bad apples from the groups and institutions they are part
of. Howe's co-author, the late William Strauss, added in reference to
events like 9/11 and Columbine, "When random (bad) things happen,
we tend to want to smell the flowers a bit." Millennials, he predicted,
will be inspired to "re-create a civil society and address the question of
how something like this can happen."[33] And it certainly seems that we
are trying to do just that.

While we have lived through attacks on our cities and our schools,
long wars, and several cycles of corporate greed throughout our formative years, we were for the most part blessed with a very good economy. We saw what the world could be like if the economy prospered.
But we weren't conscious and aware of that for long enough to take it
for granted. We've lived through the fear and terror of 9/11, but we've
also lived through the excitement and empowerment created by the diffusion of web-based technologies and social media. The combination
of a good economy and a complicated, turbulent social and political
climate—and our society's responses to all these things—allowed many
Millennials to experience the best and worst of our world simultaneously. It also showed us that we could play a role in crafting our world
to be better or worse.

One word has come up time and time again to describe this generation, both by those in it as well as outsiders: resilient. Kelsey Swindler, twenty-two, described it this way: "I see a sense of resilience in the
people I surround myself with. And I would say that's characteristic of
a lot of people in our generation. A sense that things can change and
things can happen. We haven't been jaded yet. Even though we've lived
through these terrible moments, they really shaped our consciousness."

These major moments of crisis will certainly not be the last of their
kind we will see in our lifetimes. Even today, after five years of economic
recession, the employment picture remains extremely challenging for
young people. But given what we have been through and our positive
responses, it seems that our resilience will be one of our strongest assets as we move from our formative years into our more mature years.
A New America Foundation Report noted, "Millennials are becoming
adults during a post-2000 decade bracketed by national emergencies
(9/11 and the financial crisis of 2008) which are clearly reversing" the

emphasis on individuals over communities which dominated the previous generation.[34] Dave Verhaagen, a child and adolescent psychologist and author of *Parenting the Millennial Generation*, adds to the consensus, remarking that "going through adversity is something that can potentially strengthen the character of a generation. . . . They've seen the worst terrorist attack in U.S. history, the worst natural disaster in U.S. history and the worst mass killing ever. . . . They have a more realistic view of the world than previous generations."[35]

In the face of a depressing and catastrophic recession ongoing since 2008, the Pew Center found that while Millennials are not "happy with their current economic circumstances, they remain highly optimistic about their financial future."[36] The study found that 88 percent of Millennials believed that, although they didn't earn enough at the moment, they would be able to live good middle-class lives in the future. This compared with only 46 percent of Boomers who shared such optimism. In the midst of major economic upheaval, this calm, confident, and optimistic attitude will be an important force in leading this generation out of these deep challenges.

These generation-defining events took place as we were forming our identity, consciousness, and values. As a result, they cast a long shadow of influence over who we are today. This illustrates one of the primary ways that Millennials approach the world: we understand realities as realities, while remaining determined to pursue our own goals, and to find our way regardless of what people around us might be saying. We're unfazed by faux controversies and distractions. We don't waste time on debates about whether technology is good or bad, we just maximize its benefits while acknowledging that the Internet, like everything else, has risks. We don't live in total fear because of 9/11 or Columbine; we understand the world better and remain determined to do our part to make it a more livable place. We don't write off all politicians because we've seen a string of them in sex scandals. This view of the world is another manifestation of our pragmatic idealism. It's a mindset that has allowed us to succeed throughout our very stormy formative years—and one that will allow us to succeed in the face of whatever might come next.

THREE

First Digitals

Technology breaks down barriers. . . . You can define
community and associate yourself across any sort of boundary
or divide culturally . . . my world is enriched in a way that
the past generations didn't even know was possible.
—Maya Enista Smith, twenty-nine, CEO, Mobilize.org

At 8:27 p.m. on Saturday, April 23, 2005, Jawed Karim saw a message on the screen of his computer: "Video uploaded." He smiled as he played it back. It was a nineteen-second video he had recorded during a recent trip with a friend to the San Diego Zoo. The video begins with Jawed observing the elephants as he says, "All right, so here we are in front of the elephants." Jawed aptly titled the video "Me at the Zoo." Today, this moment seems so completely unremarkable that it is hardly worth mentioning, but it actually changed the world. Like the famous moment in nineteenth-century history when Alexander Graham Bell said, "Watson, come here, I need you," announcing the birth of telephony, Jawed Karim had just uploaded the first video to a website called YouTube, a website he was working on developing with some friends.

Jawed is now thirty-four; YouTube is eight. Jawed and the other two YouTube founders, Chad Hurley and Steve Chen, sold YouTube to Google in 2006, for almost $2 billion. Jawed went on to start a fund called Youniversity Ventures, which helps students develop businesses. YouTube went from being a cool, fun idea to one of the most popular and heavily trafficked websites in the world. In an average sixty-day period currently, more video is uploaded to YouTube than the entirety of video created by U.S. television networks in the prior sixty years.[1] During the last seven years, as YouTube has progressed from the clearinghouse for stupid animal tricks to a major force in political, journalistic, and personal lives (while remaining true to its stupid pet tricks origins), YouTube's leaders and subsequently their Google owners had to learn to manage complex privacy and copyright issues and transition from a countercultural rogue video site to a major media player, partnering along the way with all kinds of traditional institutions. Jawed, YouTube, and Google all grew up together. For a company, a system, a person, or a generation, growth follows a similar general trajectory: initial creation, introduction to others, maturation, independence, and pervasiveness, even while constantly dealing with growing pains and conflict. Millennials see their lives as deeply interconnected with technology. When Millennials were asked what defines our generation, 24 percent pointed to technology as a common thread, more than any other factor.[2]

The maturation of the Millennials has occurred along a similar timeline and in concert with the maturation of the digital world. As we've grown, there have been few forces that have influenced and defined our development more than the technological revolution. And no other demographic has had a greater impact on the trajectory of that revolution than Millennials.

The actual "dawn" of the digital era occurred between the late 1980s and the early 1990s, when most of the Millennial Generation was very young and some of us not yet born.[3] Millennials became aware of the technology around us after some of the key moments in digital history, but before digital technology had been widely commercialized and popularized. As children, we used a basic set of tools used by our parents or older siblings that had already been in existence for over a decade. Green-screen desktop computers are still in our distant memory, along with big, clunky car phones and CD-ROMs. While computers existed when we were infants, their capabilities and their pervasiveness were radically different from computer technology today. The World Wide Web, broadband, commercial e-mail, handheld devices, eBooks, smartphones, and social media all lay ahead.

As first and second graders, we could write reports with a word processing program and spell check them; design our own books, posters, and journals with "clip art"; play simple games like *Oregon Trail*; e-mail "pen pals" in other countries; and look things up on an encyclopedia program from Microsoft called Encarta. Through our formative years, however, digital technology began to make quantum leaps almost daily in the variety and extent of applications and functions, as well as user access and mobility. Suddenly, millions of websites were springing up. Everything was moving to the web. E-mail became the communication tool of choice. At the dawn of the new millennium, our society was confronted with big questions about the potential and power of new digital technologies. How fast would they be adopted? Would people trust their credit cards to the Internet? What about privacy and security? What would happen to analog institutions in a web-centered world? Would society be split between digital haves and have-nots? Into the huge unknown void of the answers to these and other profound and complex questions stepped the Millennials—a group well-versed enough to craft and design websites and to use the technology that existed in the early 2000s but also able to go to the next level and serve as the architects of the new web 2.0 that was about to be born. And when you grow up together and share so many experiences, you understand each other and, on the whole, you end up sharing instincts and values.

The Millennial Generation and digital technology, like two good friends, have been there at all the important moments for each other. When we needed a last-minute solution late on the night before a school paper was due, Google was there to save us. When we graduated, we uploaded our graduation pictures to Facebook; when we met a new girlfriend or boyfriend, we texted our friends to tell them. From text messaging to Twitter, from the music revolution of the iPod to the app revolution of the iPhone, from Google to *Wikipedia*, from Instagram to Facebook, from YouTube to Pinterest, and from Tumblr to Groupon, Millennials have truly dominated the creation, early adoption, and proliferation of the majority of the most important digital technologies of the last decade. Millennials were present for the creation of and often were the creators of the blogs, social media platforms, apps, and digital content that have produced a new structure for politics, media, business, and human experience. The civic mindset and the importance of collaboration and sharing had already become major parts of our Millennial system of values. An understanding of business as a part of life— but a part that should be constrained—generated our early belief that websites should be free and that if they were to be advertiser-supported, the ads should be minimal and appropriate.

Being present at the birth of the major 2.0 tech inventions, Millennials have come to use them almost intuitively. The fact that we understand these technologies so naturally and instinctively—and so soon after their introduction—means we can innovate and apply them more quickly, and often on more meaningful and creative levels. Today's digital technology would be inherently different had it been designed by earlier generations of software engineers. By adopting that technology and demonstrating its virtues and uses, Millennials have become the catalytic force to bring in other generations and eventually diffuse the technology throughout society and around the world.

Many of the major movements and technologies in history have been created or initially adopted by the young and open-minded. But the power for the young to influence and create new technology has grown tremendously in the past decade. A century ago, young inventors had big dreams, but it took them years of work and investment to develop their mechanical ideas. Henry Ford was in his mid-forties by the time the Model T rolled off the production line; so too was Edison when the first light bulb flicked on. In the late 1970s and early 1980s, Steve Jobs and Bill Gates were college dropouts when they introduced the first Apple computer and the first Microsoft operating system. But although they both came out of a young, geeky culture, the high price points of their products, dictated by the prevailing cost of new technologies, meant that their target market was business users and affluent established households. An important factor driving the accelerated advancement of digital technology has been the way young people have become passionate users and advocates of the technologies in large part because of the way they reflect our values and worldview. In the 1960s and '70s, young people were often suspicious of the top-down power of technology. "Do not fold, spindle, or mutilate this card" was the imperious, fear-inducing rubric that came with a computer-graded test form four decades ago. Technology in the twenty-first century has been introduced in just the opposite spirit: Here, this is yours, take it and use it however you want. It's free. It's really easy to personalize it and customize it. Get creative. Make it your own.

As a result, the impact of the Millennial Generation on the past decade's technological revolution can be felt on two major levels. Extraordinary Millennials have become founders of the key companies that are powering our modern world, from Jawed and his colleagues at YouTube to Facebook, Twitter, Groupon, Foursquare, Instagram, Tumblr, and hundreds of other companies. At the same time, all Millennials help spread and shape these technologies every day. Brilliant Millennial computer scientists, software architects, designers, and visionaries of all types have been key players in building the new social-mobile-digital world. But the rest of us have not been lazy recipients or mere users of this technology. The tools we have at our disposal are not mere aids that have been laid down for us, like Henry Ford giving us an automobile to drive, or Bill Gates giving us an operating system to run. Instead, our very use and creative application of today's digital technologies make us co-creators and allows us to co-evolve with each successive digital development. In the twentieth century, big companies that managed to get control of major software architectures kept them close to the vest, refusing to open up their jealously guarded APIs (application programming interfaces) to anyone but company insiders and a small group of developers they controlled. In the last few years, however, the most visionary companies are opening up their APIs and driving a new era of innovation by making them available to the developer community. This trend allows even those without software training to write an app or create a game or design a function without having to reinvent the wheel. Millennial entrepreneurs, gamers, coders, and app developers are huge beneficiaries of an ever more open API world.

The fast future has been an environment full of constant changes and big questions, necessitating rapid adaptability. One casualty of not being able to adapt fast enough to the fast future is the social network MySpace, which launched in 2003 and for some time enjoyed the title of the world's most popular social network. By 2006, it had become the most visited website, surpassing even Google. But in 2008, Facebook surpassed MySpace and then continued its meteoric rise, exponentially increasing its dominance for the next five years. When News Corp. bought MySpace for $580 million in 2005, few could have imagined that it would be resold in 2011 for less than 10 percent of that price. Many factors are responsible for the rise and fall of MySpace. But one of the most important problems was that its founders were non-

Millennials trying to cater to a Millennial audience. That problem worsened immensely after the company was sold to News Corp. Meanwhile, Facebook rejected all efforts to move out of its Millennial leadership culture and still maintains tremendously strong bonds to the Millennial Generation, even as it has become a huge business and a social network for all demographics from middle-aged professionals to seniors.

ONE FOOT IN THE OLD WORLD, ONE FOOT IN THE NEW

There is no doubt that Millennials are the most connected and plugged-in generation in history. But in our earliest years, we saw the world without ubiquitous and dominating technology. Having grown up with the development of core elements of the new digital technology infrastructure gives us a distinct advantage in a fast future world where technological change is central to our lives. In fact, in the fast future the digital world cannot be separated from the world at large. Soraya Darabi, twenty-nine, co-founder of Foodspotting, told me candidly: "I've seen a lot of smart older generation types, people my mom's age, really adjust to technology, to make it a fluid part of their lives, to embrace it. But there's something just not cool about the way they're using it, and sometimes I cringe for them. They study like it's a textbook, while I speak the language of tech the way a native speaker does, or at least the way a three year old in an immersion school gains fluency."

There is a meaningful gap in Internet usage between Millennials and older generations. According to a 2011 nationwide survey, nearly 100 percent of college students and 92 percent of nonstudents aged eighteen to twenty-four are online, compared with 75 percent of adults.[4] But we aren't just superusers of this technology; Millennials more intuitively understand its logic, approach, interactions, and possibilities. We've also been teaching it to others for a significant portion of our lives. Many of us became our family's "chief information officer" when we were in our teens, just as first-generation American children of early twentieth-century immigrants represented their parents in all kinds of adult activities, because only the younger generation spoke fluent English.

Writing presciently about this phenomenon in a now decade-old white paper, Marc Prensky, a noted expert on the interaction of technology and education, coined the now-popular term "digital natives." He defined digital natives in contrast to digital immigrants. The latter, he said, were people who "arrived" online, after having a substantial life offline, noting, "As digital immigrants learn—like all immigrants, some better than others—to adapt to their environment, they always retain, to some degree, their 'accent,' that is, their foot in the past. The 'digital immigrant accent' can be seen in such things as turning to the Internet for information second rather than first, or in reading the manual for a program rather than assuming that the program itself will teach us to use it. Boomers were 'socialized' differently from their kids, and are now in the process of learning a new language. And a language learned later in life, scientists tell us, goes into a different part of the brain."[5] Prensky goes on to point out other quaint examples of the "digital immigrant accent," including phone calls to ask someone if they received an e-mail, printing out a document to edit it by hand, and showing people a website on your computer instead of e-mailing them a link.

Digital immigrants include our Boomer parents and even some members of Generation X, as well as most of the people who are our teachers, mentors, and employers. Like traditional immigrants, most digital immigrants are able to assimilate and become almost indistinguishable from natives, although some inevitably resist assimilation and decry the new technology, and others try to assimilate and fail. Digital natives, on the other hand, are like the children of many traditional immigrants. They have known little else but the language, culture, and reality of their birth country. Steve Emerson, the former president of Haverford College and a digital immigrant who lives among his first digital students, explained part of the paradigm shift: "As children of the Internet, they function as parallel processors, making their way by creating a personal mosaic of information and insight that they have integrated and assembled into the world as they see it . . . they do all of this on the fly, much the way a web page gets assembled by databases and the way the Web itself provides many pieces of larger pictures. . . . My generation, on the other hand, seems to prefer clear authorship and packaged sets of ideas that are of a piece and complete. Perhaps this is the fundamental difference between being raised on TV, which is largely linear and packaged, versus being raised on the Web, which is by definition fragmented."[6]

One important caveat: Millennials are not truly digital "natives." Most Millennials didn't have access to new technologies until very late in our childhood. Having cut our teeth on research in brick and mortar school libraries as young children, we can still apply that kind of skill set in foraging for information in the new media age. Many Millennials went through all of high school without Facebook. Many of us went through high school without cell phones as well, and it wasn't until much later that we used mobile apps. Millennials also didn't know what iPads were until well into their teenage years.

We are the last generation to have at least one foot in the "old" world of the late twentieth century, even if most of our body and mind are now fully immersed in the new digital landscape of the twenty-first century. We have the best of both worlds: skills that were formed in important years of our development that have made lasting impressions, combined with the ability to live just like digital natives. Thus we're probably best thought of as "first digitals." We're the first generation to grow up with digital technology and the Internet playing a dominating role in the world, yet without it dominating our lives since birth. The first generation of true digital natives is the generation after us, whose members have never been alive in a world without the web.

As first digitals, we accept new technological innovations as a constant reality of our world, and we look with open minds at how we can apply technologies to innovate and problem solve. That does not mean that we are unaware of the challenges and problems associated with new technology. Ben Cole, twenty-four, observes, "Just as we can use technology to understand the broader world, we can also use it to restrict ourselves to media that only caters to our own viewpoints, cultures, and locales. How can we get people to look further, to seek mutual understanding, and to collaborate not only with like-minded individuals but also with those from disparate backgrounds and points of view?"

With the same attitude of pragmatic idealism we have seen elsewhere in their thinking, Millennials accept the reality that technology is and will be the dominant force in our society's media, knowledge-gathering, education, culture, communication, and expression. Digital immigrants, although they are less skeptical and afraid of the web 2.0 world than they were a decade ago, have not all bought into the inevitability of the technological future. For many of them, the adoption of new technology is still imagined as a choice—perhaps an extreme pole on a pendulum that will someday swing back the other way. These new technological platforms and tools, which may be seen as amusing or novel by our older counterparts, are now utilities for how Millennials do business and live our lives. This doesn't mean, by the way, that we won't have our own version of nostalgia, in fact even in this digital era, Millennials use technology where it is practical and where it adds value to their lives, but they still hunger for physical experiences, enjoy being outdoors, and increasingly are trying to spend more time with the people they care most about in person. But regardless of technology's direction over the next few decades, Millennials will have little problem adapting to whatever comes next. First digitals, accepting the reality of the digital age, understand there is no going backward. We are focused on the opportunities the web presents, and we are willing to work constructively on its problems and challenges.

What does being a generation of first digitals mean for our future? The real revolution is not the mere existence of the web or social media. It is in the way we use new technology and media to increase the impact of our ideas, generate wholly new ideas that are now thinkable, and confront old problems that technology can now help us solve for the first time.

Today's technology infrastructure allows any person to express their thoughts, ideas, or creations on a large platform, with the potential to be heard by an audience. With ubiquitous Internet access, almost anyone can publish, share, and promote content online for free. The potential power for individuals to push their ideas into the world has never been greater or more widely shared. In another era, politically astute minds could scoff at the hypocrisy contained within the promise of freedom of speech. "Freedom of the press is guaranteed only to those who own one," said twentieth-century journalist and press critic A.J. Liebling.[7] But today, everyone has an opportunity to speak online. The participatory content movement has pushed the mainstream media to create regular opportunities for average citizens to become part of even the most elite news operations. If you go to the *New York Times* website to read an article, you can usually post a comment and become part of the discussion. CNN provides an opportunity for more direct content involvement through its iReports. During Hurricane Katrina, hundreds of people living in New Orleans witnessed the devastation caused in their neighborhoods, filmed it, and uploaded their footage to CNN iReport. Ever since then, average citizens have been able to become iReporters for key events.

Whether or not mainstream media organizations are able to adapt to the digital era and remain mainstream, the current transition period reflects both the opportunity and the limitations of the new role of citizen journalists. Ultimately, more important than broadcasting our voices into the mainstream media is the ability, demonstrated by a growing number of Millennials, to become experts and online influencers through their own efforts, and to make their voices heard through the skillful use of new platforms. There are those, like Michael van Poppel, now twenty-three, who launched Breaking News Online as a Twitter-based news service when he was eighteen and has since transformed it into a major web-based wire service. He counts among his accomplishments acquiring and selling to Reuters an authentic Osama bin Laden tape, among other journalistic coups. On the other end of the spectrum, there are personal blogs where people share stories or their opinions on that day's news.

Some 58 percent of Millennials create some form of online content every week, and 71 percent of Millennials engage with peer-created content on a regular basis.[8] In the course of their everyday lives, Millennials have become content creators and publishers. Although we must acknowledge the unevenness and sometimes limited breadth of this content, the acts of creating, publishing, and sharing ideas and images are more widespread among Millennials today than in any generation in any human society that has ever gone before. What's more, even less meaningful content can still build a sense of community. Don Tapscott, author of *Wikinomics*, writes that "the simple act of participating in an online community makes a contribution . . . whether one's building a business on Amazon . . . producing a video clip for YouTube [or] creating a community around his or her Flickr photo collection."[9]

Americans, in particular, have been famous for our willingness to form new groups and voluntary associations since at least the days of

de Tocqueville, who observed the tendency toward voluntary association as one of the defining and revolutionary characteristics of American society in the early nineteenth century. De Tocqueville observed
that for Americans, it was second nature to share ideas and form groups
around those ideas: "In the United States, as soon as several inhabitants
have taken up an opinion or an idea they wish to promote in society,
they seek each other out and unite together once they have made contact. From that moment, they are no longer isolated but have become
a power seen from afar whose activities serve as an example and whose
words are heeded."[10]

Yet in the last third of the twentieth century, a variety of social trends
conspired to take us away from traditional group associations that had
once included fraternal orders, precinct-based political clubs, shared
babysitting groups, scouting, and bowling leagues.[11] Americans were in
retreat from de Tocqueville's vision of all-pervading restless democratic
activity and joining together around common ideas. Today, however,
as Millennials have met up with social media, they are able to recreate
the kind of identification with associations and interest groups that was
once a natural part of the fabric of American life—exactly the type of
energy de Tocqueville found so quintessentially American almost two
centuries ago.

Use of Facebook provides a proxy for this process of engagement.
As of January 2012, one out of every five online page views were logged
on Facebook and the average visit to the site was twenty minutes.[12] This
is our network of associations and interest groups, and we draw from it
many of the same kind of ideas, attitudes, and inspirations that de Tocqueville found among early nineteenth-century Americans. Superficial
posts on Facebook walls or simplistic clicks to "like" something may not
change the world, but neither did neighborly greetings over the back-
yard fence in the 1950s. Yet these forms of communication provide human connection in a lonely and often alienating world, while laying the
basis for sharing ideas on important political and social questions. From
the "lonely crowd" to "bowling alone," philosophers and sociologists
of the late twentieth century were deeply worried about the shredding
bonds of community in American life. Yet few of these keen observers
who understood the pain of Americans ever more alienated from each

other could have foreseen the ways that social media would begin to provide (at the very least) an alternative, and perhaps even a solution, to this half-century slide into community oblivion.

As a society, some of us have always been content creators. From soldiers who wrote regular letters home during World War II, to those ordinary people who kept extraordinary journals and diaries of their life and times, content creation has never been the exclusive province of poets, novelists, journalists, and other professional content creators. But never before have so many people seen themselves as content creators, and neither has publishing and diffusing individual content ever been so easy. Now, technology allows many more of us to be creators, publishers, and distributors of content, and we can do it so much more frequently, and in real time.

Although we may not have used the terminology, throughout history people have been segregated into those who created and published content and those who could not. These categories were essentially synonymous with the powerful and the powerless, respectively. Even in relatively recent times, unless you were a columnist, public intellectual, or recognized authority, you could write all you wanted, but you had a hard time getting published or heard. The same was true for other forms of expression—film, music, literature. But today, you can express yourself and get a response to your content. The fact that we can be heard now gives a new dimension and potentially even new meaning to our lives and to our human experience. As technology writer Howard Rheingold said of Millennials and our passion for content creation, "They're doing it because expressing yourself and connecting with your peers is something that you want to do when you're a teenager. . . . Never before have we had ways to express ourselves that the entire world could see."[13]

The "credentials" for becoming a creator have been essentially eliminated. But with all the content that now exists—thirty-eight hours of new YouTube content being uploaded every minute—we have to ask: who will filter, edit, and curate all that content? The "removal of editors" phenomenon has many deeply concerned. Mark Bauerlein, consistent with his view of Millennials as the "dumbest generation," has observed, however one-sidedly and incorrectly: "Young people are drowning in digital diversions which pervade teen stuff, and the adult realities of history and civics simply can't break through."[14] Former Google CEO Eric Schmidt, a Boomer and someone who ought to know a little bit about how people use the Internet, has disagreed strongly, saying that Millennials are "the smartest, not the dumbest . . . they are quicker, more global, more savvy, and better educated. They are the most connected generation; they care deeper about each other than we ever did."[15]

DIGITAL BRAINS AND DIGITAL BEINGS

New media and technology have taken the historic philosophical conundrum about the dividing line between democracy and mob rule into a new dimension. Intellectuals and social theorists who would normally be expected to champion the expansion of expression are now among those who fret the most over the way young people—and everyone else—are drowning in information, misinformation, and distractions of all types, without filters, curation, prioritization, credibility, and trust.

Societies have wrestled with these issues since the beginning of time. Socrates worried that the youth of Athens were being corrupted by undisciplined thinking. Savonarola burned some of the greatest books of the Renaissance because he believed them to be immoral and corrupting of the Florentine population. And those of us who were in school performances of *The Music Man* know that, as recently as the late nineteenth century, people thought the introduction of pool halls would distract and undermine the moral and intellectual fiber of youth.

But Millennials will perhaps surprise the rest of society by being able to adjust more readily than older-generation intellectuals might fear to the new torrent of digital media swirling all around us. There can be no doubt that we now have more untrustworthy new sources than we have ever had before, as well as more sources whose trustworthiness is ambiguous. David Feldman, twenty-nine, defends Millennials. "I think what needs to be known about my generation is that we don't treat the Internet like a textbook," he says. "We treat it as this organic growing source of information, and I think we know where to find this information, and we'll question any information we're given before we take any of it at face value."[16] A site that has clout among our peers—that has been recommended by people we know personally and trust—will gain our own confidence quickly. We know how to evaluate what we can trust. Referring to Millennials, pollster James Zogby observed that "bullshit detectors are set on high all the time; like guild merchants of yore, they bite every metaphorical coin they are handed to see if the metal is real or false."[17]

As we've come into the digital age, a major social concern has been the possibility of a digital divide arising between highly educated, affluent citizens who could afford the latest technology, and the less educated and poor who could not afford a computer for their home or an Internet connection. While we have not yet arrived at the point where "everyone" is online, we are getting there quite quickly. And while technology is not necessarily a panacea for solving socioeconomic and racial divisions, in general, the new digital technology has diffused into the hands of ordinary people from all walks of life and all socioeconomic and racial backgrounds at an incredibly rapid speed. Most Millennials now have daily access to the Internet, and cell phone use is ubiquitous: 93 percent regularly go online and a similar 93 percent have cell phones.[18]

What's more, a Pew Research Center Report on the state of mobile access concluded, "Minority Americans lead the way when it comes to mobile access—especially mobile access using handheld devices. Nearly two-thirds of African Americans (64 percent) and Latinos (63 percent) are wireless Internet users, and minority Americans are significantly more likely to own a cell phone than their white counterparts (87 percent of blacks and Latinos own a cell phone, compared with 80 percent of whites). Additionally, black and Latino cell phone owners take advantage of a much wider array of their phones' data functions compared to white cell phone owners."[19] In addition, laptop ownership (the standard nonmobile device for Millennials) is even among white, African American, and Latino Millennials.[20] They aren't just going online, they are also active content creators, with 76 percent of African Americans and 81 percent of Latinos saying they used video sites like YouTube as of 2011.[21]

These numbers show that technology, cell phones and the Internet can be valuable equalizers, leveling the playing field for young people. Given the resources and assets available online, simply having this connection provides economically struggling young people with more potential and opportunity than ever before. From one computer (or a cell phone)—for free—they can launch themselves into a whole world of knowledge and engagement. Jamal, a twenty-three-year-old aspiring artist from New York, told me he would have been lost without a computer: "I make T-shirts and skateboards. I wouldn't be able to get them done without my computer." While sociologists and political pundits two decades ago thought that access to technology would be the dividing line between digital haves and have-nots, that has not been the case. As we have seen, many traditional have-nots have not had a problem getting access. Today's web can be very empowering for any individual, but there is still important work to be done to improve digital literacy among all young people so that they can all reap the full potential of technology to achieve success.

As Internet pioneer and senior Google adviser Vint Cerf has said, "The Internet provides an amazing opportunity for young people to express themselves creatively and access immense quantities of useful information. Kids are using geospatial, mobile, and social networking technologies, for example, to learn in new, interactive ways. The Internet also provides unparalleled opportunities for free expression, enabling kids and adults alike to deliver tremendous benefit to society by voicing sometimes unpopular, inconvenient, or controversial opinions."[22]

There isn't just potential. We've already made meaningful accomplishments using this technology, from the geopolitical to the mundane. Millennials have harnessed the power of technology to elect a president in America and topple dictators in the Middle East. Millennials have also used the web to crowdsource solutions to everyday problems and questions, from finding a roommate to figuring out a moral dilemma. Technology allows us to tap into the ideas of our friends and the collective wisdom of people anywhere and everywhere and put this knowledge to our own use for new purposes, big or small. In fact, more than sixty million Americans now report receiving help with major life problems via social networks each year.[23]

An overarching reality of the twenty-first century is that technology has become as essential to us as breathing and drinking water. The most essential business, economic, and social systems are increasingly Internet-based. Those who ask if we would be better off if all this technology could be taken away, or those who think we should use as little as possible of it, are advocating in favor of a choice we don't have. Because Millennials are comfortable in a fast future world, the process for us to adopt a new technology is quick and easy. If we're frustrated by new features of a device or a website redesign, we are forced to cope. Is this a sign that something is wrong? That we use our cell phones or the Internet too much? Overreliance or overdependence is not the issue. These are tools that play key roles every day in enhancing our experiences, so why wouldn't we use them extensively? Although each of us, and society as a whole, will surely develop new cultural conventions (i.e., digital "manners"), it makes no sense to go on arbitrary "technology diets" as some experts have suggested, just to make sure we can survive without our digital tools, any more than a serious person could be expected to give up driving out of a concern that someday it might be important to know how to ride a horse. There are critical debates that lie ahead over issues from privacy to standards, and from copyright law to cyber security. Millennials will be among the key participants in this debate over the next decades. But we will come at the issues from the starting point of seeking solutions to real problems and establishing policies that improve society's interactions with technology, not from today's frequent starting point of fear of the changes technology brings in its wake.

One of the most frequently voiced fears about the way Millennials' lives are so closely interwoven with technology is that the new digital way of life is somehow causing us to lose our humanism. Sociologists like Sherry Turkle, MIT professor and author of *Alone Together*, worry that with communities increasingly constructed around social media, we will lose the human desire to meet in groups and in person. Face-to-face communication is as old as humanity itself, and it has always played a key role in our personal relations and societal advancement, from prehistoric humans recounting the story of their hunts, to the dialogues of great minds in the salons of enlightenment Europe or among the American revolutionaries. In the words of an ad for Apple's iPad 2: "We'll never stop sharing our memories, or getting lost in a good book. We'll always cook dinner and cheer for our favorite team. We'll still go to meetings, make home movies, and learn new things. But how we do all this will never be the same."

But we are not losing these skills; we are adapting them to new formats, relationships, and contexts. In fact, one of the major benefits of social networks and real-time social media in a hurried, complex world is the new ability to identify, find, and meet friends, romantic partners, like minds, and people who share our interests. S. Craig Watkins, a University of Texas–Austin professor who studies the effect of Facebook on young people, concludes, "Facebook is not supplanting face-to-face interactions between friends, family and colleagues. . . . In fact, we believe there is sufficient evidence that social media afford opportunities for new expressions of friendship, intimacy and community."[24]

If a Millennial has a thousand Facebook friends, it doesn't mean they think that they have a thousand very close friends. We don't view all of our "Facebook friends" as being actual friends. It's not uncommon for close friends to have minimal Facebook interaction, precisely because these are the people we want to see and talk to every day in person. As Tim, twenty-four, told me, "I feel much closer to my friends because of Facebook and iPhones. It's much easier to talk to anyone, everyone on this planet. In fact, it's improved my relationship with my friends." The rise of Facebook friends has not changed the desire for genuine friendship or intimacy. We will still see the people we most care about in person. Meanwhile, there is great value and potential in being able to stay in acquaintance-like touch, through casual Facebook interactions, with large numbers of people from many periods and phases of our lives.

For those who question whether Millennials have sufficient social interaction to develop empathy and other positive character traits, a study by Harris Interactive revealed that 55 percent of young people believe social networks are making them more aware of the difficulties their peers are experiencing, not less.[25]

As with many other issues, the Millennial experience may not hold true for the next generations younger than we are. Just as we have at least one foot in the "old" days of brick and mortar libraries at our elementary schools and handwritten letters sent by U.S. mail to friends and relatives, we also were the last generation to develop our closest high school friendships before Facebook was much of a factor in our lives. That's not true for those who are entering their teens today. Technology writer Reva Basch expresses her concerns about what lies ahead: "I got involved in social networks as an adult. I wonder about younger people who haven't yet formed a solid web of real-life relationships or learned how to function in a meat-space [that is, a real-life] social environment. I think there's a real downside there."[26] Indeed, many members of Generation Z—the generation that will succeed the Millennials—are learning basic information and skills via apps on their parents' phones; many have their own iPads. One YouTube video shows a toddler moving her hand on a print magazine and becoming frustrated that the magazine cover doesn't change in the way that an e-magazine would. While it's too early to make a definitive prediction about how technology will affect the way Generation Z thinks and acts, it's fair to say that with this kind of connectedness so early on, it will be radically different from the Millennials.

Every era has had its naysayers on the subject of how new technology will rob us of our human essence. At the time of Gutenberg, some intellectuals were very concerned that cheap, mass-printed books would ruin society and cause the quality of ideas and writing to decline. England's first official book censor declared in the 1600s that "more mischief than advantage" had been brought to the "Christian world by the Invention of Typography."[27] And the Spanish writer Lope de Vega worried as early as 1612: "So many books. . . . So much confusion/All around us an ocean of print/And most of it covered with froth."[28] Substitute "blogs" for "books," and the criticisms leveled at the Internet today are scarcely different.

Even the telephone was not unanimously welcomed when it arrived en masse in the early twentieth century. In 1923, Virginia Woolf quipped that the telephone "interrupts the most serious conversations and cuts short the most weighty observations."[29] But in fact, telephones enabled deeper and more constant human connections in an efficient way. Today, friends can be deeply engaged with each others' lives through text messages, phone calls from anywhere, and e-mails throughout the day, every day. Whether or not they see each other more or less than they would without the advent of e-mail and the telephone is not as important as the potential for an increased ability to interact and share human emotions and experiences.

In his meditation on simple living, *Walden*, the mid-nineteenth-century transcendentalist philosopher Henry David Thoreau observed, "Our inventions are wont to be pretty toys, which distract our attention from serious things. They are but improved means to an unimproved world. . . . We are in great haste to construct a magnetic telegraph from Maine to Texas; but Maine and Texas, it may be, have nothing important to communicate." Yet few historians would dispute the notion that the development of a common technological infrastructure—telegraph, telephone, railroads, highways, and so forth, reaching from Maine to Texas and in every other direction—laid the basis for America's great economic success over the century and a half since Thoreau wrote *Walden*. In like manner, in this era of new digital infrastructure, we will create the momentous ideas and important inventions of the future as a direct result of our new hyper-connected technologies and abilities.

An extensive study of the Millennials conducted by the Pew Research Center proclaimed Millennials to be the first "always connected" generation, always plugged in and connected to at least one device, if not many.[30] In addition to being connected, we understand that we have so much of the world's vast published knowledge at our fingertips, and that this is something new in our time. And we have the power to communicate instantly with people anywhere. From Google Books to the proliferation of web video, to trending topics in Twitter feeds, we continue to gain new abilities to dive deeper into the future toward which we are inevitably headed. That future is a world where most information, knowledge, creative pursuits, business, politics, commerce, and human communication takes place through a medium that looks and feels something like today's web-based technology, even as it morphs into web 3.0, and 4.0. These trends have strengthened this generation's position in the world. Futurist Jason Silva, thirty-one, believes that "we live in a world where technology extends what we can do. It extends our reach and our ability to impact things while allowing us to live exciting, fun-filled lives."

The great thinkers of antiquity and the great creators of science fiction would be amazed to find the merger of the Library at Alexandria with Dick Tracy's wrist radio. The ability to tap into all recorded knowledge and the ability to communicate with anyone anywhere are two of the oldest dreams of civilization. No wonder our generation is fascinated, and perhaps even a little bit obsessed, with these new magical powers. Yet some digital immigrant critics think there's something wrong and unnatural about the way our lives and thoughts mesh with the new technologies. They are concerned that our brains will atrophy under the constant attack of all these distractions. Dave Morin, thirty-two, an early Facebook engineer and founder of the social network Path, couldn't disagree more: "The Internet is how we think. We have developed a way of thinking that depends on being connected to an ever-changing graph of all the world's people and ideas. The Internet helps to define, evolve, and grow us. The Internet is social. The Internet is a way of life. The Internet provides context."[31]

Winifred Gallagher, author of *Rapt*, is one of those urging us to move into our future with less technology. Gallagher wants us to tune out our screens and our connectivity and focus on what's "really important" in our lives. One reviewer noted that once Gallagher "learned how hard it was for the brain to avoid paying attention to sounds, particularly other people's voices, she began carrying ear plugs with her. When you're trapped in a noisy subway car or a taxi with a TV that won't turn off, she says you have to build your own 'stimulus shelter.'"[32]

In her book, Gallagher suggests we all build a well-focused, undistracted life, eliminating constant e-mailing and checking Facebook. "Your life is the sum of what you focus on," Gallagher contends, asserting that we cannot be focused when we are online. She is so concerned with the problem that our time spent online is our time away from "important things" (according to her definition of what's important in life), that she recommends daily meditation, even a dedicated room in your house for meditation without the temptation of electronic stimuli. While I am sure that spending time away from electronic or other stimuli can be good for many people's mental and physical health, it is unclear that regular daily meditation sessions necessarily solve the problems of priorities, focus, and values that are among Gallagher's concerns. Even if we all agreed to turn our phones off regularly or spend one day a week with no Internet, it would not address the challenges to our brain and its ability to focus.

If you have ever had to deal with a weighty problem—a death in the family, a momentous career choice, an ethical problem—then you probably know that being able to get instantaneous input and support from your friends and family can be critical to helping you make the right decisions. Without denying that there are alienating and superficial aspects to electronic communication, it is important to note that there are also ways in which social media actually make us *more social* and electronic communication makes us *more of a community*. What's more, many of the really important things to us—our ideas, our friends, our schoolwork, our job search, our careers, our causes, our interests, and our families—in short, the things Gallagher wants us to focus on, can in fact increasingly be experienced online.

Millennials are not only adept at the constant switching of focus and transitions between online and off, we relish it. As Camilla Nord, twenty-two, explains: "Growing up digital wires us for fast, efficient research, international communication, exploring infinite venues for arts and performance expression, and distraction. But occasional distraction is a small price to pay for everything technology has given me, from reading medical journal articles published yesterday—or not even published yet—to the ability to call my parents in Washington, DC, while I'm at school."[33] As Camilla suggests, the true challenge for Millennials is not how to tune out electronic stimulation and digital information, but rather, how to make maximum use of the potential for ideas, exploration, creativity, and connectedness offered to us by the new tools of technology.

When I walked into a movie theater in late September 2010 for a screening of the film *The Social Network*—the plot of which centers on the creation of Facebook, led by its primary founder, Mark Zuckerberg—I had high expectations for the experience, based on the cast and creative team behind the project, including director David Fincher and screenwriter Aaron Sorkin. Although some people cringed at the idea of a Facebook movie, assuming that it would feature the website's proprietary functionalities such as "writing on walls" and "poking," the film hardly involved the experience of using Facebook at all. In fact, the beauty of the film was that it was not really about Facebook. Rather, *The Social Network* used the narrative of the company's founding to tell a story about the Millennial Generation and the experience of creation and innovation in the twenty-first century. *The Social Network* was hailed by many critics as the definitive expression of the Millennial experience in film. So said one of America's leading film critics, Peter Travers, of *Rolling Stone*. Zadie Smith, writing in the *New York Review of Books*, acknowledged that, although she finds the experience of Facebook disappointing (but a guilty pleasure that she can also find herself immersed in), she couldn't help but admit the film's generational resonance. Sarah Bowman, a Millennial from Fruitport, Michigan, said she loved it and thought it was "such an important movie for my generation . . . such an important idea for my generation!"[34] Carly Dahlen, twenty-eight, commented in her personal review that the movie "features a riveting story, but more importantly, it comprehensively captures the millennial experience. The movie is about the quintessential 21st Century communication tool—an online socializing platform—and features characters that embody the good and bad traits of the 'aughts' generation: driven personalities, selfish attitudes, and impulsive behavior."[35]

Audiences were divided by age group regarding how they felt about the movie on leaving the theater. Older people tended to think Mark Zuckerberg came off as arrogant and hubristic, an amoral nerd who didn't care about his friends and partners, and generally a bad omen for the future. Millennials and younger audiences tended to see in Zuckerberg a passionate believer in his ideas, someone who was capable of envisioning the future and fighting against all odds to bring it into being, and someone they respected. (The reality is surely more complicated, and the debate over how the film did or didn't capture Facebook's actual history will continue.) Millennials have a strong bond with Facebook because it is a natural extension of our experiences and our life—online. We gravitate toward technologies that enhance, but do not replace, our offline activities. Facebook's simple design, straightforward functionality, practical and efficient ease of use, and its cool and authentic sensibilities fit perfectly with Millennial attitudes. Ever-morphing and changing, Facebook's future is in a host of new applications and businesses. Just as Facebook helped Zynga succeed with Farmville and the creation of an entire new class of entertainment now known as social games, Facebook is rapidly becoming the leading distributor of all manner of virtual goods and applications and is in the process of becoming a payment system for everything you order online. In addition, Facebook has established itself as an important home for social and political causes. Indeed, one of the most popular apps on Facebook is Causes, which allows friends to ask friends to make direct contributions to charities they support. In addition, a feature created by the company that allows users to publicly declare themselves organ donors launched in May 2012 and has since been utilized by more than 275,000 people.[36]

Millennials believe in sharing offline, too. Ours is a generation reared with emphasis on "sharing" when we were very young, which morphed into "collaboration," "teamwork," and "transparency" as we got older. When Facebook redefined "sharing" as being open about your life and engaging in a dialogue with friends about your experiences and feelings, Millennials eagerly embraced it. For similar reasons, the Open Source, Creative Commons, and Freeware movements have found great support and been received with excitement among Millennials. A Millennial like Mark Zuckerberg may be no less ambitious than Boomers like Bill Gates or Steve Jobs, but the changing attitudes toward open versus proprietary standards and systems has distinguished software developed by Millennials from the existing software ecosystem. Facebook will no doubt face challenges in the years ahead. It may or may not be central to our lives in the long-term future. But the fact that our generation's "growing up years" mirrored Facebook's development (I graduated from college on the same day that Facebook launched its IPO) will always be part of the cultural background that our generation carries forward into other spheres of life.

The collaborative nature of the Internet has also led us to believe that we can address offline, real world problems in new, inventive ways. Take the challenge of street harassment. Emily May, thirty-two, is tackling that very issue with her organization Hollaback! Through its website and smartphone apps, Hollaback! encourages people who have been harassed on city streets to report their location and their story of harassment. May told me technology was the most natural way she could see trying to solve a longstanding problem to which there were no good answers. "When you're street harassed, you kind of just want to forget about it and pretend like it didn't happen," she says. "That's why, even though people are street harassed so often, there really hasn't been a big public conversation about it. Technology allows us to have that conversation, because it's no longer just a few activist voices. Everyone's voice can be involved in this. And I think that's where the change happens." Over time, the stories build on each other and empower people to be part of a community, addressing a problem that exists in neighborhoods, cities, and worldwide together through collaborative action. To date, more than half a million accounts of street harassment have been submitted on Hollaback's platform worldwide. A socialized web allows Millennials the opportunity to harness their collective knowledge, wisdom, and support to address such social problems.

In September 2010, eighteen-year-old Rutgers University freshman Tyler Clementi tragically took his own life by jumping off the George Washington Bridge in New York. The circumstances surrounding his suicide were widely reported in the media the following week: Tyler's roommate, Dharun Ravi, with assistance from another student, secretly broadcast a live webcam feed of Tyler—who was gay, but not out— kissing another man. Tyler's roommate tweeted as this occurred, and then repeated this broadcast two days later. All accounts seem to suggest that Tyler was driven to his death by the fallout around campus of the broadcast. Shortly before Tyler jumped to his death, he posted his intention to kill himself on his Facebook page.[37] It was a painful tragedy for the people directly involved. And many of us all over the country and the world who did not know Tyler could feel his pain and suffering.

Commentators sought to generalize the tragedy as an instance of "suicide caused by social media." Indeed, the case did go to trial; ultimately Dharun Ravi was convicted on several counts, including invasion of privacy, and served twenty days in prison. But it was not Facebook, Twitter, or webcams that killed Tyler. It was the students who broadcast the video feed to the world, their mean-spirited behavior, their lack of moral responsibility, and, of course, Tyler's own inner struggle that contributed to the tragedy. Bullying and having "fun" at the expense of others are major problems in schools today, and have been around for millennia. Before today's technology, the same incident might have occurred as a result of secret notes or photos being passed around. The "inefficiencies" have been taken out of the process. If you broadcast something live with a webcam, you don't get the night to sleep on it and think better of it, which you might have if you were determined to make video tape copies and pass them around. Armed with technology, we can do things faster, more easily, and more impulsively. The speed and immediate scalability of technology makes the impact of hate in a case like Tyler Clementi's more public and more immediate. The same is true of the many cyber-bullying incidents that have occurred across the country in the last few years. But blaming the technology won't help. Instead, we must emphasize a new set of moral ideals and balances as we decide how to cope with a world where powerful new tools have been put in virtually everyone's hands.

One hopeful note to emerge from the Tyler Clementi case was that the same new media that was used irresponsibly by Tyler's fellow students was almost immediately used to provide a counter-message of comfort and acceptance to gay youth. A video effort called "It Gets Better" encouraged citizens and celebrities to submit video recordings with "from the heart" messages to help depressed and discouraged gay youth get through challenging times. In two months, It Gets Better generated over five thousand videos, which in turn received a collective fifteen million views.[38] In addition, an impassioned speech by Fort Worth city councilman Joel Burns about his own experiences being young and gay, first aired on a public access feed, hit YouTube and received over a half million views in its first week. With this kind of reach, it's fair to say that some solace has been given to some troubled gay youth in America and around the world. It's hard to imagine how a campaign like It Gets Better or Joel Burns's speech could have achieved so much success in an age without social media. So although bullying has become more prevalent in the digital age, the responses to it have also become more powerful. In 2012, after sending out mass texts to its list of over 1 million young people, the youth social-action organization DoSomething.org noticed that subscribers were texting back with deeply personal messages, everything from admissions that they had been sexually abused to confessions of suicidal feelings. DoSomething .org has since established a Crisis Text Line to address these distressing texts. The ability to communicate anonymously—something that is now possible through text messaging—has allowed many young people to talk about their problems and get help without having to take the often daunting step of walking into the office of a therapist, social worker, or school administrator.

As the Tyler Clementi case shows us, whether we like it or not, the nature of privacy is changing. Social network and privacy researcher Danah Boyd, who has focused her work on how young people interact with technology, described the changes in this way: "We've moved from a 'private by default, public through effort' culture to one that is now 'public by default, private through effort.'"[39] What privacy means in the digital age and how we come to terms with it is a serious issue for our generation. It goes far beyond how we present ourselves on Facebook. Large philosophical and cultural questions regarding what role privacy will play in the twenty-first century loom ahead of us, and Millennials will be at the forefront of shaping policy and practice in response. With so much of our personal data online, regularly available to be mined by corporate interests (and also available to hackers aiming to steal from our credit cards and bank accounts), the debate about who controls what data, for what purpose, and for how long is growing more pressing.

In Europe, where Internet privacy rules are generally stronger than in America, a movement has grown up around the "right to be forgotten," a code phrase for citizens, courts, and governments demanding that Google and other search engines provide you with methods for blocking searches of your name and personal information. But most of us don't even bother to exercise our ability to opt out of online databases.

Because of the power of social network platforms, we've been forced to intertwine our lives with for-profit companies. Just as TV was "free" to most American homes for the last sixty years for the "price" of being bombarded with commercials, social media and web tools are similarly "costless" to us today, at the expense of providing our information to marketers and databases that want to know more about us and sell us more stuff. Arguably, the current corporate hooks into our lives are far more powerful and more pernicious than they once were, due to the unique new ability to penetrate our online lives, follow us around, and learn about and target our interests and behaviors. Many of us missed the growing effort to use this data to increase profit, because we really liked their products and websites. By the time we began to notice they weren't exactly the companies we wanted them to be, the tipping point on giving up our private data had long passed.

In their early days, companies like Google and Facebook did behave differently than the companies of the mid- and late-twentieth century, placing special focus on social responsibility and concern for their user community. The cultural habits they prompted seemed in line with our values, allowing us to think that they would not act exactly the same as the capitalists of the early and mid-twentieth century. That may have been naive. While we hope that new digital companies will avoid doing overtly evil things with our data, we probably know that this is less than true.

Our intellectual concerns about privacy often conflict with the practical realities of living as a Millennial. Today, giving out our information is a necessity of life. We are aware that there are ways to opt out, just as there are long documents filled with legalese informing us of all the ways marketers can and will exploit our information unless we opt out. But we aren't willing to give up the easy efficiencies and the benefits that come from opting in, accepting the cookies from the websites we use, and storing all our data in the vulnerable cloud. It's too easy and too appealing to use one-click on Amazon to make purchases, get recommendations for Netflix movies and shows to watch, or socialize our experiences on sites across the web with Facebook Connect.

When polled, Millennials frequently say that they are concerned about their privacy online, but the number of Millennials who have taken action to safeguard their privacy is much smaller. On the whole, we've given the practicality of using digital technology priority over privacy. Few of us have stopped releasing our information, but that doesn't mean we don't express our displeasure.

In 2010 a group of Millennials, concerned with Facebook's privacy features, organized a "quit Facebook day" movement. A poll conducted just before the scheduled "quit day" revealed that 60 percent of Facebook users were considering.[40] But in the end, just 10,000 users quit Facebook that day. That same year, a group of NYU students

announced plans for an open source, more privacy-centric social network called Diaspora. In the Millennial spirit, Zuckerberg said that he
thought Diaspora itself was a "cool idea" and admired their philosophy
"that the world could be better and [then] saying, 'We should try to do
it.'" Zuckerberg donated an undisclosed sum to the open source seed
funding page for Diaspora on the popular fundraising site Kickstarter.[41]
However, Diaspora has since disbanded, as Facebook continues to grow
its users and traffic. Kanupriya Tewari, twenty-one, typified our generation's approach. Speaking of Facebook, she remarked that she "spent
like an hour trying to figure out how to limit my profile, and I couldn't.
I don't think they would look out for me," she added. "I have to look
out for me."[42]

The activities people and institutions can truly keep private are in
sharp decline. Even the U.S. government discovered this reality in the
wake of the WikiLeaks scandal in 2010. A generalized loss of privacy
has been the overall trend. While some companies have responded to
privacy concerns by adding features to increase privacy, most of these
initiatives have not been widely used. In 2010, Facebook created a set of
new privacy features that allowed users to share posts exclusively with
a select group of friends. In 2012, Facebook announced, along with the
debut of its app portal, that it would run disclaimers in front of all applications that were found to be pulling user data from Facebook to the
app company.[43] But only a fraction of Facebook users are actively using
these features.

One of the challenges with privacy is that much of the damage occurs
behind the scenes as our personal information is constantly gathered
by search engines and social networks without our explicit knowledge.
With so much of our commerce and communication online, giving out
private information is effectively a requirement to participate in the
digital world. Although we may not like it, as we browse the Internet,
our web history is being recorded. While we may prefer not to give out
our information to third parties, almost every website requires us to do
just that. So in order to buy the products and use the services that we
want to, we are left with little alternative but to submit our information—and just hope that it won't be used inappropriately.

By the time cyber-targeters or hackers are discovered, they've usually already caused a serious problem: your credit card has already been charged or your social security number has already been stolen. Laws, deterrents, and law enforcement will have to change in the years ahead. But we also need to sort out our philosophy on issues that can't be easily regulated by specific legislation. Millennials believe in privacy, but our boundaries and limitations have shifted. Prior to the rise of social media, people normally disclosed personal information selectively. We controlled who learned about where we lived, attended school, or worked, or who our friends were. But in the age of Facebook and LinkedIn, information once disclosed only to close friends—who we're dating, when we have broken up with someone, who we're marrying—is now online. When a woman becomes pregnant, every stage of her pregnancy is documented in public through photos, status updates, and comments. Then, as soon as the child is born, the parents begin documenting his or her life until the child is old enough to manage his or her own social media profile. These details and photos, once very personal and private, are now routinely published and shared with our friends as a matter of course and, as a result, with the public at large. Updates about our personal lives that we want to share with our friends have a way of leaking beyond our inner circles. With a simple Google search, anyone can find information about people that in an earlier era would have required hiring a private detective.

The idea of personal "branding" and "self-marketing" would have seemed outrageously narcissistic just a few years ago. But many Millennials know from experience that getting into college, finding a job, winning a contest, or just organizing a gathering of friends requires a certain amount of self-promotion. Thus, we have to have Facebook pages, websites, Twitter feeds, LinkedIn profiles, and blogs to let the world know we exist and to present our "brand." But since we also prize authenticity, we know that our digital presence can't be too far removed from the truth. This combination of factors reinforces our willingness to spill our personal information and views in a highly public way.

Some of this seems shocking to members of older generations. But Millennials seem to be triggering a long-term change in the culture to embrace sharing and make personal information about our lives more transparent. Millennials are at peace with this culture. Kitty, thirty-one, says casually, "Yeah, I am naked on the Internet." She's not worried about how she'll look back at her online profiles when she's older: "I'll be proud! It's a documentation of my youth, in a way. Even if it's just me, going back and Googling myself in twenty-five or thirty years. It's my self—what I used to be, what I used to do."[44]

In late 2009, the debut of Foursquare ushered in a new kind of "location-based" platform that encourages "check ins" when someone arrives at a certain location. Through these services, we are transparently telling the world exactly where we are and what we are doing. Location-based services, while fast-growing, have not mirrored the meteoric rise of other kinds of social media. Millennials retain a certain amount of skepticism about revealing exactly where they are at all times. We are absolutely a social and sharing generation, but the idea of regularly broadcasting where we are without commentary or explicit purpose is not perceived as valuable by many in our generation, even as there are some in Millennial circles who thrive on the chance to become the "mayor" of the neighborhood Starbucks by checking in there more than anyone else.

Platforms like Facebook, Foursquare, Twitter, and Google Plus encourage users to put forward their actual identity, almost to the point of requiring it, and most Millennials heed the call. If you don't use your real identity, friends won't be able to find you, and you won't get much out of the experience. A famous 1993 *New Yorker* cartoon depicted a dog surfing the Internet and a caption commenting on the potential of online anonymity: "On the Internet, nobody knows you're a dog." While many Millennials experiment with their expressions of identity online, most are not looking for anonymity. In general, we want to be known and to have an authentic identity on Facebook (although the debate about what constitutes the "real me" and what is actually "authentic" will continue). At the dawn of the Internet era, the online world and the "real" world were very clearly defined and different. You went online, then you left, re-entering the real world, and vice versa. Now, not only have the online and offline worlds merged in time and space, their characteristics have also grown more alike. Early on, the virtual world was marked by relative inaccessibility, an absence of guideposts and, for those who gained access, a total freedom to the point of lawlessness, inviting comparisons to the Wild West. As the Internet has been reined in by government regulation and companies trying to monetize the web, its economics, legality, and politics have begun to resemble those of the non-digital world. At the same time, the voluntary and radical transparency that the digital age has helped foist upon institutions and leaders has now begun to creep into the offline world. With decreasing separation between the two, there are more ways to hold these institutions and leaders accountable. The relationship between the real world and the virtual world will undoubtedly become more intricate as Millennials, who are driving this merger, get older.

THIS IS YOUR BRAIN ON THE INTERNET

A big, sprawling, and profound question hangs over the future of digital technology, the Millennials, and, in fact, all of human society. What is new technology doing to our brains? We know it is changing the ways we behave and communicate, but is it changing the ways we think and the content of our thoughts? And if so, what are the implications? The most articulate and outspoken of the commentators on this set of questions is Nicholas Carr, the technology and business writer whose 2008 cover story in *The Atlantic*, "Is Google Making Us Stupid?" and his subsequent 2010 book *The Shallows* (subtitled *What the Internet Is Doing to Our Brains*) served as a cautionary warning about the effects of digital technology on the human brain and its ability for rational, in-depth thought.

Carr's argument is worthy of serious attention. He has skipped the usual list of first-order concerns about the Internet (privacy, accountability, security, pornography, etc.) and chosen to focus on the way "Google" (by which he means all of digital technology) is making us "stupid" (by which he means less able to focus and think deeply, and less able to read and respond to extended long-form arguments). Despite all the beneficial attributes of electronic searching, web surfing, social media, e-books, web video, and so on, Carr believes that "Google" is essentially eroding our brain's capabilities for attention, focus, memory, in-depth analysis, deep learning, and deep thought. "The price we pay to assume technology's power is alienation," says Carr. The impact of "Google" on young brains that have been nurtured by electronic technology is to "numb the most intimate, the most human, of our natural capacities—those for reason, perception, memory, emotion. . . . While this cybernetic blurring of mind and machine may allow us to carry out certain cognitive tasks far more efficiently, it poses a threat to our integrity as human beings."[45]

For Carr, the medium really is the message. In his cosmology, the rise of print books and newspapers in the era after Gutenberg leads directly to the Enlightenment and to modern democratic, scientific, and rational thought. According to Carr, a society that grows up in the culture of print books is able to engage in a rigorous process of seeking truth and knowledge from facts, evidence, thought, discussion, and substantive debate. On the other hand, a society whose young people grow up enmeshed with electronic technology is destined to gloss constantly over the surface of truth and knowledge, dipping in only to shallow levels before being distracted away to the next idea, link, or incoming message. Under the pernicious influence of the web, we are losing our ability to think critically, Carr maintains, and will wind up as some kind of lost civilization.

Anyone who ever sat down to work at a computer and discovered hours later that they had accomplished nothing on an important project, yet had been all over the world and back many times in their web surfing, knows that there is at least some validity to Carr's concerns. But he takes genuine problems, such as the dangers of distraction and superficiality, and stretches them into a theory at odds with his own version of human history.

Carr bemoans the rise of e-books and tablets, not to mention condemns the subversive influence on our minds of Google, Facebook, Twitter, YouTube, and the rest of the web. He chooses an obvious anomaly and generalizes it. Carr worries in the opening pages of his book that "We've reached a point where a Rhodes scholar like Florida State's Joe O'Shea—a philosophy major, no less—is comfortable admitting not only that he doesn't read books but that he doesn't see any particular need to read them."[46] Carr quotes O'Shea as saying, "Sitting down and going through a book from cover to cover doesn't make sense. . . . It's not a good use of my time, as I can get all the information I need faster through the Web."[47] According to Carr, O'Shea claims that, for the skilled online hunter, "books become superfluous." Carr maintains that O'Shea's view is "more the rule than the exception."[48]

I found the story about Joe O'Shea hard to believe, so I contacted O'Shea to find out more. O'Shea told me that Carr had actually taken his quote from Don Tapscott's 2009 book, *Grown Up Digital.* O'Shea reports he had a conversation in 2008 with Tapscott, but says he was not quoted correctly by him. Carr picked up Tapscott's version, relying on another print book without checking first with O'Shea, whose contact information is easily available through searching Google. Carr appears to have eliminated one sentence that appears in Tapscott's version of O'Shea's remarks, in which O'Shea says that some of his research "comes from books." O'Shea explained to me, "I told Don that I didn't typically use books when seeking information—that I use Google and Google Books. I think that is true for most people now, especially when seeking quick information. But of course I read books! . . . Books provide a medium for a fuller discussion and argument than short articles. They are also an essential form of art and expression. We would be much worse off as a society if people didn't read books! You also can't graduate from college without reading books—much less get a PhD from Oxford." Not only is O'Shea a reader of books, but when I spoke to him in June 2012, he told me he was finishing a book manuscript for Johns Hopkins University Press. He signed off saying, "I sure hope people are still reading books!"[49]

As it turns out, Carr has misquoted his key expert witness at the very outset of his argument, while emphasizing that O'Shea's lack of involvement with books is supposed to be the "rule," not the "exception."

Since the web is such a rich storehouse of knowledge, including a vast number of books that are instantly accessible, more and more of our knowledge and learning will be web-based in the coming years. But is this really worrisome? Whether reading takes place online or in a printed book is an increasingly irrelevant fact in today's world. Most experts believe that more people are reading more total words every day as a result of the torrent of electronic information coming at them, as well as all the features of personalization, customization, and interactivity that screen-based reading brings to the reader. Yet Carr insists that the *form* of reading, not the content, is what matters most.

Millennials have grown up in a world where physicality matters less and less. What matters most is ease of access and what we can do with the material once we find it. The ability to read something on the web and then jump to deeper or related content—exactly what Carr worries about, incidentally—is a comparative asset over a print book, not a limitation. Kelsey Swindler, twenty-two, was excited by the potential of a new edition of Jack Kerouac's *On the Road* that offered interactive maps, audio recordings, and other multimedia, thinking it perfect for Millennials. Says Kelsey: "This audience will download this book to their iPad, Kindle, Nook, or smartphone and read, listen, watch, and consume the story in an entirely new way." In response to the idea that this was dangerous for our brains or somehow less valuable, she asked, "What do we do about it? Adapt. At this point there is little else we can do. I am still a lover of traditional books, and will always treasure the look and feel of an old hardcover copy, worn by many page-turns and more than a few previous readers. But I'm also a modern-day consumer, and a reader that is desperate to continue reading, learning, and experiencing books, even if it is in new, unforeseen ways."

If Carr encountered Kelsey, he would no doubt place her in the same tableau of national tragedy as O'Shea. Carr argues throughout his print book that no electronic technology can match print's benefits for critical thinking and democracy. He claims there has been degradation in the amount individuals can absorb and learn from material presented electronically versus the same material presented in a print book. Invoking numerous experts on neuroscience, Carr argues that traditional reading influences the wiring of the brain as it develops, in ways that then form the basis for the rest of the process by which modern humans absorb knowledge. His corollary is the assumption that our brains have already been optimized for knowledge-gathering through the modality of reading print books, and any adaptation is a step backward or away from the ideal. According to Carr, "For the last five centuries, ever since Gutenberg's printing press made book reading a popular pursuit, the linear, literary mind has been at the center of art, science, and society. As supple as it is subtle, it's been the imaginative mind of the Renaissance, the rational mind of the Enlightenment, the inventive mind of the Industrial Revolution, even the subversive mind of Modernism. It may soon be yesterday's mind."[50]

Carr provides an artful disquisition on all the naysayers from history who imagined that the next form of media would prove to be the downfall of society. Socrates, for example, is said to have decried the idea of writing down great ideas, because they would allow men of only ordinary minds to appropriate great ideas from men with extraordinary minds, and they would allow everyone to "cheat" by reading things instead of being forced to memorize them. Summarizing the argument of Socrates, Carr writes: "By substituting outer symbols for inner memories, writing threatens to make us shallower thinkers . . . [and prevents] us from achieving the intellectual depth that leads to wisdom and true happiness."[51] Socrates thought writing would ruin in-depth thinking, but it obviously did no such thing. Carr's argument against digital technology is merely another step in a historical pattern of the old guard rejecting transformative technologies as dangerous and civilization-threatening—a pattern that he himself documents has continued from the days of Socrates to modern times.

If it is of any consolation to Carr, the rejection of the book may not be happening as fast as he imagines. Millennials have been somewhat slower to accept e-books than some initially anticipated, although there is no doubt that e-books are a part of the future. But as of 2013, Millennials continue to find physical books valuable. In fact, the U.S. Book Consumer Demographics and Buying Behaviors Annual Review found that in 2011 Millennials bought more books than any other age group, surpassing Boomers for the first time.[52] We do not blindly accept every new technology. We appreciate functionality and usefulness, and many of us, like Kelsey, actually have affection for some of the very things that Carr assumes we disdain.

Consider the case of *Wikipedia*. Millennials now in their mid-twenties witnessed the arrival of *Wikipedia* in middle and high school, causing unprecedented consternation for teachers and administrators. As the grown-ups saw it, *Wikipedia* had made the answers to homework questions easily available. Students were imagined to be rushing home to cut, paste, and plagiarize this new online encyclopedia at the click of a few keystrokes. At least with the old print *Encyclopedia Britannica*, would-be plagiarizers had to do a little bit of heavy lifting, use an index, look something up in multiple volumes, and then retype the relevant passage. *Wikipedia* not only obviated those time-honored copying skills (which were presumed to have at least some intellectual benefit) but added the new problem of providing students with information supplied by "anyone," lacking the prestige and credibility of the *Encyclopedia Britannica*. Allegedly, many *Wikipedia* entries were wrong and the content deliberately manipulated by those with points of view or axes to grind. *Wikipedia*, which is written largely by volunteers who care deeply about the site's credibility, turned out to be quite good at self-correcting. While there have been a number of incidents in which *Wikipedia* entries have been hacked to reflect incorrect or hateful content, in general these kinds of hacks tend to get flagged and swiftly corrected on *Wikipedia*. In spite of the fear that Millennials would blindly believe everything we read on *Wikipedia*, we rapidly learned that information had to be checked and double-checked, and that *Wikipedia* was, at best, a good starting point for research. Over time, the self-organizing and self-policing policies of *Wikipedia* as a social research community have made it the best, broadest, deepest, most timely, and generally highly accurate body of reference material in the world. Today, *Wikipedia* is a poster child for the development of valuable, useful, accurate, and relevant crowd-sourced content. Had the contents of *Wikipedia* been paid for by a university or a philanthropic foundation, it would have cost several billion dollars. Instead, it was free. Having learned that we can't automatically trust any one source of information—whether *Wikipedia*, about a particular topic, or our government, about weapons of mass destruction—Millennials have developed a new kind of media literacy that has become an integral piece of our lives.

When it comes to reference material, no one can doubt the power of web-based research versus clumsy physical volumes. Not surprisingly, after continuous print publication since 1768, the *Britannica*'s owners announced in March 2012 that no new print edition would be forthcoming. The *Encyclopedia Britannica*, which *Wikipedia* itself calls "one of the most scholarly of English language encyclopedias," will continue to exist online.

Another powerful riposte to the Carr argument comes from NYU professor and author Clay Shirky, author of several important books about technology, including *Cognitive Surplus*. The book makes a revelatory observation. As a society, we are watching significantly fewer hours of television, and many of us are repurposing those marginal hours into online experiences, creating a "cognitive surplus" of intellectual time and energy that allows collective intelligence tools like *Wikipedia* to arise. Moreover, the experience of web surfing is, by definition, more interactive, more reading- and writing-intensive, more open to curiosity and serendipity, and requires more brain activity than the TV-watching couch potato experience. Shirky's work indicates Carr is making the wrong point: it is not that a nation of book readers is sadly being dumbed down into a nation of web surfers. Rather, a nation of TV watchers is becoming at least somewhat more engaged in the more interactive experience of the web. In response to Carr's argument about the alleged inherent superiority of reading print books rather than reading on the web, Shirky writes, "The anxiety at the heart of 'Is Google Making Us Stupid?' doesn't actually seem to be about thinking, or even reading, but culture. . . . Much of the current concern about the Internet, in fact, is a misdirected complaint about television, which displaced books as the essential medium by the 1970s."[53]

While Carr claims science has proved the connection between decreased brain power and technology use, others who have studied the neurology and technology data firsthand often draw other conclusions. Gary Small, author of *iBrain: Surviving the Technological Alteration of the Modern Mind*, observes, "Besides influencing how we think, digital technology is altering how we feel, how we behave, and the way in which our brains function. . . . This evolutionary brain process has rapidly emerged over a *single* generation and may represent one of the most unexpected yet pivotal advances in human history. Perhaps not since early man first discovered how to use it has the human brain been affected so quickly and so dramatically." Small sees the changes in brain use helping twenty-first century digital citizens cope better with the world around them, process more information more rapidly, and potentially solve unsolved problems with access to new ideas and tools. Like Small, Camilla Nord, twenty-two, is excited: "My generation is wired differently because of technology. I'm not worried, though: if technology is the thing that defines us, let it be the device that makes us faster, more critical, lends us the ability to share our opinions with the world. I want to be in a world where YouTube can give an isolated teen hope."

David Eagleman, the author and neuroscientist who is one of today's scientific leaders in understanding the evolution and plasticity of the brain, also provides an important counterpoint to Carr. He sees enormous value in the positive attributes of the web, likening it to the Library at Alexandria in ancient times and seeing in it the realization of humanity's long-sought dream of a shared, accessible repository for all the world's ideas and knowledge. This is a "virtuous web," where instead of our brains being distracted or fried, we get the potential benefits of interconnecting our collective intelligence through digital technology. Eagleman also believes that if the web didn't exist, we'd have to invent it, not just to improve civilization, but to save it. In his book *Why the Net Matters*, Eagleman proposes that the Internet is essential to our very survival as a society and a species. He lays out six key threats to humanity's future and how the power of the web may create solutions to these mortal dangers. For example, web-based technologies and social media may allow us to avert new epidemics and plagues of the type that previously came close to wiping out humanity.

Critics like Carr are right about one thing: we will all lose historically valuable features of our human experience in the swirl of the fast future's paradigm shift. I love print books, and that's why I wanted this book to be a print book and not simply an e-book, although I realize that you may be reading the e-book version right now. I am anything but dismissive of the value our society may lose as the vitality of the ecosystem around print (books, bookstores, the *Encyclopedia Britannica*, libraries, cultural approaches to browsing and serendipity) slips away. But the same point could be made about every era of change and transformation. The right response is not to wring our hands and worry about civilization's doom, nor to try to stop the tsunami of technology with a finger in the dike. We need to understand that we are gaining much that is positive, as well as bringing some new negative forces into our world. The questions to ask are: how can we take advantage of the new tools we have gained? How can we constrain the negative influences? How can we preserve the essence of what we might be losing in a new form?

Millennials will have to make decisions regarding a wide range of issues about our digital future, from the seemingly mundane, such as whether or not there should be sales tax on virtual goods, to the all-encompassing, such as how we protect all of our personal information as more and more of it gets pushed into the cloud. As our generation grows up and as many more of us become parents, we'll have to decide how we will incorporate technology into our children's lives, and we'll have to figure out how, as the first generation of Facebook users, we allow our children to use social networks. Hacking in all its many forms is proving to be a defining challenge. What should the penalties be for cybercrime? How far do we want to go with artificial intelligence? How will we organize, secure, and process the massive amount of data in our world that is growing exponentially every year? It will be up to our generation to answer these questions and set precedents for future generations.

If we think of the creation of the digital world we are now in like the creation of the United States, the inventors of the Internet and the World Wide Web, Vint Cerf and Tim Berners-Lee, along with modern technology innovators like Steve Jobs and Bill Gates, would be that world's founding fathers. Millennials must assume the role of framers, tasked with figuring out the rules and framework of the new digital age, just like the delegates at the Constitutional Convention in 1787. We've taken the raw materials the founders provided and have begun to apply them to solve practical and social problems. There is no going back. Our best chance of getting to a new golden age is to embrace the new technologies and navigate their difficulties and complexities. It's our responsibility to help frame the future. When combined, the experience of growing up in the fast future, our pragmatic idealism, and our unique standing as first digitals enable us to tackle these challenges.

FOUR

Twenty-First-Century Capitalism

In the past thirty years technology and globalization have
revolutionized the way that we interact with each other,
burning through any semblance of a boundary between
our jobs and the rest of our lives.

—Lisa Curtis, twenty-five, blogger and
entrepreneur, in a *Forbes* blog post

I am heading for baggage claim in the Cleveland Airport at the beginning of the Fourth of July weekend in 2010. My guide, the then-twenty-five year old—and for the moment heavily bearded—Mark Rembert greets me, sipping a large coffee. I've come to spend the weekend in his hometown of Wilmington, Ohio, just about an hour south of Cleveland.

When the 2008 recession hit, the impact was felt around the country and around the world. Small towns in the middle of America, out of the spotlight, were hit particularly hard. Wilmington, Ohio, was nearly devastated. The biggest job machine in the town—and for many miles around—a DHL plant employing eight thousand people in the area, shut down unceremoniously in 2008, triggering a cancerous ripple effect throughout Clinton County and southwestern Ohio. Small businesses from diners to suppliers were also shuttered in the wake of DHL's closing, leading unemployment to skyrocket as high as 18 percent.

Wilmington has special community spirit. People there not only know their neighbors but go to great lengths to help them. But Wilmington—and towns like it—have been at risk of disappearing since before the recession and are now an endangered species. Mark and his friend Taylor Stuckert, now twenty-seven, both grew up in Wilming-

ton, but by 2008 they were preparing to strike out into the world. Taylor
had been serving in the Peace Corps in Bolivia when a political crisis
broke out, forcing him to evacuate. Suddenly he found himself back
home in Wilmington. At the same time, Mark, just out of college, was
about to head off to Peace Corps service in Ecuador. But with the economic turmoil in their beloved hometown swirling around them, Mark
and Taylor felt they had to do something. In a late-night instant message chat, Mark suggested to Taylor that they try to take some action.
The idea was to act quickly, the exact plan still embryonic: maybe they
could "start working towards an organization" or "try to do a campaign
to help people winterize their home" and "get donations from local
businesses/banks." A few weeks later, they abandoned their plans to
leave town. Instead, they stayed in Wilmington and created an organization and a movement called "Energize Clinton County." The idea
was simple: bring young people back home and help rebuild the local
economy.

Less than two years later, with the country still in the grip of a deep
recession threatening to worsen, Mark and Taylor had already achieved
an impressive string of victories. They built a countywide campaign
called "Buy Local First" to encourage residents to buy local products.
Energize Clinton County (ECC) was instrumental in certifying the
region as Ohio's first "Green Enterprise Zone," a special classification
that garners government funding for local, environmentally sound energy sourcing and economic development. ECC has brought dozens of
young people back to Wilmington, partially through an innovative fellows program that matches young people with local businesses to help
its members learn about business and local needs, while allowing the
business community to make use of skills the young fellows possess—
everything from deploying social media to help promote business to the
engineering necessary to create green technologies and processes. Taylor and Mark are committed to this effort for the long haul. The former
chairman of the local Chamber of Commerce, Phil Swindler, says of
their efforts: "They have created possibilities. Because of the changes
that they've made, you see a very bright, hopeful future."

Mark and Taylor's work is still in progress. Wilmington has far to
go. Many young people continue to leave Wilmington, never to return,

part of the flood of talented youth leaving small towns known as the "rural brain drain" that has been going on for decades. But with one out of five young people unable to find work in America's increasingly expensive big cities, Mark and Taylor's appeal is starting to make sense: return home to find new opportunity. As Mark told me, "We're well aware of the rural brain drain, we see plugging that drain as a responsibility and a priority. If we don't do that, we're going to lose towns like Wilmington." Like many other Millennials all over the country faced with deep economic challenges and an American Dream slipping away, Mark and Taylor have chosen to channel their energy and passion into a constructive response.

In September of 2008, the fall of Lehman Brothers triggered the worst economic collapse since the Great Depression, an event which, by then, only about two percent of Americans could even remember. As financial services, hedge funds, the stock market, real estate, and banks crumbled, Main Street was hit even harder. It seemed as if overnight the world had changed, although in reality many of the contributing factors (the subprime mortgage machine, the overleveraging of the financial system, the surreal buildup of mountains of credit default swaps and other derivatives) had been brewing largely unnoticed for some time. Companies that were planning significant expansion instead announced record cutbacks. Factories full of jobs announced immediate closures. Home foreclosures skyrocketed, 401ks plummeted in value, unemployment numbers shot to their highest levels in decades. After all the available deficit spending—and political capital—that could have bailed out the financial institutions and a few select industries was spent, gridlock on Capitol Hill would not allow for sufficient additional spending to help the broad middle class, the young, and the poor who were rapidly becoming the victims of this new recession. New homeowner programs and incentives vanished in the wake of the subprime mortgage crisis. Veterans desperately in need of benefits saw deep funding cuts. Severe limits placed on student loans and higher interest rates on those loans made an already pricey college education even further out of reach for many Millennials. Teachers were laid off in large numbers, their pension plans gutted and their right to unionize threatened, seriously jeopardizing investment in the education of post-Millennial generations. Homelessness and insecurity were on the rise. The middle class—already in trouble for decades—was being squeezed even more.

Years of over-reliance on financial services, spending way beyond our means, and fiscal irresponsibility of all types had led us to disaster. We will debate the root causes of these problems for many years to come. But one thing is clear: the economic infrastructure Millennials are inheriting is not one built according to our values and our vision. The collapse was devastating for America as a whole, but in particular for Millennials. In 2010, youth unemployment (sixteen to twenty-four year olds) rose to 18.4 percent, the highest since 1948 (when numbers started being recorded), leaving a stunning one in five young adults living below the poverty line.[1] Unemployment was even worse among African American and Latino youth, at 45 percent and 35 percent, respectively.[2]

Student loan debt also reached an all-time high, crossing the $1 trillion threshold in aggregate. As of 2011, the average college undergraduate's debt was an estimated $25,250.[3] In recent decades, college graduates could afford to be less concerned with student loans than today's graduates are. Enforcement of loan repayment plans has tightened, and with graduates facing poor job prospects and their families suffering from increasing debt levels, student loans have become a real stress point in many people's lives. Credit card debt is rising as well—for those who can still get credit—and despite all the efforts to "protect" the consumer, the fact remains that Millennials are paying huge spreads for their rising credit card balances, as well as being forced to pay high fees for their increasing reliance on debit cards. Hourly wages have been in a downward spiral since late 2010.[4] A series of analyses has concluded that Millennials are the first generation in decades to be financially worse off than their parents.

Aware of these grim realities, Millennials remain optimistic and resilient. In fact, polling consistently shows that the highest levels of optimism about the American future are to be found in those who are today in their twenties. But that doesn't mean many Millennials aren't frustrated, angry, and keenly personally aware of the economic inequalities and unfairness of our society. A 2012 analysis by psychologist Jeffrey Arnett, who coined the term "emerging adulthood," found that while a majority of Millennials said they were anxious, 85 percent said they felt life was fun and exciting. Commenting on these results, Arnett said, "This fits what I've seen in interviews. It's both things! They feel excited, but they're anxious with how things are going to turn out—where they are going to fit in in the world."[5]

On October 5, 2011, just as the Occupy Wall Street (OWS) movement was beginning to reach critical mass and capture public attention in Manhattan's Zuccotti Park, a telling moment occurred. The demonstrators, who were an amalgam of Xers, Boomers, and Millennials, were perceived as "anti-business." But on that day, the crowd learned of the death of Apple founder Steve Jobs, and many of the Millennials began expressing their strong emotions about the loss of this particular billionaire and visionary, whose iPads, iPods, and iPhones they rely on in their daily life—even as organizational tools for that very demonstration. To most Millennials, Steve Jobs was a hero of business, invention, and opportunity. They saw an innovative technology company like Apple—even if highly profitable—as a contributor to the solutions needed in our culture, not as a problem that OWS was protesting.

The Millennials who were part of OWS were frustrated and trying to take meaningful action. Yet their anger was directed not at "business" in general, but quite specifically at banks and financial companies, and at the systemic ways our society has come to favor Wall Street and the wealthy at the expense of supporting young people and the middle class in the quest for decent jobs and expansion of economic opportunity. Writing in *New York* magazine, Millennial Noreen Malone suggested wryly but accurately why OWS was lacking in Millennial support and spirit: "If you look at the people on the left who have painted the darkest picture of what the economic downturn means, they're a generation ahead . . . they are unabashedly, feverishly upset. Our generation tends to prefer our dystopian news delivered with the impish smile of a Jon Stewart. . . . Reared to sponge up positive reinforcement that requires only a positive attitude as a buy-in, we are just not that into anger."[6]

In many ways, the last several years of recession have strengthened the resolve and determination of our generation. Lily Granville, twenty-five, who was laid off soon after she started her first job, says that the experience hasn't made her bitter; she thinks that "the recession will make us . . . improve our skill sets. We'll have to be more self-sufficient."[7] Similarly, Kristina Holliman, twenty-six, thinks the recession has been discouraging, but she also believes that now Millennials "will look inward to find their own resources. The fact that we learn early in life that accomplishing the things we aim to do may be 'a little harder' than we had first thought is a positive, not a negative."[8] While the challenging economy is delaying some Millennials' careers, it's also making us independent, self-reliant, and more prone to the "do-it-yourself" approach to all areas of life. Thomas Friedman has observed that, in this shifting economy, Millennials will "increasingly have to invent a job" rather than find one the way our parents' generation did.[9]

Writing in the *Harvard Business Review*, the authors of *Jugaad Innovation* (*jugaad* being a Hindi word for an innovative, improvisational way to fix a problem) compared Millennials to the protagonist of the 1980s television show *MacGyver*, "who was able to extricate himself from any predicament using a Swiss Army knife and duct tape. Like MacGyver, the resilient DIY generation believes in doing more with less."[10]

This feeling was seconded by Jeff Cornwall, director of the Center for Entrepreneurship at Nashville's Belmont University, who declared Millennials to be "the most entrepreneurial generation ever." When Cornwall founded the center in the 1980s, it was one of only a dozen or so university-affiliated centers for entrepreneurship around the country. Today, over two thousand such centers exist as a result of growing Millennial interest in entrepreneurship.[11] In fact, according to a 2012 report from the Kauffman Foundation, which focuses on entrepreneurship, more than 40 percent of young people want to start their own company, and almost a third of all U.S. entrepreneurs are Millennials.[12]

Millennials have responded to the recession and their challenging economic situation in many different ways. The OWS movement is an example of activism and street protests, showing that our generation is not as quiescent as some pundits have feared. But for every Millennial who participated in an OWS action in an American city, there were a thousand others who chose to respond to the economic crisis with innovation, adaptation, and the pragmatic idealist spirit of trying to make the best of a bad situation.

One of the accidental results of the recession years—and most novel in the history of economic downturns—is the large number of Millennials who have been forced to move back in with their parents while they pursue employment opportunities. A much-debated article about this trend, "What Is It About 20-Somethings?" appeared in the *New York Times Magazine* in the summer of 2010. It opened with what has become an all-too-familiar image, "A cover of *The New Yorker* picked up on the zeitgeist: a young man hangs up his new Ph.D. in his boyhood bedroom, the cardboard box at his feet signaling his plans to move back home, now that he's officially overqualified for a job. In the doorway stand his parents, their expressions a mix of resignation, worry, annoyance and perplexity: how exactly did this happen?"[13] The article argued that the recession was creating a new stage of development among Millennials, "emerging adulthood," with Millennials staying at home—often on their parent's dime—while they look for work, or while they simply try to figure out what exactly they wanted to do. "Why are so many people in their twenties taking so long to grow up?" the article asked. This question pops up everywhere, underlying concerns about "failure to launch" and "boomerang kids."

Trying to have an intelligent discussion about the complex nexus of underlying issues and trends over generational issues between Boomers and Millennials was made no easier by a grossly inaccurate yet widely cited graduation season report in 2011 that indicated, in the phrasing of *Time*, that a stunning "85% of New College Grads Move Back in with Mom and Dad."[14] While the lack of jobs for college graduates, the lack of affordable housing, and the challenges of young adulthood in a time of economic uncertainty are real issues, the extreme overstatement of the statistics made a prevalent trend out of a much more marginal one. Some media groups that had conveyed the wrong information at least had the good sense to correct it, as in this correction from *The Huffington Post*: "An earlier version of this story referenced a study that said 85 percent of college graduates are returning home to live with their parents. . . . PolitiFact debunked the widely cited number."[15]

A subsequent *New York Times* report parsed the data better, noting that with "just 74 percent of Americans ages twenty-five to thirty-four . . . working," it is perhaps no wonder "that 14.2 percent of young adults are living with their parents, up from 11.8 percent in 2007. Among young men, 19 percent are living with their parents."[16] Even aggregating those college grads actually living at home currently with those who had lived at home temporarily at some point in the last few years, the highest credible number reported was 21 percent—a far cry from the initial reports of 85 percent.[17]

While this trend is certainly a force in the Millennial Generation, for most Millennials it isn't a core concern. Besides, being young and living at home in 2013 doesn't mean the same thing as living at home twenty years ago. Millennials' parents don't classify having their children back home as a "failure" the way that our grandparents' generation might have. Contrary to the idea that Millennials are living at home as nothing more than freeloaders, it turns out that almost half of the Millennials living at home pay rent to their parents.[18] Arguably, an economic crisis that calls on multiple generations to pay for a college education and housing has brought Millennials and their Boomer parents closer together. In 1986, just 50 percent of all parents reported speaking with their grown child once a week. In 2008, it had increased to 87 percent. Today, 90 percent of parents report giving their children advice regularly and 70 percent of parents provide monthly direct assistance to their Millennials.[19] Young adults' emotional, financial, and sometimes physical closeness to their parents has been growing since the dawn of the new millennium. Mobile phone penetration and the economic crisis have accelerated the trend.[20]

Moving back home has also enhanced some Millennials' ability to take a little more time for their job search and to focus on meaningful, long-term goals. Reid Fontaine, twenty-seven, moved back in with his parents after he was laid off from his IT job after only six months. The experience has allowed him to "bank a significant amount of money toward savings rather than dipping into it to pay bills. My parents knew that would ultimately help me later in life." His parents appreciate his position and realize he'll move out when it makes sense. "Sure, I'd rather be in an apartment in Boston making a large salary, but I also understand that I have changed career paths and it's going to be more slow-going."[21]

Millennials have certainly been set back by the recession, but few have given up. People like Tyler Manninen, a Millennial who runs Top-Pix Autographs, an autograph business, with his wife, Jenn, told me that although the economic crisis hurt their business, it just meant that "We have to be more innovative with our techniques, and we have to differentiate ourselves . . . the recession was discouraging, but we had to just figure out a way to be more competitive. We started this business, and we wanted to follow through with it. We didn't want to just give up. We wanted to keep going."

Tyler is emblematic of many Millennials who have responded to the crisis by throwing themselves into work, trying to use technological sensibility and a resilient spirit to find unique solutions, even in an economy where finding a job after college has become a real struggle. "If I can't get a job, I'll create a job for myself," has become their new mantra. A good example is twenty-six-year-old Nick LaCava, who started a customizable chocolate bar company called Chocomize in 2008. Growing up, Nick, a self-described "candy addict," could never have imagined that one day he would actually be making chocolate. Nick had initially planned on working in finance, but after the recession, he had trouble finding a job.[22] So, with several of his friends, Nick created Chocomize, with a simple premise: go online, select your ingredients and the kind of chocolate you want, customize the design, and then get it shipped to you.

A mere thirty words of positive recommendation in *O! Magazine* led to an explosion in sales for Chocomize almost overnight. Before the article, "we were probably getting around fifteen e-mails and fifteen phone calls a day," LaCava says. "After the magazine came out, we would get anywhere from fifty to one hundred e-mails and phone calls a day, which made things really stressful."[23] In the process of filling new demand, one of their machines broke down. But LaCava and his team never panicked. They did some quick problem solving, and they were back in business. LaCava sounds quite Millennial when he says, "We really had to really figure stuff out. . . . When things were pretty chaotic, we thought, 'We've got to try new things.'"[24]

As of 2012, a little more than half of recent college graduates were unemployed or underemployed.[25] Against that backdrop, it isn't surprising that young people have been starting their own businesses in response. The *New York Times* wrote, "What do some people have to lose? The lesson may be that entrepreneurship can be a viable career path, not a renegade choice—especially since the promise of 'Go to college, get good grades and then get a job,' isn't working the way it once did. The new reality has forced a whole generation to redefine what a stable job is."[26]

The financial crisis also shifted the way Millennials view careers in finance. The financial sector had been a huge engine of job growth for young people, with financial services absorbing up to 20 percent of the entire U.S. workforce by 2007. But as jobs in finance became scarcer— and as the cause of the recession came into focus—young people had even more reason to rethink careers in finance. The Freshman Survey, a study that has been conducted annually at UCLA's Higher Education Research Institute since 1966, found that between 2008 and 2009, the rate of freshmen who planned to become business majors fell to 14.4 percent, the lowest level since 1974. In addition, only 12.1 percent of students listed business as their "probable career," an all-time low.[27] A *Wall Street Journal* article describing how Millennials think about business noted that "the financial crisis—and universal loathing it earned bankers and financiers—is making a mercenary career increasingly unappealing to the next generation."[28]

In the face of across-the-board unemployment, Millennials are much more optimistic than their older counterparts. We are the most underemployed generation in modern history, yet even in the midst of a severe recession, nine out of ten Millennials said they believed that they will eventually have (or already do have) "enough" money. This was actually an *increase* over pre-recession polling numbers.[29]

The recession has made us quite resilient. In a way, we may be akin to our grandparents' generation, who grew up during the Depression, fought in World War II, and emerged much stronger and more determined as a result of these experiences. Our country made lofty promises to our generation that it can no longer keep. But that just means we'll have to find the way to fulfill those promises ourselves. Even those who are frustrated persevere. Take Matt Handler, a Millennial who graduated in the top 10 percent of his class at Brooklyn Law School but was unemployed months later. The conclusion Matt came to after job (and soul) searching was, "After everything that's happened with the economy . . . hard work doesn't pay off like it used to."[30] But he put aside his frustrations and continued to be optimistic and aggressive in trying to find a job.

We're certainly making sacrifices. By 2010, the marriage rate for people between twenty-five and thirty-four had dropped to a historic low of 44.2 percent, the number of children born to women between twenty and thirty-four had dropped by two hundred thousand since 2000, and first-time home ownership had been declining steadily since 2007.[31] We're delaying marriage, delaying starting families, and delaying buying our first homes, in large part because we simply can't afford to take these steps. In addition, as Morley Winograd and Mike Hais, authors of *Millennial Momentum: How a New Generation Is Remaking America*, point out, this is a result of Millennials' basic caution and "unwillingness to take such an important step until they are sure that it is right."[32]

This is part of a broader shift away from the old model of marriage, an institution that has grounded civil society for hundreds of years. In a 2012 survey of single Millennials, 27 percent said they did not want to get married, 40 percent were unsure, and just 34.5 percent said they definitely wanted to get married.[33] But that doesn't mean we aren't happy, and it doesn't mean we aren't falling in love. Rob Weitzer, twenty-five, who has been in and out of work throughout the recession, sums up the changing definition by which Millennials are defining what it means to be "better off" than our parents' generation: "My parents are well-off financially, but I'm better off culturally."[34] Weitzer reflects a spirit found throughout the Millennial Generation. For decades the question "Will you be better off than your parents?" has been posed solely as an economic question. Today, while economic success remains important, happiness and fulfillment have become increasingly important to the Millennial definition of a life well lived.

NEW MODELS FOR NEW TIMES

The financial crisis, with its extreme and economic consequences, as well as the personal, political, and moral questions it triggered, accounts for part of the movement by Millennials away from a focus on traditional business and financial jobs, but it is just one of several factors. Given the desire among many Millennials to "make a difference," some have come to see business in a new light. Michael Fertik, the founder and CEO of ReputationDefender, a company that aims to help people and businesses manage and alter their representation on the Internet, described the new conceptualization of capitalism in the Millennials' minds: "The Lehman cataclysm and the Great Recession have already made their imprint on the entry-level workforce. There's been a turnaround in the culture of the graduating classes." The Millennials, he adds, "tend to view capitalism as imperfect but damn good, and their trust in merit-based systems and their first- and second-hand observations of successful entrepreneurship reinforce their basic belief in the intelligence of the market and the moral success of capitalist rewards for hard work and good insights."[35] Millennials have envisioned new models that emphasize business as a path to social change, or at least as a way to create positive, meaningful changes in the world as a by-product of for-profit business. Partly as a result of Millennial values and influences in the society as a whole, there are three distinct new trends in how business and social values are being combined and integrated: more "traditional" companies are incorporating social good and social values into their mission. Young companies are incorporating social values into their business and embracing the "second bottom line" of social impact. And newly formed companies, often founded and run by Millennials, are imbuing social values into their products and purpose from day one. These three trends make up core components of the Millennial approach to business, which we can describe as *twenty-first-century capitalism*. It's not a rejection of capitalism as we've traditionally known it, but neither is it complete acceptance. Rather, it is the Millennial Generation's pragmatic, idealistic response to the realities and resources of our world, the unavoidable impressions and experiences of capitalism we have experienced in our lifetimes, and our own hopes and desires for change.

Business involvement in philanthropic efforts has a history that dates back to the Rockefeller and Carnegie families in modern times and even back to the Medicis half a millennium ago. For decades it has been common for businesses to donate to community needs, sponsor charity events, and contribute directly to causes from cancer research to building schools. In the late 1970s, "cause marketing" began to take shape. One of the earliest such efforts was a partnership between Marriott's Great America amusement park in California and the March of Dimes, a not-for-profit working to improve infant and maternal health.[36] The partnership generated publicity for the amusement park, which was opening at the time, and raised money for the March of Dimes. The term "cause marketing" was first used in 1983 during an effort by American Express to provide support for the restoration of the Statue of Liberty, while simultaneously seeking to increase credit card use and applications for new cards. For a period of three months, American Express donated a penny for every credit card transaction and a dollar for every new card application to the restoration effort.[37] Soon it became clear to many large corporations that they could generate tremendous benefits by linking their marketing efforts to various causes.

The trend toward socially responsible business has been growing for some time. But today Millennials are increasingly demanding that the brands they buy from demonstrate a commitment to social responsibility. Since Millennials are the largest consumer force in decades, these concerns have been heard loud and clear by brands and major corporations. In a 2006 study from the cause marketing agency Cone Inc., 78 percent of Millennials said they believe that companies have a responsibility to support social and environmental causes. The same study found that 45 percent of Millennials are likely to refuse to buy from a company that does not have a social responsibility policy, 56 percent are likely not to work at such a company, and 42 percent would encourage people they know not to buy from that company.[38]

"Young people are responsible for driving this change," says David Jones, co-founder of the global youth summit One Young World and CEO of global advertising firm Havas Worldwide. "Young people are probably the fastest catalyst and the most significant group in terms of driving the change . . . the power of young people plus technology is enormous. We saw that with the Arab Spring. We're seeing the same thing in the business community: young people forcing businesses to be more socially responsible. But I think, importantly, what we're seeing is some of the world's biggest businesses actually stepping up to that challenge."

While Millennials may have been the catalyst for these changes,

this shift is affecting all people—young and old—companies themselves, consumers, the environment, and the world. Walmart, one of
the most profitable companies in America, is held in disdain by many
progressives, yet it has stepped up its environmental and social efforts
significantly in the past several years. Although many in the activist community are still skeptical of Walmart's agenda, Erin Schrode, a
twenty-one-year-old environmental activist, told me, "Walmart has the
power to change the world. I think if we don't engage with Walmart
and others [do], we're not going to see the change. We have to highlight
the good that these companies are doing, but be honest about where
they have to improve. . . . Companies need to take responsibility for
their actions, just like people."

Today, Millennials have set higher standards. They want companies
to become more deeply engaged in socially responsible practices, including going green, providing low-cost, direct impact in their charitable work, and pursuing a new agenda of responsible business practices,
from fair trade to international labor standards. Aria Finger, thirty,
COO of DoSomething.org, works closely with major corporations on
Millennial-focused cause marketing campaigns. She told me, "Companies can't just pollute for twenty years and then write a big check to
an environmental organization. Millennials won't let them; they're too
smart for that. Cause marketing has resonated so well with Millennials
because they are demanding that companies introduce socially responsible policies and giving back into the DNA of the company, not just
into some oft-forgotten foundation. This generation knows that they
have a lot of power, and they can certainly vote with their wallet."

Companies able to build a strong reputation in philanthropy and
social engagement have a demonstrated ability to attract greater Millennial customer loyalty. Companies such as Trader Joe's and Burt's Bees
have proven particularly adept at winning Millennial loyalty with their
commitment to environmental causes. The same is true of the Gap,
Starbucks, Apple, Converse, and American Express, which have all part-
nered with Project (RED), an organization that aims to help alleviate
the AIDS crisis in Africa.[39]

Even without an explicit social agenda, young companies often gravitate toward a positive kind of social responsibility. Twitter is

one such company. Although many tweets are mundane or trivial, the micro-blogging giant "gets it" about our world. Its real-time capabilities have played an important role in generating global awareness for political movements like the Iranian revolution in 2009. And it has been used by public figures from Lady Gaga to *New York Times* columnist Nicholas Kristof to raise awareness and funding for issues from bullying to the crisis in Bahrain. It's not exclusively a forum for social change, but like most Millennial-era platforms, it is a forum for expression, in which positive social action regularly occurs.

In a speech, Claire Diaz-Ortiz, head of social innovation at Twitter, explained that for Twitter's founders (two of whom are Millennials; the other is just slightly older) promoting social change is part of the company's DNA. They "don't think that we have the responsibility to create a social impact, but that we have the *opportunity* to do so," she noted.[40] Diaz-Ortiz's line of reasoning is reflective of twenty-first-century capitalism. She is explicitly acknowledging that with a great platform comes great power, and great opportunities to use that power for good. As twenty-first-century capitalists, the Twitter team isn't simply focusing on social action because they believe it will be good marketing; they do it because they believe it's the right thing to do. This hasn't hampered their monetary value: a 2012 analysis valued the company at $9 billion, making it one of the most valuable private companies in the world.

Through our lifestyles and mindset, our generation is also affecting traditional American businesses. For decades, eighteen- to thirty-year-olds have been a highly prized demographic in the eyes of brands and marketers. We are coveted both for our emerging buying power and incipient brand loyalty, as well as our role as leading pop culture tastemakers and trendsetters. So it shouldn't be surprising that big businesses have spent a great deal of time studying Millennials and what we expect from companies and brands. Millennials are pushing companies to enter into a meaningful and authentic "two-way conversation" with their customers. This conversation includes how and where a company produces its products and how they incorporate causes, environmental, labor, and human rights concerns into their global operations. Millennials are addressing these issues with companies on all their platforms, as the companies themselves become "pro-social" and learn to use Facebook, Twitter, and other tools to market their products and build brand loyalty.

At Unilever, one of the world's largest consumer goods companies, corporate social responsibility has now been embedded into global day-to-day operations. In 2010, Unilever CEO Paul Polman announced the company's sustainable living plan, pledging that by 2015 they would achieve key goals, including cutting the environmental footprint of Unilever's products by half, building a sustainable and ethical sourcing chain for all of the company's raw agricultural materials, and helping 1 billion people around the world improve their overall health.[41] The battle continues—as it does at almost all big companies—with groups like Greenpeace, which continues to criticize Unilever's shortcomings. But the reality is that the company has made very substantial progress on an ambitious set of environmental goals.

Millennials are also at the center of pioneering business models referred to collectively as "the shared economy." Zipcar, the short-term car-sharing company, represents this new kind of business. Millennials make up more than half of its users, or "Zipsters" as they are known, and the company has a presence on 250 college campuses.[42] Understanding that there is a market for people who only need cars during specific and limited time periods, Zipcar has built a business model around making small, cheap, fuel-efficient vehicles available for a few hours at a time, in effect "sharing" the resources and cost of automobile ownership, and reducing costs below those of traditional auto rental companies with their one-day minimums and high-priced locations. Within a year after Zipcar was introduced in Baltimore, 18 percent of Zipcar drivers had sold the car they owned, cutting costs while feeling safe in the knowledge that they could rent a Zipcar whenever they needed one. Some 46 percent of those registered for Zipcar had chosen not to buy new cars, 14 percent were now using their bikes more, 21 percent reported walking more, and 11 percent were now using public transportation more frequently.[43] All of these trends—and their positive impacts on the environment, traffic congestion, and health—came about because Zipcar made it possible to live in Baltimore without owning a car.

The shared economy "has the potential to be lethally disruptive," says Umair Haque, an economist and author of *The New Capitalist Manifesto: Building a Disruptively Better Business*. "If the people formerly known as consumers begin consuming 10% less and peering [sharing among peers] 10% more, the effect on margins of traditional corporations is going to be disproportionately greater," Haque argues. "Which means certain industries have to rewire themselves, or prepare to sink into the quicksand of the past."[44]

Zipcar is just one of the many reasons that today's Millennials are no longer the fertile marketing ground for new automobiles that young adults historically have been. The importance of the social goal of owning your own automobile at a young age is in decline, just as all the other twentieth-century signposts of "adulthood" are changing or arriving later. Millennials facing a difficult economy, high unemployment, record high gas prices, and the pressures of student loans are not eager to take on more expense and more debt by buying a car, so it shouldn't be surprising that car ownership is at a historic low for young Americans. But something more profound is happening as well. A growing percentage of Millennials want to own less, have fewer responsibilities related to material things, and have made a principle out of not bringing energy- and resource-consumptive items into their lives. Plus, many Millennials want to live in center cities—places where parking a car is expensive and where public transportation has been heavily improved. As a result they turn to Zipcar as a pragmatic alternative that addresses all of these concerns, leaving the auto industry with a deep need to appeal to Millennials.

The emerging model of twenty-first-century capitalism has numerous other features as well. This can be seen in a new social contract that is arising with regard to social media: companies will use social media to market to us, and we will use social media to insist on social responsibility and transparency from the brands we favor.

In late 2011, many Millennials rose up on social media after they got wind of a plan by Verizon to add a $2 fee to all one-time debit and credit card payments for customers who pay their bills online or over the phone. The pushback was so strong that Verizon was forced to abandon their plan. The top-down approach—the one-way blast of TV advertising messages—that has long dominated the relationship

between businesses and consumers is being challenged by the Millennials and the social marketplace they have created.

This shift is forcing all companies to change or face possible brand
extinction. Mark Benioff, founder and CEO of Salesforce, takes Millennial power very seriously. "The elites—or managers in companies—no
longer control the conversation," he says. "This is how insurrections
start."[45] Writing about this revolution in *Forbes*, David Kirkpatrick, author of *The Facebook Effect: The Inside Story of the Company That Is Connecting the World*, noted, "In this new world of business, companies and
leaders will have to show authenticity, fairness, transparency and good
faith. If they don't, customers and employees may come to distrust
them, to potentially disastrous effect."[46]

Netflix provided a case study in how to generate customer distrust—
a surprise considering how closely in tune the company had been with
its customers since it was founded in 1999. In 2011, the company announced a sudden switch in how customers' subscription plans were
managed. Taking customers completely by surprise, Netflix told them
that physical DVD rentals and online streaming were going to be separated in different plans. Although the DVD rental price stayed the
same, the streaming plan would cost $7.99 a month, an effective fee
hike on those who had come to rely on the site's streaming library. As
soon as the change was announced, Millennials flooded Facebook with
comments attacking the company for the unilateralism of the change.
Almost instantaneously, Netflix, a company that had been frequently
lauded as one of the smartest businesses in decades, found itself with a
serious problem. Eventually, Reed Hastings, the company's CEO, had
to apologize and reverse some of the proposed changes, but not before
the company lost billions of dollars in stock value. It was more evidence
that in today's world, businesses no longer control the customer the
way they once did. Companies and consumers today are dancing together in a complex choreography. One misstep can throw the whole
ballet off.

Today, Millennials demand that companies open themselves up to
comments and criticisms, and they expect those comments and criticisms to be listened to. Bernd Beetz, CEO of the global fragrance and
beauty company Coty, observes that today it's essential to "keep your
brand in the zeitgeist of this generation." Realizing that market research

is no longer enough, Coty has put an emphasis on creating a constant stream of feedback from their consumers, before and after new products are launched and everywhere in between. While Millennial demands for corporate social responsibility, authenticity, and transparency seem to pose a threat to the traditional business order, many companies are stepping up to the plate. Corporate social responsibility initiatives are becoming more widespread across companies big and small. In some cases, it's a single relationship with a charity. Coty, for instance, works closely with a leukemia organization called DKMS, raising money and encouraging employees to become bone marrow donors.

Aaron Pomerantz, a Millennial who left a real estate career to work for WINGS, an education-focused not-for-profit, is even optimistic about the future of the most inherently non-social companies. "Even banking and financial services are being changed. The sustaining impact to come out of this new movement is going to be socially responsible, for-profit businesses. That, I think, is where you're really going to see the lasting impact, where you can do good and be financially viable. That's the most innovative shift in the last few years." Just one high-profile example: while many valid criticisms can be leveled at Goldman Sachs for the way its policies and investments contributed to the financial crisis, some of their social responsibility initiatives are demonstrably valuable and are setting new standards of corporate involvement in improving the global business culture. In March 2008, before the economic meltdown, Goldman Sachs launched an initiative called 10,000 Women. The program's goal is to train 10,000 women in developing countries in business and management skills to help ensure a new global generation of strong female entrepreneurs.

It's also worth noting that some Millennials have come to see the corporate world as an important place to learn skills to run an efficient social enterprise. Adam Braun, twenty-nine, went to work at the management consulting firm Bain & Co. before he founded Pencils of Promise, a not-for-profit that builds schools in the developing world. Braun told me he knew if he wanted to build a great not-for-profit organization, "It couldn't be run by passion alone. It needed to be run with the same level of diligence, structure, and commitment to results that the best for-profits are run with. The best place for me to learn that was working at a top-tier management consulting firm."

■ ■ ■

In September of 2010, I traveled to Argentina with TOMS, the popular shoe company founded by Blake Mycoskie. After our group arrived in Buenos Aires, we spent several days participating in a series of "shoe drops" in and around the Misiones region in rural Argentina. In a village we visited in the San Pedro area, I was fitting a little girl for a shoe—she couldn't have been more than six years old. It was tricky to get the shoe right. Without knowing her shoe size, I had to go back and forth to the shoeboxes, getting a smaller or bigger size. I kept looking up at her to see her face to see if I was hurting her and I kept expecting her to help me get the shoe on her foot. But she didn't know how to put on a shoe. She had never owned shoes. When I finally got the shoe on, she sprung off without a word.

As I stood in that village in rural Argentina giving these children their first pairs of shoes, it was hard to believe all this was being orchestrated by a for-profit company. But as you might have guessed, TOMS isn't a traditional for-profit company. For every single pair of shoes TOMS sells, they give one away to people in the developing world, mostly to people who have never owned a pair of shoes in their lives. Mycoskie appropriately dubbed this model "One for One." They regularly give away shoes on these "shoe drops," mostly in Africa and South America, although they are constantly expanding their reach. TOMS takes great pains to document shoe drops with photography and videography, so they can clearly communicate to customers the direct power of their purchase. Few companies demonstrate the promise of social business as well as TOMS. Mycoskie, thirty-six, is just outside the Millennial Generation, but most of the company's earliest employees are Millennials, and the company is infused with the Millennial spirit. Mycoskie espouses it himself: although he performs the function of a CEO, his official title is Chief Shoe Giver.

TOMS embodies social entrepreneurship. The company has become perhaps the premier example of how a company can do well and do good at the same time. In just four years, TOMS expanded from two employees to over one hundred. They now sell shoes in thirty-one countries and conduct shoe drops in twenty-five. They boast the distinction of being one of the best-selling shoes at Nordstrom stores nationwide.[47] They've sold well over one million pairs of shoes, and they gave away their one-millionth pair of shoes on the Argentina trip. But perhaps just as important as their social impact, people really like their shoes.

The trend of social business has been emerging for the past thirty years, but has exploded in the past few years. Paul Newman founded one of the earliest social businesses, Newman's Own. It was launched in 1982 as a food company. Starting out with salad dressing, the beloved actor declared this fledgling company would give all of its proceeds after taxes to charity. As of 2012, Newman's Own had given over $350 million to charities from sales of their increasingly diverse line of food products. Other early pioneers of social business include Ben & Jerry's cofounders Ben Cohen and Jerry Greenfield, who incorporated charitable activities into their company, and went so far as to offer any Vermonters who were so inclined a stake in the company, and Anita Roddick, who founded the Body Shop, a cosmetics store which was one of the first major businesses to incorporate fair trade with developing countries into its operations.

Millennials are embracing the "socialization" of business as the new normal. Even those in the supposedly glitzy, self-involved world of fashion and design are often guided by social values. Model Lauren Bush Lauren has blended fashion with an effort to end hunger. She founded and is CEO of FEED Projects, which produces a line of fashionable bags and accessories. The bags are sold in retail stores across the country, with proceeds going to the World Food Programme. As Lauren told me, "We want to be practical, while aiming incredibly high to help tackle the tremendous problem of world hunger."

The accessibility of products like TOMS shoes and FEED Bags allows this generation to wear fashion items and feel fashionable while contributing to a greater cause. As one Millennial TOMS customer and supporter, Sara Scholin of Minneapolis, says, "It's the mission of TOMS that I am obsessed with. . . . Paying $45 for a pair of shoes is no big deal for most Americans. Why not be able to help someone out while getting some retail therapy. . . . I love that there are companies out there who are so focused on social change. That is exactly the kind of company I would love, and hope to someday, to work for."[48] The individual act of Sarah buying and wearing TOMS isn't making a huge impact in the world, but as Millennials like Sarah buy, eat, dress, and think in a more socially conscious way, the impact can scale exponentially. Bill Drayton, founder of Ashoka, described the scaling this way: "As the number of leading pattern-changing social entrepreneurs has been increasing everywhere, and as the geographic reach of their ideas has been expanding ever more rapidly, the rate of plowing and seeding therefore has multiplied."[49]

Social businesses are becoming significant social change agents alongside political action and not-for-profit companies. Bethany Halbreich, twenty-two, is one of a growing number of students who majored in social entrepreneurship, explained her passion for this sector: "Philanthropy is a good thing, but on its own, it's not sustainable for most young people. For people to make sustainable change on a widespread scale, they need a monetary incentive and more motivation than just to 'do good.' In a world that is growing more and more complex, solutions need to be more innovative. Business with a social entrepreneurship aspect can be part of the answer. For me, finding and testing those innovative twenty-first-century solutions is a challenge more exciting than any other."

In contrast to the generation before us, Millennials are likely to have had, on average, fourteen jobs by the time they turn thirty-eight.[50] Ninety-one percent of Millennials themselves believe on average they will stay at any given job for less than three years.[51] The standard life plan that dominated the twentieth century—leave home, go to college, find a good job, get married, buy a house, and have kids—is being remade by Millennials. We're looking for different experiences and values in our lives. As Mark Rembert told me, "Sometimes I think about it in terms of my personal enjoyment. I think, man, I'd be having so much more fun if I were living in Philly and making sixty to seventy thousand a year. . . . But then what always brings me back is that Wilmington, Ohio, is my home; this is where I feel happy. To me, finding that sense of place is a greater accomplishment in my life than a degree or a high-paying job."

In their search for personal fulfillment and impactful careers, Millennials are even turning down high-paying jobs in order to do things they personally value. Michelle Trahey, twenty-five, turned down three marketing job offers in order to participate in Teach for America.

Some of her friends couldn't believe her choice, calling her crazy, as did her parents. But Michelle said her "passion is helping people and making a difference. . . . This is the perfect time for me not to focus on business. . . . If I don't do this now, I may never have this opportunity again."[52] In addition, many Millennials—even some of those who are entering traditionally high-paying sectors like finance and real estate—want to work for companies that have some commitment to social responsibility. Since young people are always highly desirable candidates for entry-level positions, these Millennial values are pushing companies to make commitments to social responsibility. Aida Molineux, a senior executive at Northern Trust who has interviewed and hired scores of Millennials over the last few years, says, "Nowadays one of the first things graduates ask at an interview is about the bank's social responsibility policy. . . . To get the best people through the door, you have to mention CSR [corporate social responsibility] in the job advertisement."[53] In fact, a 2012 study conducted by Clark University found that 85 percent of Millennials were willing to take a lower-paying job where they felt they could have social impact over a higher-paying job where they knew they wouldn't make any social impact.[54]

However, not every Millennial embraces this viewpoint; plenty of Millennials are simply eager to find a high-paying job and go on with their lives. The endgame is not for every Millennial to desire or find deeply fulfilling and impactful careers and work. Rather, the hope is that this trend will continue to grow and spread throughout the generation, and that it will continue to manifest itself throughout Millennials' lives as they get older and take on more key institutional leadership positions in society.

Similarly, while there are thousands of Millennials who have started their own businesses, the vast majority of our generation will end up working for small businesses and large companies currently owned and run by people from other generations. Right now, our representation at well-established companies is still mainly at the entry and lower levels. But when we take the reins as executives and managers of these institutions, when the first few Millennial CEOs take charge of Fortune 500 companies, we may see some of these businesses display new qualities, new work habits, and new social aspects. Mint.com founder Aaron Patzer, thirty-two, sold his company for a reported $170 million to Intuit in 2009. He told me, "It's silly to start a company just for the money. . . . You have to be proud and challenged by what you've accomplished. There are millions of different ways to make money, and no one should be afraid of making a profit or making money. Having wealth is very valuable in life in many ways. But you ought to make money in a way that you're really proud of and really pleased with and that really stimulates you mentally."

But for-profit businesses have their own inherent value. Patzer says, "The primary purpose of a business is to create value, first, for its shareholders, and the way you do that is by creating real value in the world. And so a business should not be run as a nonprofit. Mint.com has found $1 billion in savings for people, which is great. It dramatically affects their lives. But I'm building a business and a product that isn't primarily altruistic or trying to save the world."

At the very nadir of the 2009 financial crisis, Jackie Ramos, a Millennial Bank of America employee in Atlanta, decided she could no longer tolerate the bank's myriad of extra fees imposed on already squeezed consumers, such as $15 "convenience" charges on late credit card payments and $39 over-the-limit fees. Ramos was a "customer advocate" whose job was to call struggling credit card customers and either encourage them to pay or show them how they could modify their accounts to avoid the fees. Not every customer qualified for the bank's modification program. Unable to sleep at night thinking of the people she was hurting by pressuring them to pay their bills, she came up with the idea of helping more people modify their accounts, even those who did not technically qualify.

"I stopped denying people," said Ramos. "I helped people get on programs that they didn't necessarily qualify for but who definitely needed the help."[55] Ramos's actions, which might be considered heroic by some, got her fired. Two days after losing her job, she uploaded a video to YouTube that has been viewed over three hundred thousand times. "There was something inherently evil about my job," the then twenty-three year old said.[56] After the YouTube message went viral, Ramos emphasized that she was not speaking out of bitterness toward Bank of America, and in fact she doesn't consider her former employer any worse than other banks—she's frustrated by the whole industry. She told *The Huffington Post,* "I feel like there's a real credit problem in this country. . . . Too many people are complacent. . . . Slavery was also legal at one point in time. It was the law. Now we have 30 percent interest rates, $39 late fees and over-limit fees. I want the laws changed. I want the federal government to protect its people and do what it's supposed to do."[57] Even though it meant losing her job, Ramos stood up for what she believed.

The companies we choose to invest in with our consumer power are also the companies we want to work for. TOMS's Mycoskie is outspoken about the dream of mixing work and passion for social causes, but he adds a note of caution for this particular career recipe: "This generation is expecting that work should be fun and fulfilling, and I think that's a good mentality. A lot of our employees are on their first job, and because of that lack of experience, they think a company like TOMS is the norm. You have to remind them that not all businesses are fun and not all jobs are something they will look forward to going to." He also worries about the sense of frustration and even disenfranchisement that might come to young people who can't find the right mix. "The good and the bad is that people in this generation don't just all want a regular job anymore. What I worry about is that if you look at the realities of business and work, many jobs remain overwhelmingly 'work' and very little else."

Mycoskie is right—not everyone can find the perfect mix of a fulfilling life and career. There simply aren't enough social businesses to employ everyone who wants to work at one. Not everyone can start their own company, and the restructuring of the global economy has made entering the workforce harder and harder for young people. Most Millennials will not end up in jobs that are as personally and socially satisfying as they might wish. But once in the workforce, Millennials are showing that their outlook has a ripple effect on the companies they work for. In addition to the emergence of more social businesses like TOMS, more traditional companies are encouraging a pro-social company culture (separate from their brand, products, and services), including emphasizing a sustainable workplace, lowering carbon footprints, and allowing employees to take a certain amount of paid time off to volunteer and work with charities.

■ ■ ■

Not everyone sees Millennials this way. Some critics have charged that
Millennials are overly self-involved, materialistic, and not serious about
changing the world. Perhaps the loudest voice among these critics is
Jean Twenge, the author of *Generation Me*. She argues that Millennials
are "entitled," "narcissistic," and even the "worst employees in history."
According to Twenge, who is also a professor of psychology at San Diego State University, Millennials have been raised in an atmosphere of
too much self-esteem building and too little discipline. The result, she
says, is that they are overconfident, believe too much in themselves, and
aren't prepared for the harsher realities of adult life. The subtitle of her
book *Generation Me* sums up her case: *Why Today's Young Americans Are
More Confident, Assertive, Entitled—and More Miserable Than Ever Before.*

Paul Harvey, an associate professor of management at the University of New Hampshire, reached conclusions similar to Twenge's in a
separate study, claiming that Millennials had a "very inflated sense of
self," leading to "unrealistic expectations" and, ultimately, "chronic disappointment." Harvey adds that even when Millennials "fail miserably
at a job, they still think they're great at it."[58] He claims that members
of our generation believe we are entitled to success, and he faults our
families and schools for raising us in ways that consistently emphasized,
"You're great, you're special."

Many Millennials may well be confident and assertive. We are also
adaptable and resilient. While some are frustrated and angry about their
inability to find a job, few are paralyzed or hopeless. It's worth noting
that although the current age of the Millennials places us in what has
historically been the second most suicide-prone demographic group,
very few of the tragic suicides among our cohort have been officially
linked to recession-specific circumstances.

Having self-confidence and being able to assert one's self are not
necessarily bad traits in an age of uncertainty characterized by the constantly shifting pressures of the fast future. Millennials know that society is not going to take care of us. We have to assert ourselves to some
degree to be successful. Moreover, we are definitely not "miserable." In
2011, some 74 percent of Millennials described themselves as "happy," a
somewhat higher number than in the rest of society.[59] While Millennials

may be more stressed and forced to cope with more challenging job and housing markets than other generations, they are actually happier, in large part because of their strong rooting in pragmatic idealist thinking.

Yes, we were told by our parents and our teachers that we were "special" when we were children and yes, some of us may translate that into deep confidence. But for most of us, that parental and community support has resulted in a strongly held belief that each of us can make a contribution—in our own lives, and in society—that we are committed to acting upon. This is a generation that believes it can and should change the world. This very belief is shared by 82 percent of Millennials worldwide, including 88 percent of American Millennials.[60]

Where Twenge and Harvey may be right is that our whole society is becoming more self-centered and narcissistic. Not a month goes by when some public figure—usually not a Millennial—is declared in the media or in a courtroom to be suffering from "narcissistic personality disorder." NPD was first proposed as a clinical psychological term in 1968—not during the youth of the Millennials, but during the youth of the Boomers. There is more than enough blame to go around for the rise of narcissism in society. As *Newsweek*'s Raina Kelly points out, many different individuals and institutions have encouraged this epidemic: "Pastors preach of a Jesus that wants us to be rich. The famously egocentric wide receiver Terrell Owens declares at a press conference that being labeled selfish is fine with him. Donald Trump names everything he owns after himself and calls his detractors 'losers.' "[61] For the record, neither Trump nor Owens—nor the "get-rich" pastors that Kelly is thinking of—are Millennials.

Long before Twenge wrote *Generation Me*, Boomers were being referred to, with the word order flipped, as the "Me Generation." Likewise, the Greatest Generation was chastised throughout the '60s and '70s for sitting idly by as the civil rights movement and the Vietnam War raged. (As both groups have aged, they have been redeemed by new analysis and opinions.) Meanwhile, the labels of the "most selfish" or "most narcissistic" generation have been passed on to our generation. In the daily reality of the American workplace, however, Millennials have become a new source of energy, innovation, and productivity. The authors of *Generations at Work* sum up key Millennial qualities in this way: "They combine the teamwork ethic of the Boomers with the can-do attitude of the Veterans and the technological savvy of the Xers. At first glance, and even at second glance, Generation Next may be the ideal workforce—and ideal citizens."[62]

This positive view of Millennials at work is reiterated by many of those who manage them. Marianne Silver is the chief human resource officer and co-founder of Coyote Logistics, a Chicago company. The company grew from three employees in 2006 to over one thousand by 2012. Silver was responsible for hiring a steady stream of new employees every week, many of them Millennials. Says Silver, "They love the concept of being able to shape not only their future, but the future of the company. They're genuine in their belief that they can make a difference. . . . They defy the stereotype." When Coyote asked Millennial employees to volunteer with Chicago's City College system, more than 350 responded to her call, eighty of them in the first hour alone.[63]

Perhaps not surprising for a generation that tends to be much closer with their parents than the previous generations, Millennial employees tend to have more respect for older employees and managers than Boomers or Xers do. A *Wall Street Journal* study found that 68 percent of Millennials viewed the performance of their older managers favorably, a statistic that was considerably higher than the number of Boomers or Gen Xers who felt that way about their older managers (55 percent and 59 percent, respectively). The split was similar on several other qualities, including viewing managers as outstanding leaders.[64]

When young people took up major positions in businesses during the '90s tech boom, they brought a new kind of company culture with them. Google, founded in 1998 by Larry Page and Sergey Brin, then both in their mid-twenties, was a leading example. Google's youth-led office culture featured a casual dress code, an open office space, and fun office perks like dozens of snack stations, a gourmet cafeteria, playrooms, and a masseuse. Since then, this kind of culture has been adopted at many new companies (in the tech space as well as in other fields), even those much less wealthy than Google.

Mark Waid, a well-known comic book author, believes attributes of youth culture that the old guard in the entertainment industry (and critics like Twenge) see as "entitlement" are in fact the seeds of a new business and intellectual property culture: "We are entering an era of sharing . . . whether or not you're sharing things that technically aren't yours to share, whether or not you're angry because you see this as a 'generation of entitlement,' that's not the issue—the issue is, it's happening, and the Internet's ability to reward sharing has reignited this concept that the public domain has cultural value."[65]

Millennials have also brought new technology and communication methods into the workplace. Once feared and prohibited forms of communication have become key tools for increasing productivity. More than a few trendsetting companies that once prohibited the use of Facebook and prevented employees from accessing corporate information through their own smartphone have now reversed themselves and are pouring corporate resources into enabling individuals to use their own devices and accessing social media securely, even at work.

The "emoticon" tells another interesting tale of the influence of Millennials in business. As the *New York Times* declared in 2011, "The emoticon has rather suddenly migrated from the e-mails and texts of teenagers (and perhaps the more frothy adults) to the correspondence of business people who pride themselves on their gravitas."[66] A global study commissioned by Cisco revealed that more than 40 percent of Millennials would accept a lower salary if it meant greater freedom to use social media while at work, their ability to work from home, and increased options with respect to what devices they would be able to use on the job.[67] This should serve as a warning sign to businesses that they must adapt to the needs of the Millennial workforce, even if those needs make them uncomfortable. Youth culture has historically become the mass culture, and that is certainly true today. The Millennial approach to work is becoming the new normal as this new generation floods into the workforce.

While Millennial entrepreneurs and young business leaders are driven by the goal of making money, the kind of avarice that has dominated the long history of capitalism is noticeably less visible. We have already looked at the prototypical example: Facebook's Mark Zuckerberg, whom his business biographer, David Kirkpatrick, has called the "role model" for Millennial CEOs. At several points along the way to Facebook's success, Zuckerberg chose to keep control of his vision and to pursue the excitement of technological challenge rather than sell out for immense sums of money. Zuckerberg, at twenty-eight, has already

joined the Giving Pledge, an effort organized by Bill Gates and Warren Buffett, to get the world's billionaires to donate half of their wealth
over their lifetimes. Indeed, in the first few months after emerging
as the world's youngest self-made billionaire, Zuckerberg established
a program to donate $100 million to Newark, New Jersey's troubled
school system.

Zuckerberg isn't the only young entrepreneur focusing on philanthropy from virtually the first moment of his success. Andrew Mason,
the Millennial CEO and co-founder of the daily deal site Groupon, has
shown a major interest in philanthropy. Groupon itself grew out of a
website called The Point, which was an effort to energize activism and
charitable fundraising with online tools. Even today, Groupon maintains a branch called the G-Team that organizes campaigns to encourage users to donate to organizations in their local communities.

While Zuckerberg, Mason, Mycoskie, and others are no doubt
exceptional people, their style as business leaders and their company
values emerge naturally out of the pragmatic idealist, philanthropic,
and civic-minded Millennial mindset. Unlike the wave of then-young
technology billionaires in the 1990s led by Bill Gates and Steve Jobs,
the current crop of Millennial business leaders seems to be building
philanthropy and social entrepreneurship into the experience of their
twenties, not waiting for middle age to adopt these important facets of
life. We don't yet know what the total impact will be, but it's telling that
we've never seen business leaders this young giving away so much so
early in their lives.

AN INNOVATION ECONOMY

There are thousands upon thousands of Millennials who are starting
their own businesses and making a living for themselves, hiring employees, and expanding the economic pie. In the fast future, it's easier
than ever for young people to start their own business. Just a year after
the iPhone was introduced, more than a thousand new businesses that
had been created to write iPhone apps were already each generating
enough revenue to support at least two full-time employees. As first
digitals, Millennials know and understand how to build websites; we can
become entrepreneurs, build online communities and apps, or become

merchants and service providers, selling e-books or providing SAT prep assistance.

When I talked to Ricky Van Veen, the thirty-one-year-old founder of comedy website CollegeHumor, he was excited by the new potential for businesses. "Right now, there are virtually no barriers to entry," he told me. "Even with the early Internet, like five years ago, there were some barriers to starting up a web business. You had to get a server, and you had to pay for custom design and programmers and stuff. Now anybody who has an idea can start a web business." Given all the success stories, it has also become more socially acceptable for a young person to start a business. Family members, potential clients, and others no longer look askance at a nineteen year old with his or her own company. These new businesses are not necessarily just about technology. Ricky notes, "There hasn't been a lot of change in businesses like paper towels for many years. There are a lot of opportunities ahead for young people in revolutionizing the way paper towels are made (green and greener), the design elements of the towels and the packaging, and even the way they are distributed. And you can multiply the paper towel problem over and over again in every traditional business. I think this generation is going to take advantage of those opportunities."

Since the late '90s, the American and global economies have been undergoing a fundamental restructuring. However, the global recession of 2008 shifted that restructuring into overdrive. The national conversation about jobs and the economy is dominated by words like "innovation" and "creativity." Both in talk and action, the world is moving toward a knowledge economy, driven by innovators with creative ideas and Millennial entrepreneurs looking for unique opportunities. Many Millennial entrepreneurs are more focused on the ideas and quality of their products than the perks and trappings of running a company. We've all heard the stories of excess from prior eras of successful business people. During the financial crisis, it was revealed that former Merrill Lynch CEO John Thain spent $1.22 million on office redecoration, including $1,405 for a trash can.[68] This is not the Millennial style. We're not as focused on big staffs and plush offices as we are on building a strong team. Millennials who create companies are also finding they can do a lot with very little. Facebook serves nearly a billion users. In a prior era, serving a market that large would have necessitated a work-force of hundreds of thousands of employees. In the Millennial era, in early 2012, Facebook's full-time staff was just over 3,500. The Facebook instant messaging platform, which sees over 1 billion messages sent every day, was managed for most of its existence by just one person at Facebook.[69] That's the power of a Millennial-led business today. These trends also mean that the economic success of companies doesn't always translate into the creations of tens of thousands of jobs, as might have happened in the past. After decades of increasing consolidation into ever-larger, ever-more integrated companies, the future now lies in the small- and medium-sized business revolution.

Culture counts for a lot in business. Consider this scene, in which Microsoft CEO Steve Ballmer, fifty-six, responded to an employee who took out an iPhone (from arch-rival Apple) during a meeting, according to one account: "Ballmer freaked out. The chief grabbed the iPhone, placed it on the ground, and pretended to stomp on it. This was typical Ballmer, whose notions of company loyalty were honed in his home-town of Detroit, where everyone drove Fords."[70] In contrast, the found-ers of Twitter and Facebook, who are competitors, have active accounts on each other's sites. At the offices of Google and Facebook, a majority of employees use and depend on the other company's services for busi-ness and personal needs every single day. While still driven by competi-tion, today's workers are not as ideological or dogmatic when it comes to using a competitor's product or service. We're also shying away from elaborate corporate hierarchies and intricate chains of command. In-stead, Millennial businesses are embracing the open and collaborative spirit of the technology we know and use so well. As Jose Antonio Var-gas said of Millennial-led companies, "Bureaucracy saddled with hier-archy is sneezed at; what's preferable is a more flattened, individually focused yet collaboration-oriented working environment."[71]

It follows that many Millennial companies are making their CEOs and executives much more integrated into the rest of the staff. Top ex-ecutives are regularly copied on e-mail chains, and often respond. They are always in the office, approachable, and ready to discuss ideas and action with employees at all levels. In order to create an atmosphere that brings out people's creative spirit, and in an effort to increase col-laboration, the physical layouts of offices often reflect these values. At many new companies, executives are even seated across from or next to engineers, developers, and entry-level employees.

While Millennials have driven cultural shifts in business thinking on hierarchy, executive access, and work environment, motivations for starting businesses are similarly changing. In fact, many of the Millennial business leaders I spoke with didn't initially think of their businesses *as* businesses. Josh Williams was a programmer who had worked on Causes, an app that allows Facebook users to show their support for not-for-profit organizations and steer donations to them. Josh had a deep passion for exploration and travel. He wanted to combine the experience of travel with sharing experiences through social media. Putting these ideas together, he founded a location-based app called Gowalla in 2009 (he sold the company to Facebook in 2011). "Initially, Gowalla was a project," Josh, now thirty-three, says. "We wanted to build a service that you could take with you regardless of where you went. So if I was at the coffee shop or a waterfall in Argentina, I could tell my friends, 'Hey, here's where I am.' Once we built the first version, I think we realized it could be bigger than just a project, that it could really be something that changes the way that people communicate with their friends. . . . We're passionate about design and exploring. So building this was a lot about expressing our passions."

Like Josh, Ben Bator started something he initially thought was just a project. In 2009, he and some of his friends thought they could do something with the odd, weird, and funny text messages they received from their friends. "What if we put those texts online?" they wondered. They decided to do just that, and launched a website called Texts From Last Night. After posting some of their own messages, they encouraged other people to share their own funny texts. Soon people from all over the country began sending text messages every day. Today, Texts from Last Night receives over five thousand text message submissions on an average day—and over ten thousand on New Year's Eve and Halloween. Ben, now twenty-seven, turned it into a real company, sold advertising on the site and launched a series of spinoffs, including T-shirts, a book, and several other media projects. "When we first started it, it was purely for fun," he says. "We started it as a way to keep in contact with our friends that had moved away. What it turned into was almost a repository for everyone's best or worst night. Suddenly more and more people found the site, wanted to be a part of it, and wanted to submit and be part of the community. Today, it's a growing business, even though no one expected that outcome at the beginning."

Josh's, Ricky's, and Ben's companies also highlight a trend of Millennial businesses that aren't necessarily utilitarian or immediately practical, but help add real enjoyment and fun to our lives. They're careful to underscore that, in a stressful and fast-changing world, "fun" is an important social contribution. They're not bringing about major political change, but their platforms are based on their passions and skills, and they've all resonated with people around the world. As Ben told me, "Everyone has their own Texts from Last Night every morning, based on the circle of friends that they are in. And this is one way to be a part of something bigger than just your night out. Instead, you're part of a collective group of people, realizing the potential entertainment in your own experience and sharing it with others. It's not world-changing, but it's fun and I think powerful." Texts from Last Night has in fact led a major disruption of the online humor space by creating a new genre of humor sites based on user submissions. These entrepreneurs are leading new kinds of businesses that place a value on sociality. They're all ordinary people who have achieved success by simply following their passions and turning simple, cool ideas into businesses. And they get to go to work every day in their jeans.

The stories and voices here belong to the entrepreneurs of today. They are a new breed. They're creating new kinds of companies influenced by the Millennial mindset and values. The companies of the twenty-first century won't be like early twentieth-century giants such as General Motors or U.S. Steel. They may not even resemble late-twentieth-century entrepreneur-founded businesses like FedEx or Microsoft. Instead, the new companies will be infused with the Millennial spirit and full of Millennial employees, more in the model of Google, Facebook, and Twitter. These new businesses will be created around new ways of thinking and curating, while they empower us, and simplify or enrich our lives. Some will bring us closer together; others will create new opportunities for collaboration and knowledge sharing. Almost all of them will consume fewer resources than the companies of prior eras. In a dark chapter for the U.S. economy, Millennial-led businesses are one of the brightest spots on the horizon and sources of hope for the future.

FIVE

Political Pivot

My generation acknowledges science, and we want to
protect our planet. . . . My generation does not hate
gay people. We don't hate any people. . . . My generation
does not fear the future. . . . We welcome change. And,
ladies and gentlemen, as a word of caution to you, my
generation is sprinting this way.
                    —South Carolina State Rep. Boyd Brown,
                        twenty-five, in his farewell speech to
                        the South Carolina General Assembly

As thousands of people—young and old—filled Chicago's Grant Park, similar groups were gathered in student lounges and tiny apartments across the country, glued to their television screens. They were waiting for Barack Obama to take the stage in Grant Park and speak for the first time as president-elect of the United States. This was 2008, and the atmosphere was electric. Obama appeared at that moment as the human incarnation of democracy's power to inspire hope, change, a better America, and a better world. Acknowledging the role that young people had played in his election, Obama proclaimed from the Grant Park stage that his campaign "grew strength from the young people who rejected the myth of their generation's apathy; who left their homes and their families for jobs that offered little pay and less sleep." On that night, young people were indeed jubilant. They had ushered in a transformational leader whom many of them deeply believed in.

For the several decades since the 1960s and '70s, young people had been viewed as apathetic, apolitical, disengaged, self-absorbed, and disinterested in social progress. But on that night in 2008, the tone changed. America's youth, with their passion, energy, intelligence, and technological sophistication, had been a critical catalyst in this election. Along with Barack Obama, the first African American president and one of the youngest presidents in American history, the Millennials had arrived at center stage in American politics a decade or two ahead of schedule.

Unfortunately, four years of often disappointing and frustrating results would follow, as Obama tried to battle the forces of an unrelentingly negative economy and a bitterly partisan Congress. However, regardless of the reasons why more progress wasn't made in the difficult years between 2009 and 2012, and regardless of the speed with which positive impressions of Obama turned negative after he took office, Millennials have retained much of the interest and enthusiasm for civic engagement and social change that resulted from their experience in the transformational election of 2008.

With youth unemployment sky-high and the wealth and fairness gaps more prominent in our society than at any time in the last hundred years, Millennials were rethinking and reconceiving what role they wanted to play in politics within the first two years of the Obama administration. Some joined up with the Occupy Movement (although, contrary to popular belief, Occupy was not a youth movement: a mere 23.5 percent of Occupy Wall Street protestors were twenty-four or younger.)[1]

Others moved more deeply into social entrepreneurship and various efforts to solve pressing problems through community and volunteer actions, as well as businesses with social goals. Some decided to run for office. And in 2012, although Millennials didn't turn out as forcefully as they did in 2008, they still played an important role. The sharp pivot in American democracy that began in 2008 is continuing; the pragmatic idealistic Millennials are here to stay, and their impact will undoubtedly be felt for the next several decades in American politics.

Throughout history, young people have often been the group affected by political developments rather than the group who shapes them. But like our activist peers in the 1960s and the 1930s, the Millennial Generation has already become a significant player in the political landscape.

During the 2008 election, when the media referred to "early Obama

supporters," they were usually referring to people who began supporting Obama at some point in early or mid-2007, when then-Senator
Barack Obama announced his candidacy. But the real "early supporters" were almost all Millennials, who began coalescing around Obama
in 2006. Millennials began encouraging him to run when most Democratic Party leaders and professional pundits didn't give him much of a
chance. In 2006, Meredith Segal—then twenty years old—launched the
Facebook group Students for Barack Obama. Although it was initially
just for her friends, it turned into a group with hundreds of thousands
of students and burgeoned into a grassroots movement to get Obama
to run. Ultimately, the Obama campaign adopted Students for Barack
Obama as its official youth outreach arm, and Segal became a national
co-chair of the campaign. For Segal, starting her efforts on Facebook
was a no brainer: "If we want to engage young people in politics," she
said, "why not bring it to the place where they do hang out and they feel
comfortable?"[2]

Young people have been enthusiastic about presidential candidates
over the years (John F. Kennedy, Eugene McCarthy, Bobby Kennedy,
Barry Goldwater, Ronald Reagan, and Howard Dean all enjoyed devoted contingents of youth supporters). But in the past, youth activism in presidential elections had usually been limited to college students
ringing doorbells, particularly in the early primaries. By contrast, the
Obama campaign was able to catalyze the election across all demographic sectors through its contagious passion as well as its sophisticated use of social media and technology.

Even Millennials—with at that point comparatively little history of
political engagement—threw themselves into the campaign. Indeed, in
a bitterly divided, polarized, and consensus-averse nation, the fact that
66 percent of Millennials voted for Obama, forming a generation-wide
consensus for a political candidate, is quite remarkable. Rarely has such
a large percentage of a demographic age group voted for the same candidate. The 66 percent of the youth vote garnered by Obama, as compared to his support among other age groups, marked the largest gap
between young voters and older voters on record.[3] Some twenty-two
million eighteen to thirty year olds voted in 2008, bringing youth voter
turnout to 51 percent, the third-highest turnout of young voters since

1972 when the Twenty-sixth Amendment was passed, effectively lowering the voting age to eighteen.

Millennials were critical to Obama's victory on many levels. In the
Iowa caucuses, they created the momentum that made it safe for other
demographic slices of the population to embrace Obama. In the general
election, Obama won states like North Carolina and Indiana specifically
because of the youth vote. According to one exit poll analysis, "Young
people provided not only their votes but also many enthusiastic campaign volunteers. Some may have helped persuade parents and older
relatives to consider Obama's candidacy. And far more young people
than older voters reported attending a campaign event while nearly
one-in-ten donated money to a presidential candidate."[4]

Campaigns are often staffed by young people, and the Obama campaign was no exception. Because of the technological capabilities of our
era, a new level of support and involvement from citizens was possible.
Millennials played a key role in these grassroots efforts, from organizing
online social media campaigns and hosting and attending self-organized
events to writing about the campaign on blogs and in local papers and
recruiting their friends to volunteer and vote. According to American
National Election Studies, an analysis group run by Stanford and the
University of Michigan, 2008 saw more people under thirty working on
campaigns than the rest of the population for the first time since 1952.[5]

Millennials also played a role in helping to convince their parents
and other important adults in their lives to support Obama. Caroline
Kennedy and Senator Claire McCaskill, both political veterans, told
stories on the campaign trail of how the arguments of their own Millennial children were key to their decision to support Obama. Similar
stories were told over and over again in households across the country. Obama turned out not just to be the "youth candidate," but the
candidate around whom Millennials could unite their parents and
grandparents.

Beginning in Iowa in late 2007 and continuing through the early
caucuses and primaries, young people played a key role in delivering
critical victories for Obama, allowing him to demonstrate to donors
and to the media that he was, indeed, a viable candidate. In a political
campaign, every decision has a range of potential ramifications for the

future. It is conventional wisdom that if Obama had lost in the Iowa caucuses held on January 3, 2008, his campaign would have collapsed in the subsequent weeks. To enhance the chances for victory, the Obama campaign carefully courted young voters in Iowa, including high school students. In Iowa you can participate in the caucuses even if you are only seventeen, as long as you would be eighteen by Election Day. Knowing this, the Obama campaign created an effort called BarackStars, recruiting "captains" for each high school who were tasked with mobilizing their peers and disseminating information about Obama and the caucus process. No other presidential campaign has ever incorporated high school students in this way.

The Obama campaign's outreach to young voters in Iowa was full of this kind of attention to detail. Since the caucuses fell during the traditional January break for college students, the Obama campaign tried to figure out how to get out-of-state students back to Iowa to participate in the caucuses. Campus supporters organized buses and group trips to get people back. At Grinnell College, out-of-state students came back to campus early from as far as Oregon and New York. Since the dorms weren't open yet, the administration allowed students to camp out in the gym. Over a hundred people did so. In a state like Iowa and a process like the caucuses, even a hundred people made a huge difference.

The efforts of grassroots Millennial organizers paid off on the night of the Iowa caucuses. More than sixty-five thousand eighteen- to twenty-nine year olds participated in the caucuses, and youth Democratic turnout increased by 135 percent.[6] Reflecting on the youth strategy, David Von Drehle wrote in *Time* that "Obama clearly knew something others didn't, and that zig where others zagged now appears to have been a shrewd move on the path to a dramatic achievement . . . these first-time voters gave him most of his margin of victory."[7] Young voters continued to deliver for Obama throughout the early primaries. Maya Enista Smith, twenty-nine, CEO of the youth civic engagement organization Mobilize.org, noted that after 2008, "You can no longer say that this generation is apathetic. We effectively got together and elected a president . . . we are the ones that carried him to victory." *Washington Post* columnist E. J. Dionne was just as blunt: "More than is often appreciated, the electoral revolution that brought Democrats to power was fueled by a younger generation with a distinctive philosophical out-look. Put starkly: If only Americans 45 and over had cast ballots in 2008, Barack Obama would not be president."[8]

The Obama campaign was widely praised for its use of new media and online organizing. In January 2007, Chris Hughes, a Facebook co-founder, left the booming social network company to lead the online outreach efforts of the Obama campaign. Specifically, Hughes's mission was to develop an internal social network for the campaign's website that would be called "myBO." Hughes left Facebook just as it was be-coming a juggernaut to join a campaign whose odds were long at best. Hughes said Mark Zuckerberg was stunned by the decision and kept saying "Really?"[9] The Obama campaign decided to hire Hughes, then twenty-three, based on his credentials at Facebook, whose power had just begun to be fully realized by the public. Hughes said in 2009 that he would not have left Facebook "for any other person or at any other time."[10] Similarly, the Obama campaign's decision to invest in new media and to hire young tech innovators such as Hughes was a bold stroke. The conventional wisdom long-dispensed by political consul-tants about how to run a campaign—heavy spending on costly TV ad-vertising and direct mail—was changing with the disruptive arrival of social media and the Millennials.

It's not surprising that it was a Millennial that conceived and ex-ecuted myBO, which turned into one of the most successful online tools for a political candidate in the digital age. As the Obama campaign pressed on through the spring and summer of 2008, it continued to in-novate with activities like building up a huge registered online database of people who wanted to be the first to know when Obama had selected his running mate.

Of course, the technologization of politics began long before 2008. In 2004, Howard Dean's presidential campaign empowered grassroots organizing through then-innovative tools like blogs, Meetup.com, and unconventional online fundraising. In 2006, a video uploaded to You-Tube caught then Virginia Senator George Allen referring to a Millen-nial of Indian descent as "macaca." The remark, deemed a racial slur, led to the demise of Allen's campaign, though he was then considered a leading presidential contender for 2008. Allen lost to his opponent

Jim Webb by a few thousand votes—almost identical to the number of young people who turned out to vote at the University of Virginia. This was the first time a candidate's political future was wiped out by viral video, still a new phenomenon at the time.

In the 2010 midterm elections, the shift toward the use of mobile phones for political engagement was dramatic. In those elections, national studies indicated that 58 percent of Millennial cell phone owners used a mobile device in some way to inform others that they had voted, and 24 percent of Millennial cell phone owners used their phones to "keep up with news related to the election or politics."[11] The increasing dominance of technology and the Internet in mainstream politics, and the status of Millennials as first digitals, means that now young people have real and immediate access to politics anywhere, anytime. When you can see the candidates wherever your life is, when you go online to chat with your friends or to your favorite website, politics becomes omnipresent, less foreign, and more integrated into your life. It seems more natural to participate, at least casually. As this trend has crystallized, it has removed some of the traditional barriers to entry to political engagement.

The 2008 election was the first in which almost all Millennials were old enough to vote. And if you wanted to engage a new generation with politics, the 2008 election was the perfect opportunity. In this way, the Obama election was a huge victory for the civic future of the Millennial Generation.

Throughout the 2008 campaign, Obama seemed to espouse pragmatic idealism in his rhetoric. He also focused on youth issues and young people, attending a record number of college campus rallies and youth events. Famid Sinha, a Millennial Obama supporter, put it well when he said that during the 2008 campaign Obama showed Millennials "that we do matter in our political system. And I don't think there are many people who have showed us that."[12] Following the Obama campaign's lead, every one of the major Republican and Democratic campaigns hired a "youth vote director." But the Obama campaign went further, establishing separate youth vote directors in key states in addition to their national youth vote team. Students for Barack Obama groups sprang up not just in big cities and college communities but in every likely neighborhood and town, and many unlikely ones as well. By Election Day 2008, there were 1,500 active Students for Barack Obama chapters. Jose Serrano, twenty, a Millennial who graduated from Truman High School in the Bronx, spoke to me about the impact Obama had on him and his generation. "Obama made history," he said. "Obama showed young people, that any kind of person, from any different kind of race, could be president. It shocked me. At that time I couldn't vote, but I campaigned for him in New York and Pennsylvania. And then on election night, when he won, do you know what it did to the young people in schools across the country? The impact it had? Many of them were sick of politicians, sick of them saying this, saying that. Obama said, 'Yes, we can. We could have change.' And he's doing it now."

Soon after the January 2009 inauguration of Barack Obama— complete with its hundreds of thousands of young people in attendance and the first-ever Youth Inaugural Ball—the politics of reality began to assert themselves. Obama had inherited the worst economic crisis since the Great Depression. He had to focus on the economy rather than many of his other initiatives. Soon there was bitter partisanship, the rise of the Tea Party, a bloody battle over health care, and all the other problems of the first years of the Obama administration that we came to know so well by the time of the 2010 midterm elections.

Did the Millennials abandon Obama in the midterms? Were they acting as the pundits had predicted—disappointed that Obama hadn't been immediately successful? Had they moved on from their brief infatuation with civic engagement? Writing of the absence of young people in the healthcare debate, *Politico*'s Erika Lovely lamented, "Young voters helped put Barack Obama in the White House, but they're not proving to be much help when it comes to the biggest push of his presidency."[13]

Early on, Obama tried to maintain and then recapture some of the youth enthusiasm that had put him in office. The first initiative was asking young people to get involved with community service. Millennials are overwhelmingly supportive of community service; some 94 percent think it's effective for solving local problems and 85 percent think it's effective for solving national problems.[14] While some young voters threw themselves into this particular presidential initiative, it lacked strong, visible youth leadership, it had little real funding, and it certainly became hard to focus on in the aftermath of the economic crisis when young people lost their jobs or couldn't find one. Moreover, after the great hope and inspiration Millennials had drawn from the Obama campaign, young people were itching for a real seat at the table on major issues that affected youth directly and indirectly. On climate change, an issue that consistently ranks among the top priorities for Millennials, the Obama administration has worked only minimally with environmentalists, and hardly at all with younger people focused on these concerns. On education, the Obama administration has pushed for major reform, but has made little effort to connect with students, focusing efforts instead on administrators, teachers unions, businesses, and individual reformers. Young people could have been tremendous fighters for Obama's healthcare bill, if we'd been asked in the same way that the administration enlisted many other groups of supporters. But he didn't reach out to Millennials until an eleventh hour rally at the University of Maryland. It was a clear last-ditch effort minimally helpful to the ultimate passage of the bill, but it was too late to begin real engagement on the issue.

Beyond the community service campaign, Obama hasn't done much work to truly engage young people in his administration. "The way that energy around the presidential election was harnessed was so important," says Maya Enista Smith. "So many people were empowered for the first time and felt real ownership over their political futures, their community, and their campuses. But it's tough to maintain that. You're not always going to win. Showing people their role in improving their community and local issues is inherently harder and less sexy." Justin Ormont, thirty-one, expresses the sentiments of many Millennials when he says, "The enthusiasm is definitely down. We still have enthusiasm but it's not at the same level. People can't live up to all your hopes and dreams. Obama made a lot of promises. Some he fulfilled, some he still has to work on."[15]

Although Millennials have become less supportive of the Obama administration, just like every other demographic cohort, they haven't abandoned him. In December of 2011, Obama still retained an approval rating of 46 percent among young people when looking at his overall job performance. Despite the low-sounding number, Millennials actually remained one of his most supportive age groups.[16]

Even after decades of skepticism about the youth vote, politicians and political operatives have begun to recognize the importance of courting young voters. Ever since the 2008 campaign, every candidate and party wants their own version of a 2008 Obama campaign. In the 2012 Republican presidential primary campaign, candidates Michele Bachmann and Ron Paul were visibly trying to emulate aspects of Obama's 2008 youth strategy for the Republican caucuses in Iowa.

What these politicians may not be as attuned to is that Millennials are just as powerful as organizers as they are at the ballot box. In 2008, young voters didn't just turn out to vote. They also played a key role as organizers within the campaign, as volunteers, and as independent activists. But in order for Millennials to exercise that muscle, we have to be passionate about the candidate, as many Millennials were about Obama. That kind of passion must start from an authentic excitement about and appreciation of a candidate. Without that, we won't be powerful evangelists, organizers, or voters. Although we're one of the largest voting blocs in history, we're also one of the most selective about whom we vote for and why we support them.[17]

One of the key lessons the 2010 midterms taught us about Millennial political behavior was that Millennials will only be political powerhouses if we believe in the candidate. There were few, if any, candidates in 2010 that spoke to or excited Millennials. By and large, it was a disillusioning election cycle, filled with an unusual level of anger brought on by the Tea Party and negative response to its tactics. Most candidates were not targeting Millennials for support. They were instead aiming their message to attract older and more polarized voters. After the low turnout in the midterms by all demographic groups that had voted for Obama in 2008, some blamed Millennials for the Republican gains in Congress that gave them back control of the House of Representatives.

Millennial turnout was low for several reasons. First, it's important to note that turnout is always low in midterm elections among all age groups. But in the case of Millennials in 2010, they simply weren't excited about the candidates. And while the logic of party-line voting appeals to other generations, Millennials weren't eager to turn out just to help the Democratic Party per se. We want to vote for candidates we believe in—not because they are the lesser of two evils, or because our vote is somehow connected to some complex algebra of how Democrats

retain power. Perhaps we are too selective in wanting to support candidates who resonate with us, but that's the "idealism" component in
pragmatic idealism. It is true that in the process of being too selective
about our participation, we may end up ceding some electoral political
power to other demographic groups. But that's part of the new approach
to politics we are focused on, in which we engage with electoral politics
when it can make a real difference, but maintain our own extra-political
path for change that focuses on progress outside of government. When
we have political leaders who share our values, we'll support them. But
we aren't waiting for them. Political strategist Ben Goddard summed
up the challenge of electoral engagement, saying that Millennials "don't
want to be limited by political party affiliation. They care about issues
important to their 'community' and will work with anyone who can
get something done."[18] In other words, we didn't reduce our engagement because we didn't care, but because we were frustrated and disappointed with the lack of seriousness and effectiveness of the existing
conversation.

As Morley Winograd and Mike Hais conclude in *Millennial Momentum*, Millennials triggered a political realignment in 2008. Realignment
elections occur every few decades, ushering in a shift in political values
that remains in place as a voter group—in this case the Millennials—
rises to power. They write:

> As the United States moves towards another political realignment
> and a new civic era, millennials' preferences for the Democratic
> Party are once again shifting the balance of power . . . millennials
> have substantially more positive perceptions of the Democratic
> Party than the Republican Party. In a 2006 national survey . . . a
> slightly larger number of millennials said that their impressions of
> the Democratic Party were more positive than negative. By con-
> trast, a clear plurality of millennials had unfavorable rather than
> favorable attitudes towards the Republican Party . . . millennial at-
> titudes toward the two parties appear to be a bit more firmly set in
> place than those of older generations as well . . . only two percent of
> millennials were not sure how to evaluate either party . . . for the
> first time in the last forty years, a plurality of an American genera-
> tion is willing to call itself liberal.[19]

Like any habit, participation in elections is a practice that, if formed early, will tend to stick. Gideon Yago, who ran MTV's political coverage for several election cycles, told me, "If you decide when you're eighteen that you like Coke not Pepsi, you're going to be a Coke drinker until the day you die or your teeth fall out. And yet politicians don't approach it in the same way. There's very little effort to do what the private sector does, which is aggressively market toward young voters, aggressively make them brand loyal, aggressively bring them into the process—because even if you don't win this election, you're talking about a massive demographic swell."[20] The Obama campaign reversed that tendency and brought Millennials into the electoral process. This has set in motion a powerful force: the voting habit. What's more, consider that youth's big impact on Obama's 2008 victory was produced with only about half the Millennials having then turned eighteen. Through at least 2028, today's Millennials will be moving ever more centrally into the heart of American life. A growing number of Millennials will be elected to office at every level. Millennials will make up an increasing portion of the constituency for every cause, issue, and fundraising effort.

However, in order to get the most out of Millennials, the political parties need to encourage young voters to get involved, register, and vote. But they need to do much more as well. Peter Levine, executive director of the Center for Information and Research on Civic Learning and Engagement, observes: "Since 2004, young voters have been one of the strongest Democratic constituencies. Democrats need to engage them better than they did in 2010, and Republicans need to make inroads in a generation that continues to prefer Democrats."[21]

Historically, youth vote organizers have seen that the two best ways to get a young person to vote are to register them and to ask them for their vote. In the past few election cycles, more and more young voters have been registered, but even assuming continued growth of registration and engagement of young voters, turnout will suffer unless politicians ask Millennials for their votes. In 2008, Obama spent a considerable amount of time meeting young people where they were, in communities and online, and then asking those young people to vote, and to vote for him. He was the first modern politician to approach young people in this way. Future youth voter turnout will struggle to live up to its potential unless future politicians similarly engage with young voters like they do other age cohorts.

Many professional political operatives failed to understand that Obama had personally appealed to many of these voters and that they had voted for candidate Obama, not the Democratic Party. Obama brought many new people into the political process, but Millennials tend to be independent minded, and the Democratic Party would do well to understand how much of the 2008 enthusiasm for Obama was for a specific candidate, and not for the Democratic party at large. Sarah Buck, twenty-three, who voted for Obama in 2008, said in 2010 that she still supported Obama and his agenda and would vote Democratic in the midterms primarily to support him. "I'm voting the same way for support at the top."[22] However, even Sarah, who is more willing than some other Millennials to see the connection between supporting Democratic congressional representatives in the midterms and support-ing Obama in a presidential election, wouldn't accept being labeled as a Democrat. She says simply that she is an "Obama supporter."

Sarah's feelings are reflective of young people across the country. As pragmatic idealists, we are more interested in specific candidates, issues, and ideas for the long-term future than being wedded to a particular party. The leaders of the Democratic and Republican National Com-mittees don't seem to understand Millennial voters yet. Although more Millennials identify as liberal than as conservative, and more identify as Democrats than as Republicans, the Democratic Party shouldn't assume that they can always control the Millennial vote. Political leaders need to engage meaningfully with us. They need to engage with us on policy and issues, and do so on a regular basis, not just during election season.

The face of the Republican Party is also changing in the Millennial Generation. While National College Republicans are still regarded as ultraconservative, the group has made steady moves to become more inclusive and capture wider student support. In 2011, many of the lo-cal College Republicans in Maine went against their state party to sup-port an ultimately successful referendum in Maine that would allow same-day Election Day registration—a step that was widely believed to mostly benefit young voters (and, by extension, Democrats). College Republicans also pushed back against Chip Saltsman, a candidate for RNC chair, when he sent out a Christmas card that featured a racist song about then-president-elect Barack Obama. The Log Cabin Republicans, a moderate, pro-LGBT wing of the GOP, have gained a stronger following within the College Republicans and, in no small part backed by growing college-age membership, have gained a stronger foothold nationally.

In 2012, a Pew Center poll showed that the percentage of Republicans between the ages of eighteen and twenty-nine who supported same-sex marriage had climbed by 9 percent from 2004. Another Pew analysis found that Millennial Republicans are more likely than other age groups to agree that "more people of different races marrying each other" and "more women in the work force" are positive improvements in America.[23] Speaking about this trend to the *New York Times*, Matt Hoagland, a Millennial Republican from North Carolina, commented, "When it comes to what you do in your bedroom, or where you go to church, or where you want to put a tattoo, we just couldn't care less."[24] Similarly, Zoey Kotzambasis, nineteen, vice president of the University of Arizona College Republicans, remarking on how her conservative peers feel about homosexuality, said, "I think people have become much more at ease and comfortable about it. Honestly, there's about zero judgment from the people in our club, and I think that reflects the direction my generation wants to take the party in."[25]

While few of the major 2012 Republican primary candidates appealed to young voters, the campaigns of former Utah governor Jon Huntsman and Congressman Ron Paul drew a disproportionate amount of their strength from young enthusiasts. Huntsman's more liberal positions on social issues—and Paul's radical libertarianism—had clear appeal to young voters. Indeed, Paul captured almost half the Republican youth vote in the Iowa caucuses and the New Hampshire primary in 2012. While the 2012 Republican presidential nominee Mitt Romney ultimately failed to catch on among young voters, he knew their power early on. In April 2012, Romney endorsed a plan to keep the current interest rates on student loans. Obama had endorsed the same plan, making it one of a small number of policy issues on which Romney and Obama had found broad agreement.

Millennial Republicans may not succeed in making the party significantly more liberal on social issues, but through small actions like these, their voice pushing in this direction is louder than it has been in decades. The Republican Party will have to confront these issues as Millennials come to make up a larger percentage of the Republican Party and the electorate.

The creation and rise of the Tea Party in 2009–2010 provides an illustration of the stark divergence between the pragmatic idealism of Millennials and the polarized sentiment of older age cohorts. Interestingly, the Tea Party movement was birthed in large part by a Millennial, Texas native Brendan Steinhauser, now twenty-nine. He'd been a Ron Paul supporter during the 2008 campaign and was working at Freedom-Works (one of the major organizing groups behind the Tea Party) when he saw CNBC commentator Rick Santelli's now-legendary speech on the floor of the Chicago Mercantile Exchange in February 2009, just one month after Obama had taken office. With unusual populist fervor, Santelli attacked what were still only nascent plans by the Obama administration for mortgage bailouts: "The government is promoting bad behavior. . . . How about this, President and new administration? Why don't you put up a website to have people vote on the Internet as a referendum to see if we really want to subsidize the losers' mortgages; or would we like to at least buy cars and buy houses in foreclosure and give them to people that might have a chance to actually prosper down the road, and reward people that could carry the water instead of drink the water?" As floor traders joined in cheering Santelli's remarks, he provocatively asked, "President Obama: are you listening?" After Steinhauser saw it, he began to share the Santelli video, which spread virally. After an overwhelming response, he found himself shortly thereafter leading the very first Tea Party rally. He would later go on to assume a leadership role in FreedomWorks as their federal and state campaigns director. In this capacity he continued to organize Tea Party events. He spoke of the Tea Party in its early days as a pragmatic effort to address spending and deficits, and viewed the movement like a family, cautioning other members not to "forget the social aspects, these ties that bind us all . . . there is something very powerful about that."[26] Steinhauser, who had been a leader of the Young Conservatives in college, shared the widespread view among Millennials that government is spending too much and borrowing from our future to pay current bills.

But he differed from the mainstream of Millennials in wanting to solve the deficit problem through radical spending cuts and deficit reduction on a current basis, even in the middle of the country's worst economic crisis in eight decades. He envisioned the Tea Party movement as a way to tap into the anger of ordinary Americans about fiscal issues. However, as the Tea Party steered away from the principles that Brendan was interested in, became more negative, and began to focus on social and fringe issues that distracted from their main message, it failed to attract much Millennial support. According to the Harvard Institute of Politics, Tea Party support among eighteen- to twenty-nine-year-olds is at merely 11 percent. Another report indicated that among participants at a typical Tea Party rally, 97 percent were over thirty.[27]

Many Millennials share the Tea Party's stated concern about America's fiscal future. But for the majority of Millennials, the Tea Party's approach is not the right way to go. Patrick Kelly, a self-described Millennial Tea Party supporter, acknowledged the challenges to engaging young people: "A lot of young people, whether it's from the media, professors, or other sources, come to the opinion that the Tea Party is just a bunch of right-wing extreme radicals, racists—whatever. That's the biggest deterrent."[28] As a diverse generation, inclusivity is important to us, and the Tea Party, by and large, is not inclusive. In general, polls tend to show Tea Partiers are more likely to be white, male, married, older than forty-five, more politically conservative, and wealthy.[29] The negative nature of the Tea Party continues to discourage Millennials from engaging with its political agenda, even though we share concern about the deficit from a policy perspective.

The Tea Party and the broad base of Millennials do have other commonalities. While Millennials and Tea Partiers have different beliefs and expectations about the proper role of government, the reality is that Millennials are not able to count on government for the exact kind of support the Tea Party is criticizing government for providing. As a result of the economic crisis, Millennials are experiencing a world without government support. For the millions of young people who can't find jobs and have never been in the work force, so can't count on unemployment insurance, we are living the lives of self-reliance the Tea Party would prescribe. We are learning how to find and create our own jobs and make our own way. While the Tea Party talks about "getting government off our backs," Millennials are actually living and thriving in a world without that government support (while many of the older Tea Party supporters are benefitting from Social Security, Medicare, and other government programs). Millennials are supportive of many government assistance programs, but we have been acculturated to the idea that we had better plan to work longer and harder and have no false vision of a golden retirement in our '60s. In fact, 50 percent of Millennials do not believe social security will exist when we are sixty-seven and ready to retire, and an additional 28 percent of Millennials believe that while Social Security will exist, it will be much smaller.[30] With that knowledge—despite the reputation of Millennials as entitled—we are actually saving and planning our retirement more aggressively than our parents or grandparents.[31]

Our pragmatic idealist mindset means that Millennials will be active in electoral politics without putting all their political energy into the quadrennial electoral battle. Activists like Mark Rembert and Taylor Stuckert will keep working to rebuild their Ohio hometown economy, regardless of who is running for president. The same is true for Marvelyn Brown's continuing crusade for awareness of HIV/AIDS. Millennial activists like these all follow electoral politics closely and care about it deeply, but their work will go on regardless of presidential elections and congressional debate. They don't require an election cycle to make progress. As Mark points out, "We're in Wilmington for the long haul, to make a real lasting impact. We observe politics for sure, we're political junkies, but whether Obama gets re-elected or not, whether our mayor gets re-elected or not, we're here. Will those things have an impact on our work? Definitely. But what we're doing is bigger than elections."

Mark is practicing hyper-relevant politics. This concept, borne out of our pragmatic idealistic mindset, identifies the most important issues in our lives and recognizes that the ways to address those issues exist at the intersection of our individual abilities, passions, ideals, and networks. Then we act.

Millennials were excited by the potential for the federal government to become more effective and responsive after the 2008 election, especially in this time of serious economic crisis and unemployment. Instead, the frustration Millennials felt at the continued—perhaps even worsened—ineffectiveness and irresponsiveness of government led to a renewed focus on the importance of independent, local, and non-electoral actions on key issues, including the environment, deficit, employment, labor rights, social policy, international issues, civil rights, and human rights. These issues are too big and too important to leave in the hands of a dysfunctional government. In Millennials' hyper-relevant politics, when we say, "We can't wait," we mean we're going to start fixing the big problem right now. More and more, it seems that government isn't addressing the most relevant issues, so we have to dig in and start somewhere.

Many of these hyper-relevant efforts often start small, in local geographic or demographic communities. Mark was already practicing the art of hyper-relevant politics when I met him in 2010. He couldn't wait for the government to jumpstart economic recovery, so he started taking action outside the system. In 2011, in addition to his role with Energize Clinton County, he was named director of the Wilmington-Clinton County Chamber of Commerce, one of several Millennials who have become local chamber of commerce directors in the past few years. Mark was appointed as a result of the town establishment recognizing his proven ability—outside the system—to affect the ailing economy. Mark can now effect change from the inside *and* the outside.

Hyper-relevant politics also drove the Occupy Wall Street protests. Millennials have long been concerned about the economy and the deficit. We are aware that the ever-rising, broadening, more inclusive middle class—the building block of the American dream—has become more elusive. The 2008–2009 financial collapse, with its mortgage crisis, bank bailouts, and attendant deep anxiety and uncertainty in our own families made the reality more palpable for many of us. High unemployment rates, mounting student debt, and the decreasing affordability of college have combined to hit Millennials ferociously. But for most of the recession, Millennials were too busy trying to find a job, or working long days at multiple jobs, or working at the job they were lucky enough to get, to organize and express their outrage.

So they began to gather in Zuccotti Park, in the heart of New York's

financial district in the fall of 2011. As the Occupy Wall Street movement grew, it opened a new chapter in the national political discussion.
With the Occupy movement came a tonal shift in the national conversation to the broader, systemic challenges facing the country as a whole.
The extreme weight of the accumulated unfairness, hypocrisy, and injustice finally broke through and became part of the national conversation. There was no accountability, no movement for significant reform,
no one going to jail or being prosecuted for hundreds of billions of
dollars lost to risky financial engineering that was clearly tantamount
to fraud.

Occupy expressed the inchoate feelings of virtually all demographics in the society. In particular, Occupy's focus on the so-called 1 percent
of the population, who account for an estimated one-third of the aggregate wealth in the country—as well as its focus on the growing disparity
in wealth between the top 1 percent and everyone else—made for very
compelling issues. "Occupy" was voted the official word of the year for
2011. "The Protestor" was *Time* magazine's "Person of the Year," standing in for protesters from the Arab Spring at the beginning of 2011
and the Occupy movement in the fall to the biggest demonstrations
in modern Russian history that December. But the great failing of the
Occupy movement was its collective anarchic decision not to stand for
any particular goals or reforms, to be a cultural statement rather than
a political change agent, and as a result, with so much idealism and so
little pragmatism, it could not sustain itself long enough to actually accomplish anything specific.

The majority of the Occupy movement's participants were actually Boomers. And while the movement likes to pretend it doesn't have
leaders, the two most prominent figures whose ideas and actions caused
people to know about and join Occupy Wall Street were Kalle Lasn,
a seventy-year-old Estonian-Canadian designer, author, and magazine
editor, and David Graeber, a fifty-two-year-old academic anthropolo-
gist and anarchist. Furthermore, any support the movement had from
Millennials had dwindled to just 14.9 percent in 2012.[32]

On my visits to Zuccotti Park, the Millennial protestors I spoke to
were divided over whether or not they should have any goals—and if
they did decide to adopt goals, what their goals should be. "We've got

to change the system," Max, twenty-three, told me. "We have to stop the banks." But when I tried to get his ideas on how to stop the banks, or whether he envisioned a society without banks, or what one or two laws Congress could pass that would most restrain the naked greed of the banks, Max had no specific views he cared to share. Pat, twenty-one, who stopped by Occupy Wall Street, was concerned about the issues, but favored a different approach. "I agree with the goal," he said. "I think it's really important. I'm not sure maybe this is the best way to do it. I think sometimes you have to get up and play ball, you can't always just have a sit-in. You kind of have to meet everyone in the middle."

Caitlin, twenty-one, was also at the protests and was concerned about their structure: "I feel it's kind of a nebulous movement, which is nice in some respects, but in others it's hard to pin down their actual mission."[33] While specificity was often lacking, one concrete outcome of the movement was a renewed national focus on the economic disparity between the so-called 1 percent and the 99 percent. The nation became acutely aware of just how wide the wealth gap has become and how many people are concerned about it.

Although Occupy was not truly a Millennial movement, our spirit and sense of pragmatic idealism did have at least an occasional influence on the protests. For one thing, the Occupy protests developed an intriguing hybrid model somewhere between a "sit-in" and a demonstration. While the protestors wanted action, they were also building a new community. In New York and the other cities Occupy spread to, encampments became intricate physical communities, with Millennials often figuring out how to establish battery-charging stations and Internet access points, while blogging and tweeting about all the developments. In New York, a makeshift restaurant and commons emerged alongside the tents, and shifts for various clean up and maintenance duties were assigned collectively.

Millennials also helped make the Occupy protests the most technologized protests to date. Immediately upon my first visit to Zuccotti Park, I found the official "live stream" tent that broadcast daily interviews and scenes from the protests. The people in this tent were almost all in their twenties. They ran a savvy website, activated social networks, and used the group payment site WePay (also founded by Millennials) to collect contributions for Occupy, as well as for individual protestors with legal troubles. The tent served as a command center, with protesters being dispatched to film at locations around the park.

While the Occupy movement received extensive media coverage, many Millennials had been working on hyper-relevant politics in New York City for years before OWS was blessed with the media spotlight. Millennial Divine Bradley has been working in the Canarsie neighborhood of Brooklyn for a decade building community centers for neighborhood youth. As the leader of an organization called Team Revolution, he works with these young people to turn them into leaders and entrepreneurs. He's working in a neighborhood and with a population—underprivileged youth—that federal, state, and local government have been discussing and claiming to help for years. But Divine can't wait. He views his work as essentially independent from politics, and he's skeptical of the change that can come from the federal government. "My feeling about Obama is the feeling I have for just a president in general," he says. "He's a black man, yeah. The impact it had on African Americans in regards to them seeing change appear in a suit, and that suit is filled by a black man may have created this mystical experience for these folks, thinking, 'Well, Obama is president. That means all black people are changed.' It's not the truth." Divine understands and appreciates the importance of small, relevant action: over time, those smaller actions can scale while addressing the bigger national issues in a hyper-relevant way.

In the 1960s, many Boomers believed that working with or within the government could never produce meaningful change. But in the Millennial era, leaders like Divine and Mark Rembert appreciate the coexistence of governmental forces and external activism. Sometimes they work toward the same goal in a coordinated effort, at other times they work independently in concert, and at still other times they work independently in conflict or competition. All of these avenues are acceptable to Millennials. We want government to be involved in solving the big problems of our time, and we believe there is an important role for government. We don't hope or wait for or expect government to take the lead, but we are ready to embrace any role we can get from government in actually solving a problem.

THE CULTURE WARS ARE OVER!

Millennials are emerging as one of the largest and most energetic demographic forces in American life; they are also reconfiguring the ethnic and racial landscape. Millennials are statistically the most diverse generation in history. Only 61 percent of Millennials are white. This contrasts dramatically with Americans over sixty-five, who are 84 percent white. Moreover, the "minorities" among Millennials are visible and present throughout the country, no longer concentrated in specific geographies. Some 17 percent of Millennials are Latino, 15 percent are black, and 4 percent are Asian.[34] Even the "other" 3 percent comprises over two million people. Millennials are not only diverse; they are also the most educated generation in history. During the three decades between 1970 and 2004, the college enrollment rate among eighteen and nineteen year olds went up from less than half the population (48 percent) to almost two-thirds (64 percent). And from 1972 to 2003, the percentage of students enrolling in college right after high school similarly shot up from 49 percent to 64 percent.[35] By the 2016 election, today's Millennials will make up more than one-third of the total electorate.[36]

Given the unique and diverse demographic makeup of this generation, our experiences of the world we've grown up in, and our pragmatic idealistic mindset, we bring a new approach to the culture wars that have wrenched American society since at least the 1980s. These "wedge" issues—same-sex marriage, abortion, "traditional" moral values—have exercised an overbearing presence in American politics for three decades. The culture wars—and their manipulation by certain politicians—have also been a major factor giving rise to the current period of deep political polarization.

In this environment, Millennials are less polarized, less focused on what divides us, and more open to intelligent compromise. Almost every opinion poll demonstrates a striking openness, and even consensus, among Millennials on issues that have been at the center of the polarization of American politics. Not only have Millennials declined to engage with divisive movements, they also are less divided on the social issues that have played a key role in the country's polarization. A study by the Pew Research Center concluded, "The political leanings of this youngest group of voters may be linked to their outlook on politics and society. Analysis of long-term political values finds that Millennials are far more liberal in a number of areas than are older Americans. This is reflected in Millennials' views on contemporary policy issues as well, from their widespread belief that gays should be allowed to openly serve in the military to their reservations over the use of U.S. military forces in Afghanistan and Iraq and their continued preference for a more expansive role for government."[37]

Even those Millennials who take a traditionalist view on the right to bear arms see no reason not to restrict assault rifles and machine guns. And many devout Christian Millennials believe that government should have common sense policies on issues like contraception and abortion. As the Right and the Left continue to fight the culture wars, the Millennial mindset is bringing an end to certain divisive issues. As we saw in the 2012 presidential election, hot-button issues like gay marriage and abortion which were in the political conversation in the earlier part of 2012 actually played a minimal role on the campaign trail, thanks in large part to the generational shift ushered in by the Millennials. And as Millennials expand their role in society, their positions on these issues will be absorbed into the mainstream.

Although many Millennials are still ineligible to serve in Congress, overall there has been a huge surge in local and statewide elected officials under thirty-five across the country. A number of headline-making young people have been elected to a variety of civic offices. One of those is Alex Torpey, who was elected village president of South Orange Village, New Jersey, in May of 2011 at age twenty-three. Torpey has brought a fresh approach to local government. In his words, he ran because "Coming from outside, I think I understand people's frustration and apathy. So I said, 'You know what, why don't I just jump in and see if I can get the ball rolling in our town, and maybe even larger than that?' I wanted to get people more interested in government as a means of making change. I really don't think people see government as a way of doing that right now." With his Millennial sensibility, Torpey has used social media to give constituents quick service and to help fight crime in town. He's optimistic about the future of his generation in politics, including at the local level. "I think when people see what we're doing here, this can spread. This generation wants to make change."

The numbers of young elected officials do not yet translate into political power on the national scene. But over the next decade, Millennials will begin to increase their role as candidates and lawmakers. They've mastered the technology and social media that are increasingly important to the political process, and they've brought their optimism and pragmatic idealist mindset when it comes to civic engagement. When the majority of politicians—on both sides of the aisle—running for and holding office are Millennials, our disregard for culture war politics will create the opportunity to return to real policy debates and decrease political polarization. There will always be hyper-partisans and divisive characters in any generation of political leaders, but if Millennials remain true to their pragmatic idealism, those types of political influences will likely be less prevalent.

In today's Washington, the average age of members of Congress between 2009 and 2011 is actually the oldest in history.[38] Before the 2012 election, there was only one Millennial member of Congress, thirty-year-old Republican Aaron Schock from Illinois. While Schock is generally in line with mainstream Republican views, he is noted for his civil approach in a hyper-partisan Washington. Schock told me that, as a Millennial, he is able to bring a beneficial fresh voice and perspective to the political conversation. In his first term in Congress, Schock pushed to be on three committees (freshmen members are usually only given two committee assignments). On his list was the powerful Ways and Means committee, an assignment rarely given to freshmen. When the Republican leadership initially denied him a spot on Ways and Means, he told them that it was essential to have the voice of his generation on such a critical committee. The Millennial Schock prevailed and now serves on the committee that has jurisdiction over taxes, Social Security, and Medicare.

Current politicians have noticed that our generation is gaining political power and are beginning to change their tune in response. The "Don't Ask, Don't Tell" repeal provides a telling example. In a statement explaining his decision to vote for repeal of Don't Ask, Don't Tell, longtime North Carolina Republican senator Richard Burr said, "Given the generational transition that has taken place in our nation, I feel that this policy is outdated and repeal is inevitable." Burr was

one of only two conservative Republican senators to support the repeal. Such a vote marks the beginning of a real tonal shift. Political
columnist Ben Smith noted, "If the Republican from North Carolina
is talking like this, opposition to homosexuality has, in some broader
sense, lost its political juice. That generational transition marks a shift
away from the old political order of both social conservatism on issues of sexual morality and—on both sides, I think—activism around
abortion."[39]

In May 2012, when Barack Obama endorsed same-sex marriage, he
attributed much of his change in thinking to the Millennial Generation and our mindset, saying, "This is also generational . . . when I go
to college campuses, sometimes I talk to college Republicans who think
that I have terrible policies on the economy, on foreign policy, but are
very clear that when it comes to same-sex equality or, you know, believe
in equality. They are much more comfortable with it. You know, Malia
and Sasha, they have friends whose parents are same-sex couples. There
have been times where Michelle and I have been sitting around the dinner table and we're talking about their friends and their parents and
Malia and Sasha, it wouldn't dawn on them that somehow their friends'
parents would be treated differently. It doesn't make sense to them, and
frankly, that's the kind of thing that prompts a change in perspective."[40]
Peter Baker, writing in the *New York Times*, noted that "the emergence
of same-sex marriage as a mainstream issue in less than a generation
has upended convention, scrambled long-held assumptions and defied
history. The kind of change that took other social movements decades
or longer to achieve has accelerated in an era of instant communication
and universal information."[41] For Millennials this was a no-brainer. In
the fast future digital world, a strong view on a social issue held by a
majority of such a large demographic has an incredible ability to per-
meate the rest of the society.

The Millennial Generation is also more tolerant when it comes to
race, ethnicity, and sexual orientation than any generation in history.
This isn't a triumph of the Millennial Generation; rather, this tolerance
exists in large part as a consequence of how we grew up. We have grown
up going to school with a diverse group of people; we have seen diverse
people as leaders in politics, entertainment, and business.

While Millennials are not blind to the continuing effects of racism, sexism, and homophobia in our culture, we are a generation that has grown up with the forces for openness and tolerance gaining currency. No matter how progressive our parents' generation may be, they grew up in an era where segregation was still the norm and had to be overturned. They have the visual images of racial intolerance and injustice in their minds. Millennials, white and black, have witnessed a very different racial reality than our parents' generation saw. The long-term effects of this as we age, and as the generations behind us grow up in the same manner, may be even more striking.

The support and election of Barack Obama is just one example of this new Millennial racial and ethnic attitude. Supporting an African American candidate was not the nonstarter for Millennials that it might have been for many older people. Even in the South, where Obama lost most states by fairly healthy margins, he won the youth vote in many states, including Alabama, Mississippi, Tennessee, North Carolina, and South Carolina. In Georgia and Louisiana, he lost the youth vote by only one point. Alisha Morgan, a thirty-three year old from Georgia, characterized the change this way: "Rather than just being tolerant of race, we embrace and accept our differences. We all recognize that racism still exists. But I think younger people are much more willing to get over it."[42]

As advocates for openness and diversity have noted ever since the historic *Brown v. Board of Education* ruling in 1954, nothing integrates society so much as the actual integration of society. Huge problems remain, but more Millennials have a greater diversity of friends, acquaintances, classmates, and peers than at any prior time in the history of the American melting pot.

Our openness and eagerness to break down barriers applies to many domestic and even foreign policy issues as well. For several decades, the United States has maintained a staunch pro-Israel policy. Efforts by politicians on the Right or the Left to deviate from pro-Israel positions have been deemed political suicide, as they almost guarantee losing the powerful Jewish vote. Meanwhile, little progress has been made in actually solving the fundamental problem of Israelis and Palestinians living together in the heart of the Middle East.

However, Millennials—even Millennials of Jewish faith concerned for Israel—see the issue differently and are beginning to question axiomatic U.S. support for Israel. A 2007 survey of American Jews found that more than 40 percent of non-orthodox American Jews under the age of thirty-five agreed with the statement that "Israel occupies land belonging to someone else," and over 30 percent said that they sometimes felt "ashamed" of Israel's actions. The percentages of those under thirty-five who self-identify as pro-Israel, Zionist, and those who are "comfortable as supporters of Israel" are all substantially lower than in older generations. Simone Zimmerman, a Millennial at the University of California, Berkeley, who is active in Jewish life on campus, thought about this issue during a debate about Berkeley divesting from companies doing business with the Israeli army. While Simone didn't end up supporting the divestment, it had an impact. "They were sharing their families' experiences of life under occupation and life during the war in Gaza," she recalled. "So much of what they were talking about related to things that I had always been taught to defend, like human rights and social justice, and the value of each individual's life."[43]

The shift in attitudes toward Israel since our parents' generation can be attributed to a number of factors. Perhaps chief among these is the fact that we did not live through the 1967 and 1973 wars, when sympathy toward Israel was more universal. But it is also due to the Millennial mindset. There is hardly anything the Millennials view as untouchable. Every issue should be re-examined in light of today's realities and the need for workable solutions to enduring problems. That doesn't mean we're unprincipled—far from it. It means we're openminded. Most of the American Millennial Jews who are beginning to question Mideast foreign policy say they do so out of concern for Israel's survival, not because they are anti-Israel. They are looking for ways to generate peace and stability, and end a long cycle of wars and terrorist attacks.

Our political system has been held hostage to ideological preconditions and a lack of open-mindedness for too long. Without open minds, how can you tackle giant challenges? The Millennials have no preconditions for trying to achieve progress. So whether it is Israel or fiscal policy, Millennials ask, Why support something just because it's what we've always done? If and when "everything" truly gets put on the table, we are likely to have the kind of progress everyone hopes for when they speak about an American renewal or an American resurgence. Without that spirit, it's hard to imagine breaking out of the polarization and stagnation that define our times.

SIX

Globalized

> You don't need your parents' permission, money
> to buy a plane ticket, or a passport and a visa to
> be able to interact with people of other societies.
>
> —Jared Cohen, thirty-one,
> director, Google Ideas

In June 2010, Khaled Said, a twenty-eight-year-old Egyptian, was pulled out of an Internet café by Egyptian police and beaten to death. When Wael Ghonim, the director of marketing for Google in the Middle East and North Africa, saw the gruesome pictures of his beaten face, he was horrified. He decided to act. Ghonim, then thirty, created a Facebook page called, "We Are All Khaled Said" that would serve to call his fellow Egyptians to action. Fearing the Egyptian state police, Ghonim created the page anonymously, concealing his identity as the page's administrator. He suspected many people would share his feelings, but he didn't guess that the page, as well as a subsequent event page asking people to come to Tahrir Square to protest on January 25, 2011, would draw hundreds of thousands of people and launch a revolution. But that's what happened.

Ghonim's story is emblematic of the young people throughout Egypt who rose up to demand change, an end to repression, the sanctity of basic human rights and freedoms, and economic opportunity in the Egyptian Revolution of 2011. Ghonim is reluctant to accept the mantle of hero that people all over the world have thrust upon him. Months after the revolution, Ghonim insisted what had happened was one of the first leaderless revolutions. "There's no 'I'm the leader; I'm the one who tells people what to do.'" He went further, adding, "In the next few years we're going to experience a new wave of leadership, or what we call the hero where the cause is actually the hero."[1]

The Egyptian people had lived for three decades in a country that was ever more impoverished each passing year, with decreasing economic opportunities and increasing political suppression. President Hosni Mubarak sapped the strength of the economy through massive profiteering for personal gain. Meanwhile, Mubarak became steadily more dictatorial. His police routinely arrested, tortured, and jailed political opponents; all efforts to hold genuinely free and fair elections were blocked.

In the first weeks of January 2011, events in Tunisia added another spark to the incipient flames of the Egyptian revolution. A twenty-six-year-old street vendor, Mohamed Bouazizi, barely scraping together a living selling fruit, was hassled and humiliated one too many times by a corrupt and abusive police force. In response, he set himself on fire, sacrificing himself to make a dramatic statement about corruption and lack of opportunity for young people in the increasingly repressive Tunisian state. Bouazizi's death triggered an almost immediate wave of demonstrations organized in no small part through social and mobile technology, including Twitter, Facebook, and SMS messaging—the biggest demonstrations Tunisia had ever seen. They began shortly after his self-immolation in December and grew stronger day by day after Bouazizi's death in early January. By January 14, the protest movement had grown so big and vibrant that it succeeded in bringing down the government and sending President Ben Ali, the despotic ruler who had ruled the country with an iron fist for twenty-three years, into exile in Saudi Arabia. The demonstrators were almost entirely unarmed. Their only weapons were their cell phones, Facebook accounts, Twitter feeds, and their just and popular cause. With these simple tools, they sent Ben Ali packing and took power into their own hands, creating the first possibility in their lifetimes for a more democratic Tunisia.

Tunisia set the stage for Egypt, while Egypt set the stage for Libya and the sweeping movement that would become known as the "Arab Spring." The real genesis of the success in toppling the long-time dictators in both Egypt and Tunisia lay with the millions of young people who were at the forefront of these movements demanding freedom and opportunity. More specifically, the successes of the Arab Spring can be attributed to the unique worldview held by Millennials in the fast future—as well as to the technology they have led the way in developing and popularizing.

Some 60 percent of the Egyptian and Tunisian populations are under thirty. In Egypt, more than half of that youth population was unemployed in January 2011. In addition to the sheer numbers of unemployed young people frustrated and angered by the lack of opportunity, Egypt also had the highest percentage of unemployed college graduates anywhere in the world. Well-educated and globally minded, Egypt's youth knew intuitively that, with their whole lives in front of them, they had a chance to act now to restructure their society and make it a better one.

Around the region, youth population statistics are equally stunning. The youth bulge is especially pronounced in Yemen, Bahrain, Lebanon, Turkey, Iran, Afghanistan, and Libya. In most of these countries, no matter how traditional, theocratic, and ossified the national culture and political system may be, young people have emerged with new ideas, new courage to stand up for democracy, and new technological and cultural tools to spread their ideas and to organize.

For at least the last two decades of Mubarak's rule in Egypt, there were dissidents who occasionally rose to prominence calling for free elections or exposing corruption or political repression. Illegal political parties have operated underground; movements for political change have at various times looked like they might take hold in Egypt. But none of these efforts managed to make any significant progress in democratizing Egypt until 2011. One key difference was the youth constituency for the January 25th movement. It was the energy, passion, and forward-looking nature of Egypt's youth combined with their technology and media savvy that allowed them to outflank and outsmart the repressive political machinery. No prior effort at change or reform had the tools that Wael Ghonim and dozens of other young leaders brought to the public square: a global information and communications infrastructure, Facebook pages, Twitter feeds, cell phone cameras, and an ability to command the global stage. Butul Taufik, twenty-two, a Libyan who supported the revolutions across the Middle East, spoke of the deep effect of social media. "Since social media has become so popular, young people started to compare themselves to other people in their situation," he said. "It opened things up. We made friends on Facebook, we could look at pictures online and compare. Our parents didn't have that; they were very closed off. Now we could see how we compared to America, to the UK, and to other Arab countries that were living well while they had the same resources. We had the same potential."

Almost a year after the protests began in Egypt, I spoke with Wael Ghonim and asked him about how he and others used technology to power the protests. Referring to his initial Facebook posts calling for people to go to Tahrir Square, he told me, "I did not discuss anything with anyone about going to the streets on the twenty-fifth of January. It was just a very spontaneous action. And because of the nature of the Internet, people started to subscribe. And because I was anonymous at that time, no one felt someone was taking credit for this or was benefiting from this. It was just a random post in the cloud. Pretty much the same thing happened in every other country. Someone happened to set a date and people subscribed."

The "Facebook Revolution," as some dubbed the movement in Egypt, proved to be a powerful new model integrating social media tools together with real-life physical action. The physical and the digital, the online and the offline, were completely bound up with each other: just as Tahrir Square could not have happened without technology, it could not have happened without the pragmatic idealist mindset of the determined and courageous youth of the country, who showed up in person by the tens and hundreds of thousands, with the crowds swelling larger each day. They did not riot. They did not throw rocks. On the whole, they did not commit acts of violence except when attacked by the thugs of the regime.

The concept of "soft power," championed by former U.S. assistant secretary of defense Joseph Nye, holds that culture, in the form of films, music, new technology, and political ideas, among other forces, can have a powerful impact on international diplomacy. This theory is especially true when it comes to young people in the Middle East. Even where there is strong resentment against U.S. foreign policy—and we should not be so naive as to think resentment of America is not still very strong in Egypt—the society as a whole, and particularly young people, have been exposed to influential Western concepts and ideas. Even a silly romantic comedy expresses American ideals and possibilities. Someone's ability to quit their job by choice, start a company, take a road trip, fall in love, fall out of love, start their life over again— these are all common arcs in American films, suggesting the great spirit of freedom and personal empowerment that typifies our culture. Upward mobility, independence, free expression, individualism, and entrepreneurship—these values run through many American films seen all over the world, yet these values are also novel concepts to young people in a society like Egypt.

In this vein, it's quite interesting to note that *The Social Network*, the 2010 film about the creation of Facebook, did quite well in Egypt, where it played in the months immediately preceding the January protests.[2] The Egyptian Millennials who saw the film were exposed not only to the story of Facebook and Mark Zuckerberg personally, but to the ideas of innovation and starting a company around a big idea. Wael Eskandar, writing in *Al-Ahram*, one of Egypt's largest news outlets, described the connection: "The question of what Facebook can be has been settled by Egyptians, becoming an unprecedented form of expression and a catalyst to activism. . . . In a way, we've come full circle; *The Social Network*'s Facebook took the realm of social interactions to the web and in return Egypt has taken Facebook beyond those pages into the world."[3]

Indeed, Facebook and Twitter were essential to the increased success and organization of the protests. People have always used the latest technology to advocate their causes. The invention of the copying machine in the 1960s played a key role in activist movements. In some campus towns, like Berkeley, anti-war groups formed alliances with sympathetic local printers who would allow use of their copying machine to make up flyers and newsletters for their causes. The fax machine was important in China's Tiananmen Square events in 1989 as well as the Velvet Revolution led by Vaclav Havel in Czechoslovakia at the same time. In 2011 and 2012, the Internet was not just one factor among many. Instead, the use of its tools and powers was actually decisive and central to the outcome. The Internet and social media provided a platform for smart power—among other things—allowing the Egyptian people, and particularly the youth, access and exposure to ideas, a global community, dialogue, transparency, and the sensibility of an open society. These ideas also contributed to building a mindset that prepared Egyptian youth to be catalysts for a movement. Young people revolted in Egypt partly because they knew they could do it, and partly because they knew a better future was possible. They'd seen that possibility around the world, not necessarily in person but online, on television, and in the global culture. It's no coincidence that the murder of Khaled Said, the spark that ignited the revolution, took place at an Internet café.

Even as they were pouring into the streets en masse, the Egyptian young people were pragmatic idealists. They didn't go beyond the scope of what most Egyptians broadly supported: forcing Mubarak out of office. Although they were revolutionaries, they were pragmatic in the process they used to achieve their goals. Throughout the turbulent days of protests, they continued to distinguish between the police and the military, for example. The police state had to be ended—there was no compromising on that point. Mubarak had to go. There was no compromise to be made on this point, either. But pragmatically, the young leaders of the January 25th movement were willing to ally themselves with the military.

Past youth movements against autocratic regimes have succeeded in stirring passion for freedom and democracy all over the world. But in recent times, many of these movements have also failed to bring down repressive governments. In most cases, tragically including the 2009 uprising in Iran, the governments stay in power and students and youth face harsh repression. But Egypt has arguably experienced the most significant modern success of a youth movement in overthrowing a major government.

In parts of Mexico, where the drug cartels have gained extraordinary power, serving as an officer of the law can be either a recipe for death, if you are honest, or a quick way to get rich if you are corrupt. It might be the toughest place to be a police officer anywhere in the world. In many high-crime Mexican towns, the job of police chief is so undesirable that no one will even take it. In October 2010, city officials in the border town of Praxedis G. Guerrero in the state of Chihuahua put out one of their increasingly frequent calls for a new police chief. Only

one person applied: Marisol Valles, then a twenty-year-old criminol-
ogy student. Even though she hadn't yet completed her degree and her
predecessor had been gunned down by the cartels, she signed up for the
task. She began work, saying, "We're all afraid in Mexico now. We can't
let fear beat us."[4]

Millennials don't always "win," although powerful forces are con-
verging that make the possibility of success in tackling large social
problems more likely. Valles is a case in point. She saw a problem tearing her city and her society apart. She was quite aware of the dangers
and the complexities. Nevertheless, she believed somebody had to try
to help. Why not her? While some called Valles naive and feared for
her safety, her bold actions led the Spanish newspaper *El País* to declare her "the bravest woman in Mexico." Yet a few months into her
job, she was forced to recognize it was no longer safe to be the police
chief of her town, and fled to the United States seeking asylum. Even
so, she remains optimistic: "As long as we're breathing, we can dream
for a better world." She speaks for the people she's left behind in her
beautiful but violent Mexican valley. "Don't ever lose hope," she said
in a message to them. "Continue fighting for your children. I'm sorry
I had to leave, but it's better to be safe and alive here . . . than to be
dead in Mexico."[5] Although Marisol Valles didn't win an instant victory
against the drug cartels, she was idealistic enough to try to change her
town's reality, and also pragmatic enough not to become a martyr in
the process.

Marisol Valles shares the Millennial mindset of pragmatic idealism. She is just one of many Millennials outside of America who share
this philosophy. This mindset is found even in those parts of the world
where it hasn't yet infused the country's general populace. One of the
principles that the Arab Spring demonstrated was that young people all
around the world are on the front lines of political and social change, reshaping our global future. Millennials are leading new political actions
with a unique mixture of idealism and pragmatism, making full use of
new technologies as a means toward mass empowerment.

Millennials around the world have also experienced the 2008 global financial crisis and recession. As of early 2011, some 81 million global
youth found themselves unemployed, leading former British prime min-

ister Gordon Brown to declare global youth unemployment a problem of "epidemic proportions."[6] Around the world the numbers are staggering, with many record highs: 20 percent youth unemployment in the United Kingdom, 25 percent in Egypt. In 2012, the global unemployment rate for those twenty-four and younger was 12.7 percent.[7]

Just as in Egypt, Millennials in many countries are simultaneously the most educated and unemployed generation. We've seen different responses to this predicament around the world. In the United States, many Millennials, although disappointed by the job market and the opportunities available to them, have demonstrated resilience and entrepreneurialism, creating their own opportunities. In Greece, as the economic situation grew worse and worse after the 2008 financial crisis, Millennials were among the most aggressive street protesters. They were also leaders of cross-generational coalitions to demand relief. The Millennial message was that young people refused to bear the full brunt of international bank and bondholder demands for cutbacks of social services. In the months following the Arab Spring, Millennials around the world, inspired by their counterparts in the Middle East, became more vocal in their anger over their economic situation. The success of young Egyptians in changing their political reality became a palpable inspiration for Millennials everywhere. In the months that followed the Egyptian uprising, a series of Millennial-led movements broke out around the world, including flash mobs in Philadelphia protesting a 9 p.m. curfew for minors, hunger strikes, love-ins, rallies in Chile advocating economic reforms, and the building of a tent city in Tel Aviv to protest the housing crisis there.

All over the world, Millennials increased their participation in electoral politics in the wake of Barack Obama's 2008 election campaign. Indeed, ever since the 2008 elections, in the United Kingdom, France, Brazil, India, Germany, Uganda, Liberia, Pakistan, and elsewhere, a common theme has been unusually high participation by young people, resulting in major political realignments. Greater personal freedom, jobs for an unusually highly unemployed global cohort of young workers, and greater economic opportunity have been demands voiced in all these elections. Millennials have also shared other bonds of generational experience. The 2010 events in Haiti and Pakistan—a massive earthquake in the former, and unprecedented flooding in the latter—

made impressions on the young people coming of age in those countries in much the way Hurricane Katrina had done five years earlier in the United States.

In elections in every region of the world, race, culture, fundamentalism, religion, the cost of education, and the need to deal with terrorism without turning our societies into permanent war machines have also emerged as common issues and rallying points for Millennials. And in just about every circumstance, a heady mix of Internet, social media, mobile phones, and video have brought people together in new ways, spreading the news faster, tearing down the barriers of repression and media control. Regardless of the immediate outcomes, Millennials have demonstrated that they intend to become active participants in their societies and will push for change and reform even in countries, such as Egypt, where only a few years ago change seemed impossible. As the recession deepened and spread around the globe, frustrated young people increasingly went online to organize and make their voices heard, and in the Millennial era, that has a real effect. As Nicholas Kulish observed, writing in the *New York Times*, "The critical mass of wiki and mapping tools, video and social networking sites, the communal news wire of Twitter and the ease of donations afforded by sites like PayPal makes coalitions of like-minded individuals instantly viable."[8]

While this effect has been most pronounced in autocratic states like Egypt, Tunisia, Iran, and Libya, it is also playing out in democratic countries. The British election of 2010 and the protests there provide an interesting example. Most young voters tended to favor the Liberal Democratic Party candidate, Nick Clegg. The party itself is of "Millennial age." It was founded in 1988 and is therefore one of the newer political parties in the United Kingdom. Youth support for Clegg was mainly attributable to his pragmatic idealism on many issues, which made sense to the Millennial voters. Indeed, Clegg declared he was a "radical" (that is, an idealist) of the "center" (that is, a pragmatist). He summarized his party's view by critiquing both Left and Right, saying, "For the Left, an obsession with the state. For the Right, a worship of the market. But as liberals, we place our faith in people. People with power and opportunity in their hands. Our opponents try to divide us with their outdated labels of Left and Right. But we are not on the Left and we are not on the Right. We have our own label: liberal. We are liberals and we own the freehold to the centre ground of British politics. Our politics is the politics of the radical centre."[9]

Beyond the appeal of a Liberal Democratic worldview to a Millennial audience tired of both left and right dogmas, Clegg was also a consummate user of social media, which he used in particular to appeal to young voters. In one of the most closely watched elections in recent British history, his party polled a stunning 24 percent in the 2010 election, and ultimately entered into coalition with the Conservative Party headed by David Cameron.

Millennials strongly disliked Cameron and his stated plans to raise education fees and eliminate community and youth programs. When Cameron won the prime minister post, he forged a coalition with Clegg, who became deputy prime minister. (Some of Clegg's fascination with social media has rubbed off on Cameron, who has become a passionate Facebook advocate, regularly using it to communicate with constituents, putting more government services online, and even meeting with Mark Zuckerberg multiple times.) True to his campaign promises, shortly after coming into office, Cameron enacted major austerity measures that have included huge cuts to education spending at all levels, leading to outrage from British Millennials, who have demonstrated and organized to overturn the cuts.

That outrage was still on full display in the late summer of 2011 when police killed Mark Duggan, a twenty-nine-year-old Afro-British Millennial in South London. In the wake of Duggan's death—a situation perceived by some as not unlike events in Egypt and Tunisia a few months earlier—a series of protests, violent demonstrations, and near-riots broke out. The police killing of Duggan proved to be a tipping point for the build-up of frustration many Millennials felt as a result of the Conservative party's deep cuts in social programs, which disproportionately affected young people. While the violence and looting that ensued was condemned by most Millennial activists, there was also a widespread recognition that young people in the United Kingdom are far angrier and more frustrated than Cameron's government had assumed. Cameron's insistence on attacking all the angry young people as "hoodlums" eroded his credibility even further among younger voters. Commenting on the string of 2011 uprisings, journalist Ben

Wallace-Wells noted that all were born out of "generational energies, and they have all the variability of the politics of young people everywhere. Sometimes, as in Tahrir Square, they can be stirring. But sometimes, as in England . . . they can be nihilistic, and terrifying."[10] Anger and frustration about specific issues as well as overarching anger at being denied opportunity can and will explode onto the streets. The social contract is being rewritten in many countries today, and those whose political leaders believe the youth are apathetic about these changes may be unpleasantly surprised.

These same feelings were on display in the fall of 2011, when Occupy Wall Street protests began in New York before spreading around the world. Nicholas Kristof described the deep global interconnectedness of these youth movements: "My interviews with protesters in Manhattan's Zuccotti Park seemed to rhyme with my interviews in Tahrir earlier this year. There's a parallel sense that the political/economic system is tilted against the 99 percent. Al Gore, who supports the Wall Street protests, described them perfectly as a 'primal scream of democracy.'"[11]

Among the many commonalities shared by global Millennials is our role as "first digitals" in our respective societies. We've all shared the experience of being present for the technological explosion, and living through revolution after revolution from laptop to cell phone to iPad in our short lifetimes. The impact that young people have been able to make with technology has been on display in political movements around the world. What's more, since platforms like Twitter and Facebook are themselves essentially global, all of the mass movements for social and governmental change in the past several years were seen instantaneously by Millennials all over the world. For the first time, Millennials in one country could see other Millennials taking action in real time in another. They could take inspiration from these actions and spread the message even further.

One of the early global displays of the power of social technology in Millennial-led social movements came in January 2008, when social media became a key tool in the movement against FARC, the terrorist organization in Colombia. Colombian Oscar Morales was the unlikely activist who led that movement. As he told me, "I wasn't supposed to be the person that I am. I started as a civil engineer, nothing to do with applications and mobile Internet. When you are aware of the political situation and the social situation of your own country, it's hard not to become an activist. It's hard to ignore that something is wrong." Oscar had been an early Facebook user in Colombia, so it seemed like a logical platform. He was frustrated with the terrorist group's power, and the seeming public complacency in the face of FARC's hold over the country, so he created a Facebook group one night in January 2008 called "One Million Voices Against FARC."

At the time, Oscar's goal of making a million voices heard on Facebook was just a dream. But the group exploded in its first week, attracting 100,000 members, and then served as the main organizing tool in creating a mass protest several weeks later. Describing the rapid explosion of attention and support three years later, Oscar told me that at first, "It was a very shy call. But then came the avalanche effect where we found a connection, like a symphony with an audience that was hearing us . . . thousands and thousands and hundreds of thousands. So we were really excited that we were gaining more and more attention and people were trusting us that, 'Yeah, let's do this. Let's go outside. Let's protest.'" Oscar and his Facebook group turned out massive demonstrations in the streets of Colombia, which led FARC to release a group of hostages, including prominent politician Íngrid Betancourt, six months later.[12]

The pragmatic idealism of today's global Millennials is characterized by a greater orientation toward utilizing moral suasion and political persuasion than toward using violence. This is not to say there are no more armed revolutionary movements or that taking up arms will never again be important to bring about certain kinds of changes in certain countries. But the young demonstrators in Egypt and elsewhere have emphasized organization, media, technology—and have held the moral high ground in order to effect change. Since the leaders in these Arab countries were deposed in 2011 and 2012, real democracy has still eluded much of the region, and there are worrisome signs of increased power and influence for Muslim fundamentalists and members of the old regimes. Millennials do not expect all of their actions—

even dramatic and successful ones such as overthrowing a dictator—to lead to wholesale democratic change overnight. Young people in the Arab world hope their countries are on their way to democracy and a path that will ultimately lead to a better future. But whatever happens in the future of Egypt, Tunisia, Libya, and the other countries that were part of the Arab Spring, one thing remains clear: young people in these countries, newly empowered, will continue to make their voices heard.

In Iran, almost 70 percent of the population is under thirty.[13] These millions of young Iranians are not as isolated as the fundamentalist veil of the Ahmadinejad regime would make them seem. In fact, they share many similarities with their American contemporaries. In mid-2009, Iranian Millennials were thinking about change and the potential for democracy in their country. They were frustrated by the Ahmadinejad regime and saw the potential for change on the horizon with presidential candidate Mir Hossein Mousavi. As the election approached, a strong youth following built around the elder statesman. Iranian Millennials thought this could be their shot at real political change after Iran's long, suffocating, repressive rule by religious zealots and theocrats. When the election results were announced, with Ahmadinejad declared the winner in a fraud-riddled election, millions of protesters took to the streets of Tehran, most of them young. The world watched as the historically authoritarian regime faced its first serious uprising.

Much was made of the real-time updates—particularly on Twitter—of the protests and activism on the ground. Activists and journalists from around the world were retweeting posts by Iranians. For several days, CNN displayed a constantly updating feed of Iranian Twitter posts. This activity quickly got the attention of Americans and raised awareness in the United States about the situation in Iran. But most importantly, it served to turn people out into the streets of Tehran, in a country where the media is not allowed to function freely and people are highly constrained in the ways they can communicate. Twitter did not bring about the revolution: the repressiveness of the regime and the courage of its opponents were the key ingredients. But Twitter was a valuable tool that for the first time allowed the world to peer into a

closed-off society and offered that society itself a rudimentary toolkit
for organizing to express itself. Technology became such a powerful
tool that the Iranian government tried to shut down the Internet and
mobile phone networks during the revolution. To this day, many of the
same lines of communication are still open between global activists and
Iran. Even several years after what was ultimately a thwarted revolution,
Facebook remains the main way that Mousavi communicates with his
supporters. He counts over 150,000 supporters from around the world
on his Facebook page.

Iran's Green Revolution, as it came to be known, hit a turning point
after the tragic and horrific death of Millennial Neda Agha-Soltan,
a philosophy student who happened to walk into a protest and was
shot and killed on June 20, 2009. The impact of twenty-six-year-old
Neda's death in Iran was amplified around the world, caught on video
and then broadcast online. According to *Time*, Neda's death was "probably the most widely witnessed death in human history."[14] In the days that
followed, the name Neda and the phrase "For Neda" became frequent
cries among the protesters and global trending topics on Twitter. While
Neda's murder had an impact on all people, for Millennials—both those
protesting in Iran and engaged Millennials around the world—seeing
one of their peers shot and killed for the simple act of participating in a
peaceful protest reminded us of how serious the stakes sometimes are.

Over the weekend of June 13, 2009, in Washington, as the revolution was mounting in Iran, Millennial Jared Cohen closely monitored
the situation. Jared was initially hired by Condoleezza Rice to serve
on the secretary of state's policy planning staff, known as the State Department's internal think tank. His directive had been to help understand and "counter-radicalize" Muslim youth in the Middle East, based
on what he'd learned while traveling in the region a few years earlier
to research his book, *Children of the Jihad*. When Hillary Clinton became secretary of state in 2009, she shifted Jared's focus, making him a
key advisor on the use of technology in international diplomacy. With
these dual responsibilities, Jared sat at the intersection of two key forces
fueling the Iranian revolution, new media and youth. And just as the
protests were moving to a critical juncture, Jared learned that Twitter
was due to shut down later that day for regularly scheduled mainte-

nance. Twitter's maintenance was traditionally scheduled for the middle of the night in the United States, which happened to be prime daytime hours in Iran. Realizing the important role that Twitter was playing, Jared asked Twitter to postpone its maintenance. Twitter agreed. On the surface, this might seem to be a small action. But it was the first of its kind. The *New York Times* described this as a watershed moment, a "recognition by the United States government that an Internet blogging service that did not exist four years ago has the potential to change history in an ancient Islamic country."[15] Jared, thirty-one, who is now the director of Google's think tank Google Ideas, explained the decision to me this way: "Our belief was that we should be for the free flow of information, not just the free flow of information with the exception of times where it's politically controversial. No matter what, we are for the freedom of information and the freedom to connect." While noting the role that platforms like Twitter played, Jared is careful to distinguish between technology's support role and the courageous actions of individuals and social movements in making change happen. "I'm not arguing that Twitter was how people organized. . . . But, because everything was shut down, the handful of people that were still able to get stuff out of Iran, were able to do so via Twitter. . . . Where Twitter was most valuable was for millions of people all around the world to take part in it and disseminate it and make sure that a tweet here and a tweet there got the attention of presidents and prime ministers and the media."

The Green Revolution was as close as Iran has come in over thirty years to real reform and change. The regime's limits had never been tested so aggressively and so powerfully. The revolution was brought about by the pragmatic idealism of young people throughout the country, who were not content to live under authoritarianism. Without a free society, young people pragmatically realized the only way they could be heard would be if they protested. Ultimately, Iranian Millennials suffered huge losses—hundreds of young people died, were beaten, wounded, tortured, jailed. They didn't succeed—this time—in getting Mousavi elected or Ahmadinejad deposed. But with a large, determined, pragmatic youth population, change is much more likely to come to Iran soon.

■ ■ ■

When then-seventeen-year-old Eric Glustrom graduated from Fairview High School in Boulder, Colorado, he left to go on an Amnesty International trip to Uganda. His plan was to make a film about education there. Shortly after he arrived, he came to the realization that he wanted his work in Uganda to go much further. Eric wanted to bring about fundamental change in Uganda's education system, so he began working to create what would later become an organization called Educate!, which he runs to this day. The mission of Educate! is to train young people in Uganda, where people under twenty-four make up nearly 70 percent of the population, to become leaders and social entrepreneurs.[16] The group's work has become so respected that the Ugandan government commissioned Educate! to write the first-ever countrywide social entrepreneurship curriculum in Africa, which Uganda adopted in 2012.

Technology—and particularly new, low-cost, potentially ubiquitous mobile telecommunications technology—has the potential to accelerate Africa's economic growth and its integration with the rest of the developed world. As Eric explains, by the end of 2013, Kenya will reach 100 percent "teledensity," meaning just about everyone will have a mobile phone. South Africa will reach this important threshold even before the United States will. All across Africa, the proliferation of mobile technology could be the puzzle piece needed to fix the challenges that have handicapped Africa for decades. "This could be the tipping point. The game changer," Eric says. A decade ago, experts worried about the growing divide between digital haves and have-nots. Some specifically cited the challenge of Africa, where the majority of people had never made a phone call in their lives, let alone seen a computer or experienced the web. It is a stunning thought that, just a decade later, Africa is well on its way to having ubiquitous cell phone service. Almost every international aid organization working in Africa now has big plans for how to use mobile phone applications to update health records, track the spread of disease, improve the productivity of planting and harvesting, and provide remote education. International companies and organizations with strengths in technology have used this groundswell to scale their impact. Google has developed text-messaging systems with vital health and pandemic information that can be sent out en masse. In countries that already have economic and cultural obstacles to taking HIV medication, the lack of wristwatches frequently undermines the goal of taking medication at the same time every day, even for those who are able to get the medication they need. Even the mobile phone's simple functionality as a digital clock with alarm settings is beneficial. These small steps build a network on which change can be programmed. Cell phones whose use may have started with health applications are quickly becoming tools for banking, microfinance, and education, while opening up pathways of communication that once looked like they would require centuries to build.

As Eric and hundreds of others like him help unlock the entrepreneurial spirit of Africa and provide basic infrastructure for twenty-first-century development, the dynamic will change. We'll see more people like William Kamkwamba, a Millennial from Malawi, who, at age fifteen, used a library to research how to build a windmill to provide power to his town. He has since become a world-renowned inventor and author. For the first time in many years, the youth of Africa are working for and dreaming of a future that envisions their countries as a vibrant part of the world economy, not a region written off as being a hopeless land of famine, disease, disaster, and war.

Pollster John Zogby has applied the term "first globals" to Millennials because we are, in his words, already leading the world "into a new age of inclusion and authenticity. These are our internationalists, our multilateralists."[17] Technology has enabled us to be more connected to our peers around the world than any young generation before us, and as a result, a Millennial culture is growing and spreading around the world. More than 50 percent of Millennials use the web to listen to music from across the world, and more than 60 percent are likely to use the Internet to view art from other countries.[18]

Millennials know from our own experience that the fast future world is inherently global. We are keenly aware of just how quickly we are globalizing. A quarter of American young people think they'll end up living for a significant time period in a country other than the United States.[19] Nick Anderson, twenty-six, pointed out the impact of this shift in thinking. "If you compare our generation to our parents' generation, for example, I think that we spend a lot more time thinking about the rest of the world," he says. "Part of that is interest, part of it is that there's access now, so it's possible to watch a funny Japanese commercial on YouTube, which our parents obviously couldn't do. And I think part of it is just understanding that global power is shifting away from the West, and we have to understand the new forces."

While many of us are still America-centric in our thinking, we recognize that we're playing on a global stage in terms of communication, addressing problems, and our own competitiveness. The latter is perhaps the biggest negative impact of globalization on the American Millennial Generation. We're competing for spots at colleges and for jobs, especially manufacturing and entry-level jobs, with our global peers. When we go into a job interview, we're often competing theoretically or in actuality with people all over the world. Even those who are entrepreneurs trying to create their own companies are in competition with their global counterparts. The United States, once the undisputed leader in tech startups, has lost ground to India, China, Brazil, and other countries that have seen a proliferation of startups in the past several years. We are continually and keenly aware of our international counterparts. It's easier than ever to travel internationally. Anyone on a college campus in the United States is likely to meet at least a handful of people from other countries, if not become friends.

Largely because of globalization, American manufacturing has been in a deep and steady decline since the 1980s. The once-expected course for many young high school graduates—going to work at the auto, steel, or electronics plant—all but disappeared years ago. This will not come as a shock to Millennials, although it may to older politicians and pundits. Education and skills, entrepreneurialism and flexibility, and above all, understanding how to use technology will be the lifeblood of economic opportunity for Millennials as we get older.

Millennials have shown resilience in the face of the most challenging economic crisis since the Great Depression. Yet it is not clear that high schools and even colleges are preparing America's young people to work in the new global economy. For the last several years, even as youth unemployment has soared, Millennials have continued to innovate and create our own opportunities. Near downtown Washington, DC's Old Ebbitt Grill, a watering hole for government officials, the Millennial-founded daily-deal site LivingSocial managed to create four thousand new jobs in the first two years of its existence. Many of us are accessing the entrepreneurial spirit—found in America and now in many other countries as well—to create the next generation of businesses and capital. In fact, some Millennials are using that exact spirit to look to other countries as a logical place for their first job, such as Corrie Hulse, who found work in South Korea and has already returned there three times. "For millennials, right now, there is greater opportunity for us internationally," she says. "We were built for this international market. We are mobile, adventurous, tech-savvy, and grew up knowing the world was at our fingertips. More importantly, the international market wants us!"[20]

However, in the longer term, navigating the waters of globalization will be difficult, even after the ultimate recovery of the global economy. There is no denying the disorienting and destructive impact of globalization on old industries, employment patterns, and assumptions about the world. China and India have educated their Millennials in a very different way, with extreme focus on math, science, engineering, and information technology. In fact, many of the best and brightest students from emerging market economies attend U.S. colleges and PhD programs, then go back to their own countries and apply their knowledge in their own companies, leading to the boom of tech startups in India and China. At Grinnell College in Iowa, nearly one of every ten applicants being considered for the class of 2015 is from China.[21] What's more, over half of them have perfect 800 scores on their math SATs. In the leading American engineering programs at the graduate level, it has been estimated that close to half the students are from other countries and that, given U.S. immigration policies, even many of those who wish to stay in the United States and contribute to the American economy will end up going home, effectively to compete with us.

In 2011, a controversial book called *Battle Hymn of the Tiger Mother* by Amy Chua became a best seller in the United States, crystallizing, even as it oversimplified, the global challenge for American parents and their Millennial and Gen Z offspring. The book lionized the stereotypical Asian parenting style—forcing children to spend hours doing homework, berating poor performance, setting extremely high expectations and accepting nothing less, focusing on academics to the exclusion of sports or hobbies, and rejecting American emphasis on building up self-confidence and self-esteem. As one reviewer noted, "Chua's efforts 'not to raise a soft, entitled child' will strike American readers as a little scary—removing her children from school for extra practice, public shaming and insults, equating Western parenting with failure—but the results, she claims somewhat glibly in this frank, unapologetic report card, 'were hard to quarrel with.'"[22] For the last two decades, Americans have witnessed the rise of China and India and comforted ourselves with the notion that, while the average Chinese student is better at math than the average American student, the American is more creative, flexible and entrepreneurial. While this may have been true in the past, the world is changing before our very eyes. If Americans are to retain our creative, entrepreneurial leadership—and the global economic wealth it confers—we need our educational system and our governmental and social institutions to continue to invest in creating the infrastructure that leads to the flourishing of those traits of our society.

The rise of China and India has had an ever-growing impact on all Millennials. Both countries have huge total populations (about four in ten people in the world are Indian or Chinese), as well as huge Millennial populations. There are actually some significant comparisons to be made to American Millennials in terms of pragmatic idealism. Even in a country with a history of revolutionary youth movements, Chinese young people are putting their efforts into incremental reform and change. In fact, 83 percent of Chinese Millennials believe their generation has the power to change the world.[23] They are slowly and steadily changing their country through increasing economic opportunity, technology, and business, rather than trying to overthrow the system. Today, the Chinese have returned to the historic pragmatism of a successful, ingenious five-thousand-year-old civilization, tinged with much of the idealism that comes from their long Confucian and Buddhist cultural histories. Pragmatic idealism is on display among young Chinese artists as well. Xu Bing, the MacArthur Award–winning Chinese artist and vice chairman of the Central Academy of Fine Arts in Beijing, says, "We can see in the work of the younger generation of Chinese artists a uniqueness and creative potential that could be much, much more interesting than the work of the already world-famous artists, in terms of the art market and the work itself. . . . We can see real seeds of contemporary art—a real sense of future."[24]

In the United States, more Millennials are studying Mandarin than ever before. "Chinese isn't the new French—it's the new English," says Robert Davis, director of the Chinese-language program in Chicago's public school system, which has eight thousand students studying Mandarin. "It's not romantic. It's not because you're going to have a great time in Paris," he says. "It's very pragmatic."[25] Yet even with over five hundred American public schools now offering Chinese language programs and over fifty thousand American students participating in them, these numbers are dwarfed by the laws of large numbers on the other side of the Pacific. The number of Chinese students in China studying English exceeds the entire enrollment of all American students in all levels of K–12 schools. And given the extent of Chinese college students studying in the United States, there is hardly an American college student today who has not had the chance to get to know Chinese young people personally.

While political leaders have spoken for decades about an interdependent, multipolar world, it is only with our generation that this idea has become reality. Millennials also seem to understand that China, India, and other countries have their own distinct culture and economic and political systems, and that globalization is not a process of Americanization, but a push-and-pull, give-and-take, compete-and-cooperate process of change. We'll be the first generations to live our whole lives in this reality. It does not occur to us to even try to "un-globalize." We are all about figuring out how we can maximize the benefits and minimize the problems of globalization.

Millennials are also the first generation to grow up hearing about the problems of global climate change for our entire lives. Almost everywhere in the world, Millennials take climate change much more seriously as a global problem than any other generation. Perhaps that's because we are the ones who will live with the consequences for the longest time. Many of us have become environmental activists, and most others tend to be positively disposed toward "green thinking," consuming less energy, driving more efficient cars, and taking steps to reduce our individual carbon footprint. Erin Schrode, twenty-one, tries to help the environment in her everyday actions: "Global warming and all the science on climate change are hugely affecting my generation . . . and now it's second nature to us to 'go green' and to be 'eco-friendly.' The statistics are alarming. How can we not pay attention?" Schrode is in step with her Millennial peers: 69 percent of Millennials report paying more attention than in the past to the environmental or social impact, or both, of the products they buy.[26]

American young people interested in new green technologies often face a double frustration in terms of politics and policy. While alternative energy has finally established a toehold in the American economic landscape, other countries from China to Germany are much more focused on wind, solar, and other non-carbon-based energy solutions. Indeed, green industries represent the first major technological revolution in the last seventy-five years for which the companies and the levels of technological sophistication are more advanced in China than they are in the United States. There is deep concern among Millennial entrepreneurs and emerging business people that the very technologies that could help us solve our energy problems—and in doing so create hundreds of thousands of jobs—are not able to thrive in the domestic American economic and political ecosystem.

The universality of the Internet—with the exception of some countries where access remains restricted—allows us seamless experiences and communication with our fellow Millennials. We live in a time where physical borders mean less and less and do not inhibit collaboration and communication. This is a cause for optimism among non-Millennial leaders who are trying to tackle global challenges. Andrew Ho, who manages the Global Philanthropy arm of the Council on Foundations, observes: "Now there are the tools to not only know what's going on, but know who else is passionate about global issues of the environment, poverty, global health, and education at a speed and on a scale that wasn't previously achievable." Millennials, he adds, have "higher levels of knowledge about the world but, more importantly, a higher commitment to solve challenges in today's world."[27]

The Millennials are one of the largest generations in American history, and we are even larger globally, with approximately 1.7 billion Millennials around the world. Although we can never describe all American Millennials, or all global Millennials, as stepping in unison, this is a generation that has grown up together, been shaped in similar ways, and is, by and large, responding to their respective local and global issues in similar ways. There is far more that unites Millennials around the world than divides us.

Today, Millennials are more likely to engage with people from around the world on a semi-regular basis than any prior generation. While in and of itself this is a shift from our parents' generation, the real benefit of this experience comes from what Millennials take away from their experience of global interactions. To draw a parallel from European history, from 1870 to 1945 the Germans and the French fought three wars with each other. In each of those wars, the number of soldiers who had ever been in the other's country prior to being there in combat was negligible. But over the last six decades, the interactions between French and German people have become almost seamless. In fact there is essentially no border anymore between Germany and France, and despite gnawing growing pains of common economic policy, the Euro remains their common currency. Americans are now following a similar path in our relationships with other countries, even those where our relationships have not always been good.

Along with new global hopes come new global fears. Even with the growing legions of engaged, forward-thinking, and hopeful young people around the world, Millennials also are the backbone of the forces that struggle against modernization and progress—terrorism, fundamentalism, and other backward-looking trends in global society.

In many parts of the world, there is no strong sense of opportunity, no personal space for self-expression or self-actualization, and there are no jobs. Without encouragement to focus on their future, unemployment often skyrockets. Even those who are employed are often living in poverty or near poverty. In Middle Eastern and African countries, these disenfranchised Millennials are often prime recruitment targets to become suicide bombers and jihadists. The Internet has aided the ability to dramatize these feelings and capitalize on them, leading to higher recruitment by terrorist organizations and even the creation of new "web celebrity jihadists" like the cleric Al-Alwaki who, after accruing a large audience of young jihadists for his web videos, was killed by a U.S. drone strike in Yemen in October 2011.

There is no question that certain aspects of the Internet—anonymity, wide diffusion of once-classified knowledge about bomb-making, etc.— make it easier for terrorists to develop followings and stage actions. Jared Cohen puts it well: "Technology is just a tool. It doesn't choose sides, people do. . . . It creates space for certain leaders to promote democracy, and it creates space for others to create terror."

Yet even among fundamentalists and terrorists, their lack of success is weighing on young people's enthusiasm for fanaticism. Pragmatic idealism is emerging as an increasingly strong countercurrent. In the wake of the death of Osama bin Laden it was widely reported that he had lost the resonance he once had with many young Muslims who had previously been jihadists. The average age of al-Qaeda is going up, not down; the young people are often no longer interested in what is perceived as a failed path.[28]

In the United States, we've seen our own deeply troubled Millennials instigate national tragedies. Consider Jared Loughner, who shot and wounded U.S. congresswoman Gabrielle Giffords in a rampage that left twelve others wounded and six dead in January 2011 in Tucson, Arizona. Or James Holmes, the twenty-five year old who killed twelve people during a 2012 shooting rampage at a movie theater in Aurora, Colorado, not that far from Columbine. We cannot be naive. Along with all the hope and promise of our generation and our times, there is also a dark side—and it is very dark and dangerous indeed. Troubled people— Millennials or otherwise—will always exist, and such people will always be prone to taking extreme, dangerous, and destabilizing actions. Our generation has learned to become somewhat more conscious and proactive about dealing with these individuals. We are less likely to stand aside and say we "don't want to get involved" or "it's not my problem."

It's important to remember that in tragedies where a Millennial is a villain, there is often also a Millennial hero. In the case of Gabrielle Giffords, that hero was then-twenty-one-year-old Daniel Hernandez, wise and mature beyond his years, who tended to Congresswoman Giffords after she was hit in the shooting spree. By many accounts, he saved her life in those first minutes. Even as suicide bombers—some of whom are Millennials—continue to attack innocent civilians in the Middle East, there are young people fighting for a solution to the decades-long conflict. OneVoice, an organization of thousands of activists around the world, anchored by Israeli and Palestinian youth, are working together in a grassroots effort. Leaders in the Middle East peace process, including former British prime minister Tony Blair, have heralded their efforts. Blair views the largely youth movement as an important part of the process. In order "to change the realities on the ground, the grassroots need to be involved in the process, and that is exactly what OneVoice is doing," he says. "For the outside world, when they see young people prepared to reach out to one another, it gives the rest of us hope."[29]

Coming of age in the twenty-first century, Millennials are sometimes better able to see the suffering and problems in the world—and to be motivated to do something about them. What's more, the ability to travel to distant regions is arguably easier than it has been in prior eras. For our parents' generation, traveling to Africa over a spring break would have been unlikely. Today, young people are frequently members of NGO delegations or local church missionary trips to remote impoverished countries. They go for short and extended periods of time; they go for specific home-building or well-digging trips, for junior years abroad, or for long-term aid programs.

Maggie Doyne graduated in 2005 from high school in New Jersey before deciding she wanted to go to Nepal. After seeing the number of orphans there and the lack of social services for them, she asked her parents to send her life savings to her—money she had accumulated from years of babysitting jobs. At just nineteen years old, she had made her decision: she would stay and help. In just a few short years, Maggie became the legal guardian for thirty children and built them an orphanage and a school. Eventually, she built a school for the children. Says Maggie, now twenty-six, "When I went to Nepal and met children in need of a home and decided to build one for them. I wanted it to be the kind of home and the kind of childhood that I thought every child in the world deserved."

In 2010, Nicholas Kristof wrote a *New York Times Magazine* article about what he called the "D.I.Y. Foreign Aid Revolution" in which he profiled Maggie. Kristof pointed out that traditionally, foreign aid has been doled out in grant form by the United States and other governments and agencies in an effort to address specific problems in various parts of the world. Usually, there is little involvement after the aid is granted, and there is often a high level of bureaucracy and waste involved, as a result of the nature of government-to-government interaction. Kristof wrote enthusiastically about Maggie as part of a trend of young people who are working on small, yet high-impact international aid projects independently.[30] Millennials led record volunteer rates for the Peace Corps over the past several years, including an 18 percent rise in volunteers from 2008 to 2009 and rising to a forty-year high in the number of Peace Corps members in 2010.[31] In addition, more American students are studying abroad than ever before, with the latest statistics showing the numbers at well over 200,000. At the same time, almost 700,000 international students are studying in America, also a record.[32]

Unwilling to wait for a complex government aid system to "get around" to helping the children of Surkhet, Nepal, Maggie is taking direct action every day, performing all the necessary activities to run an orphanage and a school, from finding architects to build and design the project to hiring teachers and developing curriculum. Maggie doesn't know how to do everything perfectly. She'll be the first to admit that. But she has pragmatically developed a network of supporters, partners, and volunteers and continues to contribute to the well-being of the children in the orphanage.

Maggie isn't trying to change the world. She's just trying to improve the lives of orphans in the Kopila Valley. But if there are enough Maggies, they will add up to a world-changing force. As Maggie puts it, "I can't personally do something for every single child in the world struggling to survive. I focus every day on the sanctity of our home at the orphanage and making sure that my children feel safe and loved. . . . When I feel overwhelmed by the big picture of the world or the political situation in Nepal or the extreme poverty I see around me, I stop and try to focus on the smaller things that I know are in my control: bathing my children, trimming their fingernails, cooking a meal together, and reading a bedtime story."

Millennials have also become key leaders in disaster relief and philanthropy. Combining our socially minded worldview with the new methods of giving, Millennials can easily become micro-philanthropists and repeat donors, despite our limited personal wealth. After global disasters from the earthquake in Haiti to the nuclear disaster in Japan, Millennials have been in the forefront of international efforts to raise money and provide support to survivors. After the Japanese nuclear disaster, the Bezos Family Foundation asked for citizens to send them paper cranes for Japan. For each crane, the foundation would donate $2 to the recovery efforts. The foundation expected a hundred thousand cranes, but Millennials banded together and sent in over two million paper cranes in just four months.[33]

WILL WE KNOW THE FUTURE IF WE SEE IT?

In the spring of 2011, I was in Abu Dhabi making a documentary about the idea behind a brand new institution: New York University Abu Dhabi. The campus is designed to be a full university, linked to NYU's New York campus and serving as a portal in NYU's Global Network University. The brainchild of NYU president John Sexton, the Global Network University is meant to allow students to enter the NYU system through any one of these portals (another portal will open in Shanghai later this year) and then seamlessly move through other portals, making it, in Sexton's words, "as easy to register for a course as for a continent." Sexton's overarching thought is that education needs to be global in a global world, and that university education is one of America's great strengths. He wants to see America exercise its intellectual leadership and contribute to turning the process of globalization into a positive-sum game, improving exchanges between peoples and enhancing shared global values and interests and the desire to succeed together.

NYU Abu Dhabi is designed to be a "world honors college." Its students hail from thirty-nine countries. The average student speaks three languages, and the median SAT score is 1470 out of 1600, with students taking the SAT in English, even though it is a first language for less than half of the students.[34] Interest in this new NYU program was so great that in its first year, the Abu Dhabi acceptance rate was lower than at any American college. The experience affords unparalleled opportunities to people like Musbah Dilsebo, an Ethiopian orphan who is now at NYU Abu Dhabi on a full scholarship. He is not unlike the Millennials in America and abroad who have used the fruits of modernity to propel themselves to greatness. To be sure, Abu Dhabi is a unique place with unique resources to make an experiment like this possible, so it won't become the norm around the globe. But it is a vision that resonates on both the pragmatic and idealistic sides of the equation and is being mirrored by dozens of other American and European universities that have opened campuses in other countries.

NYU Abu Dhabi is also a physical model of the way Millennials can and are connecting anytime and anywhere with their global peers. Millennials from all over the world, every day, attending classes together, sharing their experiences, adapting, learning, and ultimately laying the foundation for a world in which birthplace may no longer matter. It's an appreciation of the connected and open society that Millennials want to be a part of and share. Sitting in his New York office, John Sexton reflected on the fast future we are all headed into. The fundamental theme of the Global Network University, he said, is the ability to take in the cultures around you and soak them in, to listen, to embrace, and engage. With that spirit, this is a generation—from Wilmington, Ohio, to Abu Dhabi, and from Egypt's Tahrir Square to New York's Washington Square—that is embracing the world and each other.

There was a moment in February 2011 that symbolized the transcendent impact of this generation and the virtuous circle it has made around the globe. State workers in Wisconsin were protesting against proposed cuts to their pension and benefit plans and efforts to break their unions by Governor Scott Walker. The public employees marched on the state capitol in Madison along with supporters, including many Millennials, in a group estimated at tens of thousands. In the midst of this Wisconsin protest, among all the Wisconsin Badger T-shirts and other colorful local paraphernalia, there were signs bearing an unusual phrase: "Walk Like an Egyptian." These words alluded to the Millennials in Egypt who, just a few weeks earlier, started a revolution and overthrew a thirty-year-old dictatorial regime, seizing their destiny in their own hands and defining a new model for citizen empowerment and social change. Millennials around the world are all fighting for something. The causes are different. Some may be deeply personal; others may be for the benefit of a community, country, or the world at large. Yet we all realize and sympathize with each other's feeling about the need to stand for something and to stand up.

The Millennials are a generation of change agents. And we have arrived. We are ready, willing, and doing, already working on the changes we believe our world needs. Perhaps even more important than the headline-making accomplishments of the Millennials, from the 2008 American presidential election to the Arab Spring, is the capacity for each member of this generation to bring their own ideas and vision into the world, to create their own business or organization, to become an advocate, or to solve a problem. It's never been more possible for young people to turn ideas into action, and Millennials have certainly taken advantage of this exciting new offering on the menu of our world.

Our sophistication about enacting change is exemplified by our belief in pragmatic idealism. This worldview has already helped us get through some of the worst political, economic, and foreign policy challenges in decades, emerging focused and undeterred in our mission to make the world a better place. We are and will continue to be guiders and shapers, ushering our peers and the members of other generations through the fast future. The good news is that we are up to the task.

Epilogue

Throughout the nearly two years of permanent campaigning that led up to the 2012 election, the conventional wisdom seemed to be that Millennials—who had played such a decisive role in Barack Obama's 2008 election—felt the president had failed to deliver on his promises of change and economic opportunity and, as a result, were going to be much less enthusiastic about voting in 2012. But as the numbers came in on election night, it became clear that young voters were, once again, defying the experts' predictions. Over twenty-two million people between the ages of eighteen and thirty voted, putting the youth turnout on par with 2008. As a share of the total electorate, the percentage of young voters actually rose by one point, a small but important increase from 2008.

Obama handily won the support of 2012's young voters, who broke 60 to 39 in his favor. In Florida, Ohio, Virginia, and Pennsylvania—four states essential to the president's ability to win the election—the youth vote actually was one of the key factors that put him over the top. Put another way, if no one under thirty had voted, Obama would have lost those states and, thus, the presidency.[1] Millennials also influenced many House and Senate races; races that resulted in sending a historic number of women to the halls of Congress, as well as the first openly gay senator and the first Hindu and first bisexual members of Congress.

However, it is important to note that neither Obama nor Republican nominee Mitt Romney truly engaged young voters in relevant policy conversations during the course of the election cycle. The Obama campaign deftly turned out young voters, but without the big rallies attended by thousands that were a staple of the 2008 campaign. If Millennials believed in 2008 that Obama could make big changes overnight, far fewer believed that in 2012.

As I hope I've made clear, Millennials do not place a huge emphasis on electoral politics. They understand its importance—and that's why they can be counted on to vote. But they spend far more time on other civic and social engagement activities as advocates, activists, and entrepreneurs. In fact, in a pre-election survey of young voters conducted by the Harvard Institute of Politics, 40 percent of Millennials said the winner of the presidential election didn't matter that much because Washington was so broken.[2]

That number doesn't mean Millennials have given up on electoral politics. It simply means they know they have to do other things with their lives and their beliefs to influence the changes they wish to see, *in addition to* electoral politics. Nonetheless, after sustained increases in youth turnout in every presidential election since 2004, it's almost impossible to ignore the Millennials as a major force in the American political future.

Still, some Boomers and seniors profess disappointment that only a little more than 50 percent of Millennials eligible to vote do so. However, our national voter turnout encompassing eligible voters of all ages has hovered between 49 and 56 percent in presidential elections over the last several decades, and there has been a continued tendency for age-cohort turnout numbers to increase the older the age cohort is. What's more, if we look at the youth vote in historical context, it turns out that Millennials actually follow the same participation pattern that our Boomer parents did when they were young. In 1972, the first election after the 26th Amendment effectively lowered the voting age to eighteen, only 54 percent of then-young Boomers turned out to vote, despite the strong anti–Vietnam War youth movement. In 2004, the comparable election for Millennials, 49 percent of Millennials turned out. In the 1976 election, 50 percent of Boomers participated as compared with 2008, which saw 51 percent of Millennials vote. In 1980, youth voter turnout came in at 52 percent versus Millennials in 2012 (our third election), where at least 49 percent voted (it may end up being as high as 51 percent when final numbers are revised).[3] Today's Millennial voters are *not* more apathetic or less interested than the Boomers were when they were our age—the voting patterns in each generation's first, second, and third elections are comparable. So it would follow that as Millennials age, they will probably repeat the historical and current patterns of older voters, increasing their turnout to even higher numbers.

Much of this book is about what's different about the Millennials from other generations. But the Millennials also share much with prior generations. One of the failings many Republican strategists acknowledged in the days after the 2012 election was that their party did not do enough to reach out to new kinds of voters that reflect our country's changing demographics. Though part of that failure was due to their policies, part of it was also a result of focusing on television advertising as opposed to more creative approaches using new technologies. To be sure, I want to be careful not to understate the value that Millennials place on physical space and the in-person experience of real life. I wrote earlier about Millennials' continuing interest in print books; even more recent analysis has borne this idea out. A Pew study published in October 2012, found that 83 percent of Millennials had read a book in the past year and that, of those, a whopping 75 percent had read a print book.[4] We are also seeing more and more Millennials unplugging, amid a broader movement of people of all generations unplugging, leaving their devices behind to spend time with friends and in nature.

Online communication tools have proven to be extremely useful for organizing important physical world events, from events in Tahrir Square during the Arab Spring to rescue efforts from the beaches of New Jersey to the streets of Manhattan during Hurricane Sandy. But, technology and physicality do not have to exist separately. Like idealism and pragmatism—once viewed as opposite philosophies—these two forces have also been merged by the Millennials. In the aftermath of Sandy, for instance, Millennials banded together, using technology to share photos and stories of those in need and tell the tales of those who were everyday heroes. They also used technology to help connect those outside the affected region with information about how and where to help those in need. Throughout New York, scenes of Millennial strangers talking for the first time as they met in a Starbucks where they had come to charge their devices, spoke beautifully to this new blend—and also to a new understanding about how fragile our technological infrastructure can be.

Despite Millennials' proclivity for maintaining a balance of the physical and the virtual, Millennials are still often perceived as techno-consumers who spend all their time on cell phones idling away in a new virtual world with little human contact. Similarly, despite sustained high turnout among young voters and the fact that our turnout mirrors that of our parents, many will still see young voters as politically disengaged.

It's easy to criticize young people and blame them for trends in our society that are seen as negative. But when we adopt an assumption that seems right or convincing enough, we start telling ourselves a story about how a whole group of people behaves. As that story gets told more frequently, more of us start to believe it, and it becomes difficult for us to pause and reconsider the underlying facts, especially in a world where our known truths are changing so rapidly. Our society has developed a new knack for embracing narratives that apparently explain complex phenomenon with simple stories—but actually don't explain very much or are not factual to begin with. Critics have called us shallow, self-involved, apathetic, narcissistic, and even the "dumbest generation." But I live in this generation, and I can assure you that we are engaged, optimistic, passionate, and deeply committed to the humanistic values that are at the core of our world.

Our generation is writing our own story, with marked differences from other groups of young people that have preceded us. We are at the forefront of shaping the fast future we are all living in. Just as we have achieved a balance of pragmatism and idealism, we are also working on achieving other necessary balances in society and in our lives. This fast future world that we are speeding into is not some kind of techno-dystopia; it's one where once-intractable problems can be solved and the best of our new ideas, innovations, technologies, and diverse experiences can yield a new kind of American and global Renaissance. And the Millennial Generation is in the driver's seat, shifting the gears into forward.

Creating a book isn't easy, and you certainly can't do it alone. This book would literally not be in your hands without Heather Baror Shapiro, my tireless agent, who believed in this project from day one and did not rest until it was sold. I also owe my deepest thanks to Danny Baror, without whom there would truly be no book. You couldn't ask for two better people to be in your corner when you're trying to publish a book.

At Beacon, my greatest appreciation to my editor Joanna Green, who championed this book and guided me gracefully through the challenging and often daunting process of being a first-time author. She challenged me to go deeper and further on my own ideas, and the book is stronger and better for it. Thanks also to Helene Atwan, Jessie Bennett, Beth Collins, Travis Dagenais, Tom Hallock, Susan Lumenello, Pam MacColl, Caitlin Meyer, Kristie Reilly, and the rest of the incredible team at Beacon who saw what this could be and took a chance on a first-time, then twenty-year-old author. They have all worked so hard to make this a success.

Special thanks to Scott Korb who provided his critiques, suggestions, and input into the manuscript over a multiyear period while he was hard at work on his own book. He's one of the most dedicated people I know and is deeply committed to teaching young writers how to be great ones.

I will always be especially grateful to Brian Edelman and Nick Godfrey, who embraced me and my idea to make a documentary when I was just sixteen. They have stuck by my side ever since in a series of seemingly crazy endeavors. I am deeply grateful for their friendship and support. My thanks also to the Rain and Crossborders team, past and present. They have been like a second family to me through the years, and I'm so appreciative of all they have done for me.

While I was writing this book, I was also working on a documentary film in Abu Dhabi. The team there, Landon Van Soest, John Rosenblatt, Freddy Shanahan, and Dan Morris, were patient and flexible with me and my insane schedule. Chris Casey was also on the team in Abu Dhabi. Chris and I have been friends since before I remember, and we have been partners in crime for just as long. He has believed in every crazy idea I have had and has been the first one to sign up.

Arne, Helen, and Hannah de Keijzer have been friends and so much more to me for my entire life. They were with me throughout this process, from the hatching of the idea all the way to the finish line. Arne advised me on my initial proposal and has provided me with everything from line edits to bad puns to get through the slog. Helen was the first person who ever told me about social entrepreneurship. She is always a wealth of optimism and eager to discuss the latest on Millennials; I would always leave our conversations with new ideas, many of which ended up in these pages. My fellow Millennial Hannah, who has always given me sisterly love, was a constant source of inspiration and moral support.

Throughout this process, Kim Kirschenbaum has been a patient lover, muse, researcher, confidant, and so much more. For all your support and love, I am eternally grateful.

In writing this book, I had the opportunity to talk to some of the most amazing people in my generation. While I wasn't able to include each of them, the conversations I had with each of them helped shape this book. They include Sarah Al-Fayez, Nick Anderson, Bettina Aptheker, Ben Bator, Divine Bradley, Adam Braun, Marvelyn Brown, Lauren Bush Lauren, Brian Bordainick, Jared Cohen, Robert Cohen, Ben Cole, Soraya Darabi, Michael Davidson, Maggie Doyne, Chris Eigland, Mahmoud El-Refai, Aria Finger, Wael Ghonim, Olivier Gaillard, Eric Glustrom, Tom Grace, Eric Guindon, Bethany Halbreich, Mark Hanis, Scott Harrison, David Jones, Anya Kamenetz, Nancy Lublin, Max Lugavere, Kate Lupo, Jennifer Manninen, Tyler Manninen, Emily May, Tarrell McCraney, Seth Moulton, Joe O'Shea, Oscar Morales, Blake Mycoskie, Christopher Nulty, Summer Rayne Oakes, Aaron Patzer, Doug Piwinski, Aaron Pomerantz, Mark Rembert, Erin

Schrode, Matt Segal, Jose Serrano, Jason Silva, Maya Enista Smith, David Smith, Taylor Stuckert, Phil Swindler, Kelsey Swindler, Butul Taufik, Michael Teoh, Alex Torpey, Ricky Van Veen, Amanda Warren, Amelia West, Josh Williams, and Mary Yonkman.

My friends, colleagues, and family have provided insights, advice, inspiration, new ideas, counsel, introductions, and support throughout the two years I have been working on this project. Many of them have been doing such for my entire life, I could write pages about each of their accomplishments, but for now you should all know that you all made this possible. My thanks to the Aires-O'Connor family, Jeanie Bennett, Johanna Berkson, Craig Buck, Karina Buck, Zoe Buck, Leslie Bluhm, Kassidy Brown, Ryan Brown, Jim Carlisle, Haley Cohen, Micaela Connery, Mark Costello, Alissa Curran, Howard Dean, Colin Doody, Alex Edelman, Marty Edelman, Marty Edelston, Andy Ellwood, James Elboar, Annie Fitzsimmons, Jordan Fraade, Judy Friedberg, MeraLee Goldman, Tyler Gray, Rachel Grimmelmann, Lisa Gruber, Matt Heineman, Liz Heller, David Helfand, Ed Hurley, Ina Werdinger Hurley, Shana Hurley, Michelle Horowitz, Terssa Iezzi, Ed Kaufman, David Kline, Eric Kuhn, Mark Korshak, Jess Lord, Sam Magida, Jessica Malkin, Nathan Maton, Casey McCormick, Anne McGuire, Doug Miller, Samantha Moray, Jarrett Moreno, Peter Nelson, Jessica Posner Odede, Kennedy Odede, Naomi Hirabayashi Ousley, Maureen Isern Papale, Fabian Pfortmüller, David Porzio, Mark Read, Noah Robischon, Eileen Rosen, Fred Rosen, Nathan Rostron, Miguel Sal, John Sexton, Rachel Shechtman, Elizabeth Shreve, Melanie Stevenson, Bill Stewart, Suzen Stewart, Nick Troiano, Barbara Wallner, Rob Wallner, Linden Wallner, Melanie Wallner, Sandy Warkentin, Maggie Weinberg, David Wilk, David Witter, and Allix Wright.

I'm incredibly lucky to have my grandmother Joan Aires O'Connor in my life. She was my first babysitter and she's been there at every step watching me grow up. Her vivacity, wit, and elegance inspire me each and every day.

Though they are no longer with us physically, my grandparents Leon Burstein and Dorothy Burstein are always in my heart and my mind. Their spirit was with me throughout the entire process of working on this book, and I often wished I could have asked them for their thoughts about the ideas in this book. While I didn't get to do that, I know they are smiling somewhere reading this.

Finally, I am lucky to have the best parents in the world. They raised me to dream big, think, and care about the world around me. They've never once told me no. They supported this book in every way possible, from late-night strategy chats to research assistance and literally everything in between. I truly could not have done this without their tremendous wisdom, sage advice, love, and unconditional support. My mother and father are simply the two most incredible people I know: I love you both so much, I'm nothing without you.

NOTE ON SOURCES

For this book I conducted interviews with Millennial leaders, older thought leaders, and ordinary Millennials across the country. I also drew on material I gathered in my role as a contributor to *Fast Company* and *The Huffington Post*. In addition, I drew from numerous studies, articles, films, and books. Wherever a citation does not appear following a quote, it is a quote from an original interview I conducted. In some cases where only a first name is cited, the subject did not want to be identified in full.

INTRODUCTION

1. Joyce Maynard, "An 18-Year-Old Looks Back On Life," *New York Times Magazine*, April 23, 1972.

2. Thomas Jefferson to John Waldo Monticello, August 16, 1813, "The Letters of Thomas Jefferson, 1743-1826," *American History: From Revolution to Reconstruction and Beyond*, University of Groningen (Netherlands), http://www .let.rug.nl/.

3. John F. Kennedy Commencement Address, June 11, 1962, Yale University, New Haven, CT, http://www.jfklibrary.org/.

ONE: Pragmatic Idealists

1. Matthew Segal, executive director, Student Association for Voter Empowerment, "Testimony on Lessons Learned From the 2008 Election," hearing before the U.S. House of Representatives Committee on the Judiciary, Subcommittee on the Constitution, Civil Rights, and Civil Liberties, March 19, 2009, Washington, DC, http://judiciary.house.gov.

2. After searching for a phrase to describe the Millennial theory of change, in June of 2009 I began using "pragmatic idealism" in my articles for *The Huffington Post* and elsewhere. In my view, both words signify their common usage meanings: today's Millennial Generation is, in my opinion, highly idealistic about the changes they'd like to see in society at the same time that they are

highly pragmatic about how to achieve these changes. This notion of pragmatic idealism is unrelated to the philosophy known as pragmatism, and also unrelated to the theory of knowledge presented in the early 1990s by political philosopher Nicholas Rescher in his three-volume work, *A System of Pragmatic Idealism* (Princeton, NJ: Princeton University Press, 1994).

3. Marci Baranski, Facebook post, n.d.

4. Paul Taylor and Scott Keeter, eds., *The Millennials: Confident. Connected. Open to Change*, Pew Research Center, Washington, DC, February 24, 2010, http://www.pewsocialtrends.org/.

5. "Romney Trails Among Young Adults," Center for Information and Research on Civic Learning and Engagement, Tufts University, Medford, MA, July 31, 2012, http://www.civicyouth.org/.

6. Taylor, *The Millennials.*

7. Damla Ergun, "Strong Support for Gay Marriage Now Exceeds Strong Opposition," ABC News, May 23, 2012.

8. Taylor, *The Millennials.*

9. Andrea Stone, "'Civic Generation' Rolls Up Sleeves in Record Numbers," *USA Today*, April 13, 2009.

10. Thomas L. Friedman, "Generation Q," *New York Times*, October 10, 2007.

11. "A Quiet Generation? Now Hear This!" letter to the editor, *New York Times*, October 12, 2007.

12. Ibid.

13. Bill Drayton, "Everyone a Changemaker: Social Entrepreneurship's Ultimate Goal," *Innovations: Technology, Governance, Globalization* 1, no. 1 (2006): 80–96.

14. Caroline Preston, "Generations X and Y Make Up Majority of Potential Donors, Study Finds," *Chronicle of Philanthropy*, March 14, 2010.

15. Matt Hamblen, "Text Donations Raise Millions for Haiti Earthquake Relief," *Computerworld*, January 16, 2010.

16. Sam Dillon, "Praise, Advice and Reminders of the Sour Economy for Graduates," *New York Times*, June 16, 2009.

17. Mark Bauerlein, *The Dumbest Generation: How the Digital Age Stupefies Young Americans and Jeopardizes Our Future (Or, Don't Trust Anyone Under 30)* (New York: Penguin, 2009).

18. Center for Information and Research on Civic Learning and Engagement, "New Census Data Confirm Increase in Youth Voter Turnout In 2008 Election," news release, April 28, 2009, http://www.civicyouth.org/.

19. "World Internet User Statistics," InternetWorldStats.com, accessed March 31, 2012.

20. Ruy Teixeira, "Public Opinion Snapshot: Millennials Are a Progressive Generation," Center for American Progress blog, May 10, 2009, http://www.americanprogress.org.

21. "SDS Statement," December 1968, Records of the Office of the President (Dr. James McNaughton Hester), New York University Archives, New York University Libraries, http://library.nyu.edu/.

22. Russell Simmons, "Social Media Is the New Hip-Hop," *Huffington Post*, April 21, 2010, http://www.huffingtonpost.com.

23. Jonathan Kalan, "Generation Y and the Great CSR Shift," *Causecast*, January 21, 2010, http://www.causecastfornonprofits.com/blog.

24. Ibid.

25. Bruce Nussbaum, "Facebook Privacy Flap—Gen Yers Demand Control," *BusinessWeek*, February 18, 2009.

26. People Against the New Terms of Service (TOS), Facebook group, Facebook.com.

27. Justin Smith, "Facebook Announces First-Ever User Vote on Terms of Service Changes," InsideFacebook.com, April 6, 2009, http://www.insideface book.com.

28. Mark Zuckerberg, "Update on Terms," Facebook blog, February 18, 2009, http://blog.facebook.com.

29. "Mike Arrington Interrogates Mark Zuckerberg," video from the 2010 TechCrunch Conference via UStream, January 8, 2010, accessed April 14, 2010.

30. Jose Antonio Vargas, "Our Facebook—Led by Mark Zuckerberg, We Define an Era," *Huffington Post*, May 14, 2012, http://www.huffingtonpost.com.

31. Mark Zuckerberg, "Letter from Mark Zuckerberg," Facebook Form S-1 Registration, SEC filing statement, February 1, 2012, http://sec.gov/.

TWO: Fast Future, Present Shock

1. Steve Ballmer, speech, View from the Top lecture series, Stanford Graduate School of Business, Palo Alto, CA, May 12, 2005, http://www.gsb.stanford.edu/.

2. John Brockman, "The Third Culture," *Edge*, 1991, http://www.edge.org.

3. Alvin Toffler, *Future Shock* (New York: Random House, 1970).

4. Matt Palmer, "The Generation that Can Change the World: Millennial Series Debut," *Catholic Review*, March 2011.

5. Guy Bensen, "Poll: Birtherism Shrivels after White House Releases Birth Certificate," *Tipsheet*, May 5, 2011, http://townhall.com/tipsheet.

6. Michael Hirschorn, "Truth Lies Here," *Atlantic*, November 2010.

7. Linde Wolters, "Generation Y Brings Hope for the Future," *Epoch Times*, April 14 2010; Hugh MacKay, "Social Disengagement: A Breeding Ground for Fundamentalism," Manning Clark Lecture, National Library of Australia, Canberra, March 3, 2005, http://manningclark.org.au/.

8. Cadie Thompson, "Facebook Will Disappear in 5 to 8 Years: Analyst," CNBC, June 4, 2012, http://www.cnbc.com.

9. Greenberg Quinlan Rosner/Polimetrix, *Coming of Age in America: Part I*, report, Greenberg Quinlan Rosner Research, October 1, 2005, http://www.greenbergresearch.com/.

10. "America's Long Vigil," *TV Guide*, January 25, 1964.

11. "Growing Up in the Shadow of 9/11," American University School of Communication website, April 29, 2011, http://www.growingup9-11.com.

12. John Zogby, *The Way We'll Be: The Zogby Report on the Transformation of the American Dream* (New York: Random House, 2008).

13. Ruy Teixeira and David Madland, *New Progressive America: The Millennial Generation* (Washington, DC: Center for American Progress, May 2009).

14. Amy McRary, "The Millennial Generation: Destined to Succeed," *Knoxville (TN) News Sentinel*, May 21, 2006.

15. Jaime Holguin, "9/11 Grads Choose Public Service," CBSNews, September 10, 2009, http://www.cbsnews.com/.

16. *College Students Helping America* (Washington, DC: Corporation for National and Community Service, October 2006), www.nationalservice.gov.

17. Holguin, "9/11 Grads."

18. Dakarai I. Aarons and Christina A. Samuels, "For Students, Obama's Victory Offers Lesson in Civics," *Education Week*, November 12, 2008.

19. Paul Taylor and Scott Keeter, eds., *The Millennials: Confident. Connected. Open to Change*, Pew Research Center, Washington, DC, February 24, 2010, http://www.pewsocialtrends.org/.

20. Teixeira, *New Progressive America*.

21. Peter Singer, "Millennials Will Change the World," video, Brookings Institution YouTube Channel, March 13, 2011, http://www.youtube.com.

22. Paul Rieckhoff, personal Facebook status update, May 2, 2011.

23. David Goldman, "Bin Laden Death Sends Internet Traffic Soaring," *CNNMoney*, May 2, 2011.

24. "Editorial: The Columbine Generation," *State Press* (Tempe, AZ), April 19, 2010, http://www.statepress.com/.

25. Sharon Jayson and Maria Puente, "Gen Y Shaped, Not Stopped, by Tragedy," *USA Today*, April 20, 2007.

26. Neil Howe and Reena Nadler, *Yes We Can: The Emergence of Millennials as a Political Generation*, New America Foundation, Washington, DC, 2009, http://newamerica.net/.

27. Jayson, "Gen Y Shaped."

28. Ibid.

29. Timothy Egan, "Profiles in Cowardice," *New York Times*, *Opinionator* blog, December 23, 2009, http://opinionator.blogs.nytimes.com.

30. Eric Kleefeld, "Young Voters' Approval of Obama Historically High—Can Dems Keep Them?" TalkingPointsMemo.com, March 5, 2010; "Where Does Obama Stand among Young Voters?" *Peoples World*, March 8, 2010, http://www.peoplesworld.org/.

31. Jeffery Smith, "A Golden Age for Civil Servants: How Generation Y Will Change Government," *CivSource*, June 17, 2009, http://civsourceonline.com.

32. Howe, *Yes We Can*.

33. Jayson, "Gen Y Shaped."

34. Howe, *Yes We Can*.

35. Jayson, "Gen Y Shaped."

36. Taylor, *The Millennials*.

THREE: First Digitals

1. Alex Pham, "YouTube Turns 5, Can't Wait to Grow Up," *Los Angeles Times*, May 17, 2010.

2. Paul Taylor and Scott Keeter, eds., *The Millennials: Confident. Connected. Open to Change*, Pew Research Center, Washington, DC, February 24, 2010, http://www.pewsocialtrends.org/.

3. Historians of technology generally date the birth of the digital era to August 6, 1991, the day when Sir Tim Berners-Lee uploaded the first HTML web page to what would become the World Wide Web.

4. Aaron Smith et al., *College Students and Technology*, Pew Research Center, Washington, DC, July 19, 2011, http://www.pew.org/.

5. Marc Prensky, "Digital Natives, Digital Immigrants," *On the Horizon* 9, no. 5 (2001): 1–6.

6. Stephen G. Emerson, "Can Helicopter Parents Learn to Let Their Children Soar?" *Washington Post*, November 26, 2010.

7. A.J. Liebling, "Do You Belong in Journalism?" *New Yorker*, May 4, 1960.

8. *2007 State of the Media Democracy Survey*, Deloitte & Touche and Harrison Group, April 16, 2007.

9. Don Tapscott and Anthony D. Williams, *Wikinomics: How Mass Collaboration Changes Everything* (New York: Portfolio, 2006).

10. Alexis De Tocqueville, *Democracy in America: And Two Essays on America*, Gerald E. Bevan and Isaac Kramnick, trans. (New York: Penguin, 2003), 599.

11. Robert Putnam, *Bowling Alone: The Collapse and Revival of American Community* (New York: Simon & Schuster, 2000).

12. Margaret Bonner, "10 Key Statistics about Facebook," *Hitwise* (Experian blog), February 2, 2012, http://weblogs.hitwise.com.

13. Howard Rheingold, "21st Century Literacies," keynote speech, Reboot Britain Conference, London, July 6, 2009.

14. Mark Bauerlein, *The Dumbest Generation: How the Digital Age Stupefies Young Americans and Jeopardizes Our Future (Or, Don't Trust Anyone Under 30)* (New York: Penguin, 2009).

15. Don Tapscott, *Grown Up Digital: How the Net Generation Is Changing Your World* (New York: McGraw-Hill, 2009).

16. "Mark Bauerlein and Emory College Grad CNN Debate," YouTube video, September 28, 2008, http://www.youtube.com/.

17. John Zogby, *The Way We'll Be: The Zogby Report on the Transformation of the American Dream* (New York: Random House, 2008).

18. Amanda Lenhart et al., *Social Media and Young Adults* (Washington, DC: Pew Research Center, February 3, 2010), http://pewinternet.org/.

19. Aaron Smith, *Mobile Access 2010* (Washington, DC: Pew Research Center, July 7, 2010), http://pewinternet.org/.

20. Ibid.

21. Cecilia Kang, "YouTube Use Explodes, and Minorities Lead the Way," *Washington Post*, July 26, 2011.

22. Vint Cerf, "Google's (and Parents') Role in Keeping Kids Safe Online," *Google Blog*, December 7, 2007, http://googleblog.blogspot.com/.

23. Lee Rainie et al., *The Strength of Internet Ties*, Pew Research Center, Washington, DC, January 25, 2006, http://pewinternet.org/.

24. Bernd Debusmann Jr., "Facebook Makes People More Social: Study," Reuters, November 24, 2010.

25. Ileana Llorens, "Social Media Makes Teens Aware of Others' Needs, Study Says," *Huffington Post*, February 16, 2012, http://www.huffingtonpost .com.

26. Janna Quitney Anderson and Lee Rainie, *The Future of Social Relations*, Pew Research Center, Washington, DC, July 2, 2010, http://pewinternet.org/.

27. Nicholas Carr, *The Shallows: What the Internet Is Doing to Our Brains* (New York: Norton, 2010).

28. Ibid.

29. Virginia Woolf, "How It Strikes a Contemporary," *Times Literary Supplement*, April 5, 1923.

30. Taylor, *The Millennials.*

31. David Morin, "Context Is King," *Edge*, 2010, http://www.edge.org/.

32. John Tierney, "Ear Plugs to Lasers: The Science of Concentration," *New York Times*, May 4, 2009.

33. Camilla Nord, "Growing Up Digital. And Proud Of It," *YPulse.com*, December 8, 2010, http://www.ypulse.com.

34. Sarah Bowman, "What Did You Think of 'The Social Network'?" Facebook post, November 25, 2010.

35. Carly Dahlen, "'The Social Network' Review: A Definitive Portrayal of the Millennial Generation," *Big Vision Empty Wallet*, October 8, 2010, http://bigvisionemptywallet.com.

36. David Schultz, "The 'Facebook Effect' On Organ Donation," National Public Radio online, September 20, 2012, http://www.npr.org/.

37. Lisa W. Foderaro, "Private Moment Made Public, Then a Fatal Jump," *New York Times*, September 29, 2010.

38. "It Gets Better Project: About Us," ItGetsBetter.org, accessed December 3, 2010.

39. Danah Boyd, "Publicity and Privacy in Web 2.0," keynote address, WWW2010 conference, Raleigh, NC, April 29, 2010.

40. Sam Diaz, "Facebook Fallout: Survey Finds 60 Percent May Quit over Privacy," *ZDNet*, May 21, 2010, http://www.zdnet.com.

41. Ryan Singel, "Mark Zuckerberg: I Donated to Open Source, Facebook Competitor," *Wired*, May 28, 2010, http://www.wired.com.

42. Laura Holson, "Tell-All Generation Learns to Keep Things Offline," *New York Times*, May 8, 2010.

43. "Facebook Signs Apps Privacy Agreement," *Tech Talk* (blog), CBS News, June 22, 2012, http://www.cbsnews.com.

44. Emily Nussbaum, "Say Everything," *New York Magazine*, February 12, 2007.

45. Carr, *The Shallows*, pp. 211–12.

46. Ibid.

47. Ibid., pp. 8–9.

48. Ibid.

49. Joe O'Shea, e-mail message to author, June 11, 2012.

50. Carr, *The Shallows*, p. 10.

51. Ibid., p. 55.

52. "Generation Y Leads in Book Buying," *Publishers Weekly* Facebook post, August 15, 2012, http://www.publishersweekly.com/.

53. Clay Shirky, "Why Abundance Is Good: A Reply to Nick Carr," *Encyclopedia Britannica* blog, July 17, 2008, http://www.britannica.com/.

FOUR: Twenty-First-Century Capitalism

1. Zachary Roth, "Only 55 Percent of Young Americans Have Jobs, Lowest Since WWII," *The Lookout* (blog), September 22, 2011, http://news.yahoo.com/blogs; Heidi Shierholz and Kathryn Anne Edwards, *The Class of 2011: Young Workers Face a Dire Labor Market without a Safety Net*, Economic Policy Institute, EPI Briefing Paper # 306, April 20, 2011, http://www.epi.org/.

2. U.S. Bureau of Labor Statistics, August 2011, http://www.bls.gov/.

3. Project on Student Debt, *Student Debt and the Class of 2010* (Oakland, CA: Institute for College Access and Success, November 2011), http://projectonstudentdebt.org/.

4. Howard Wial, "The Geography of Our Falling-Wage Recovery," *New Republic*, September 16, 2011.

5. Meredith Bennett-Smith, "Generation Y Suggests Another Look At 'Generation Why Bother,'" *Huffington Post*, July 30, 2012, http://www.huffingtonpost.com.

6. Noreen Malone, "The Kids Are Actually Sort of Alright," *New York Magazine*, October 16, 2011.

7. Gregory Rodriguez, "The Millennial Generation Test," *Los Angeles Times*, March 2, 2009.

8. Ibid.

9. Thomas Friedman, "Average Is Over" speech, Chicago Ideas Week, Chicago, October 10, 2011.

10. Navi Radjou et al., "Millennials Are the MacGyvers of Business," *Harvard Business Review* blog, March 13, 2012, http://blogs.hbr.org.

11. Rebecca Walker, "Gen Y Grads More Likely to Launch Start-ups," *USA Today*, May 8, 2012.

12. Ibid.

13. Robin Marantz Henig, "What is It About 20-Somethings?" *New York Times Magazine*, August 18, 2010.

14. Erica Ho, "Survey: 85% of New College Grads Move Back In with Mom and Dad," *Time NewsFeed* (blog), May 10, 2011, http://newsfeed.time.com.

15. Amanda M. Fairbanks, "2011 College Grads Moving Home, Saddled With Historic Levels Of Student Loan Debt," *Huffington Post*, May 13, 2011, http://www.huffingtonpost.com.

16. Catherine Rampell, "As New Graduates Return to Nest, Economy Also Feels the Pain," *New York Times*, November 16, 2011.

17. "Fact Checking Data On The Boomerang Generation," *Morning Edition*, National Public Radio, May 15, 2012, http://www.npr.org/.

18. Ibid.

19. Karen L. Fingerman and Frank F. Furstenberg, "You Can Go Home Again," *New York Times*, May 30, 2012.

20. Ibid.

21. Michelle Hirsch, "The Boomerang Generation: More Reasons to Move Back Home," *Fiscal Times*, June 12, 2010, http://www.thefiscaltimes.com/.

22. Julie Curtis, "Choose Your Own Chocolate Bar," *Daily Voice* (CT), August 3, 2010, TheDailyWeston.com.

23. Laura Petrecca, "Fast Growth for Your Small Business Isn't Always Good," *USA Today*, September 9, 2010.

24. Ibid.

25. Emily Cohn, "In Weak Job Market, One in Two College Graduates Are Jobless or Underemployed," *Huffington Post*, April 22, 2012.

26. Hannah Seligson, "No Jobs? Young Graduates Make Their Own," *New York Times*, December 11, 2010.

27. John Pryor, "Financial Concerns of First-Year College Students Have Wide Impact, Annual Survey Finds," *UCLA News*, January 20, 2010, http://newsroom.ucla.edu/.

28. Tara Loader Wilkinson and Maryam Omidi, "Greed Is for Wimps," *Wall Street Journal*, December 13, 2010.

29. Taylor, *The Millennials*.

30. Ronald Brownstein, "Children of the Great Recession," *National Journal*, May 8, 2010.

31. Roth, "Only 55 Percent of Young Americans Have Jobs."

32. Morley Winograd and Michael D. Hais, "As Millennials Reject Gender Roles, but Embrace Marriage, They're Changing Society," *Christian Science Monitor*, May 24, 2012.

33. Rachael Levy, "Only 1 in 3 Americans Wants to Get Married," *Slate*, February 2, 2012, http://slatest.slate.com/.

34. Malone, "The Kids Are Actually Sort of Alright."

35. Michael Fertik, "The Kids Are All Right: Why New Graduates Should Give You Hope," *Harvard Business Review* blog, November 19, 2010, http://blogs.hbr.org.

36. Anis Salvesen, "The Cause Marketing Catalyst," *PhilanthroPost* (blog), February 26, 2010, http://philanthropost.wordpress.com.

37. Jocelyne Daw, *Cause Marketing For Nonprofits: Partner for Purpose, Passion, and Profits* (Hoboken, NJ: Wiley, 2006).

38. AMP Agency/Cone, "The 2006 Cone Millennial Cause Study: The Millennial Generation: Pro-Social and Empowered to Change the World," white paper, http://www.greenbook.org/.

39. Ibid.

40. Claire Williams Diaz, "Twitter in Times of Crisis: History of Venezuela, Chile, Mexico, and Colombia," speech, Personal Democracy Forum Latin America 2010, Santiago, Chile, November 19, 2010, http://personaldemocracy.com/.

41. "Sustainable Living Plan," Unilever website, accessed November 15, 2010, http://www.unilever.com/.

42. Zipcar, "Zipcar's Second Annual Millennials Study Finds 18-34-Year-Olds Increasingly Embrace Collaborative Consumption and Access Over Ownership," news release, December 12, 2011, http://www.zipcar.mediaroom.com/.

43. Zipcar, "After One Year, Zipcar Drives Transportation Change in Baltimore," news release, July 11, 2011, http://www.zipcar.mediaroom.com/.

44. Danielle Sacks, "The Sharing Economy," *Fast Company*, April 18, 2011, http://www.fastcompany.com.

45. David Kirkpatrick, "Social Power and the Coming Corporate Revolution," *Forbes Techonomy* (blog), September 7, 2011, http://www.forbes.com.

46. Ibid.

47. Interview with Doug Piwinski.

48. Sara Scholin, "My Newest Obsession . . . and the Evil That Is Sketchers," *Taking Chances: A Peace Corps Journey* (blog), April 9, 2011, http://takingchancesapeacecorpsjourney.blogspot.com.

49. Bill Drayton, "Everyone a Changemaker: Social Entrepreneurship's Ultimate Goal," *Innovations: Technology, Governance, Globalization* 1, no. 1 (2006): 80–96.

50. *Mapping Global Talent: Essays and Insights*, *Economist* Intelligence Unit with Heidrick and Struggles, September 2007, http://www.heidrick.com/.

51. Jeanne Meister, "Job Hopping Is the 'New Normal' for Millennials: Three Ways to Prevent a Human Resource Nightmare," *Forbes* blog, August 14, 2012, http://www.forbes.com.

52. Andrea Stone, "'Civic Generation' Rolls Up Sleeves in Record Numbers," *USA Today*, April 13, 2009.

53. Wilkinson, "Greed Is For Wimps."

54. Bennett-Smith, "Generation Y."

55. Jackie Ramos, "Why Bank Of America Fired Me," YouTube video, uploaded November 25, 2009, http://www.youtube.com/.

56. Ibid.

57. Arthur Delaney, "Jackie Ramos, Bank of America Employee, Fired after Helping Customers," *Huffington Post*, December 7, 2009, http://www.huffington post.com.

58. Richard Alleyne, "Young Adults Believe in the Age of Entitlement, Claim Researchers," *Telegraph* (UK), May 24, 2010.

59. *Millennials: The Challenger Generation, Prosumer Report* 11 (2011), Euro-RSCG Worldwide, http://www.prosumer-report.com/.

60. Ibid.

61. Raina Kelley, "Generation Me," *Daily Beast*, April 17, 2009, http://www.thedailybeast.com.

62. Ron Zemke et al., *Generations at Work: Managing the Clash of Veterans, Boomers, Xers, and Nexters in Your Workplace* (New York: AMACOM, 2000).

63. Katherine Lewis, "Recent College Grads: They're Not So Bad at Work," *Fortune*, June 7, 2012, http://management.fortune.cnn.com.

64. Joe Light, "Keeping 'Overqualifieds' on Board," *Wall Street Journal*, November 15, 2010.

65. Mark Waid, "Delivery, Content, and the Gulf Between," keynote address, Harvey Awards, September 1, 2010, http://www.comicbookresources.com/.

66. Judith Newman, "If You're Happy and You Know It, Must I Know, Too?" *New York Times*, October 23, 2011.

67. Austin Carr, "Half of Young Professionals Value Facebook Access, Smartphone Options Over Salary: Report," *Fast Company*, November 2, 2011, http://www.fastcompany.com.

68. "Ousted Boss John Thain Gored Merrill Lynch's Bull with a Gold-Plated Office and Stealth Bonuses," editorial, *New York Daily News*, January 23, 2009.

69. Kara Swisher and Walt Mossberg, "Facebook CEO Mark Zuckerberg at D8: The Full, Uncut Interview," video, *AllthingsD* D8 Conference, June 2, 2010, Rancho Palos Verdes, CA, http://allthingsd.com.

70. Farhad Manjoo, "The Comeback Kid," *Fast Company*, June 2010, http://www.fastcompany.com.

71. Jose Vargas, "Mark Zuckerberg: Our First Millennial CEO," *Huffington Post*, December 9, 2010, http://www.huffingtonpost.com.

FIVE: Political Pivot

1. Sean Captain, "Infographic: Who Is Occupy Wall Street?" *Fast Company*, November 2, 2011, http://www.fastcompany.com.

2. Edward D. Murphy, "Obama Girl? Bowdoin Student Was Way Ahead," *Portland (ME) Press Herald*, March 13, 2010.

3. Scott Keeter et al., *Young Voters in the 2008 Election*, Pew Research Center, November 12, 2008, http://pewresearch.org/.

4. Ibid.

5. *2008 Time Series Study*, American National Election Studies, http://www.electionstudies.org/.

6. Bret Schulte, "Youth Vote Tripled in Iowa," *US News & World Report*, January 4, 2008.

7. David Von Drehle, "Obama's Youth Vote Triumph," *Time*, January 4, 2008.

8. E.J. Dionne, "Time to Reawaken Young Voters," *Washington Post*, October 19, 2009.

9. Ellen McGirt, "How Chris Hughes Helped Launch Facebook and the Barack Obama Campaign," *Fast Company*, April 2009, http://www.fastcompany.com.

10. Ibid.

11. *Post-Election Tracking Survey*, Pew Research Center, Washington, DC, November 3–24, 2010.

12. *18 in '08*, directed by David Burstein, Redirection Films, 2007.

13. Erika Lovely, "Young Adults Sit on Sidelines of Health Debate," *Politico*, September 10 2009, http://www.politico.com.

14. Morley Winograd and Michael D. Hais, "Obama's Millennial Moment: President to Sign National Service Bill Today," *Millennial Makeover*, April 21, 2009, http://www.millennialmakeover.com/.

15. Suzanne Malveaux, "President Obama Tries to Fire Up Young Voters, but Faces a More Subdued Crowd," CNN.com, September 29, 2010.

16. *Survey of Young Americans' Attitudes Toward Politics and Public Service*, 20th ed., Harvard University Institute of Politics, Cambridge, MA, December 15, 2011, http://www.iop.harvard.edu/.

17. Ben Goddard, "Millennials—Yes, They Can," *Hill*, March 3, 2010, http://thehill.com/.

18. Ibid.

19. Morley Winograd and Michael D. Hais, *Millennial Makeover: MySpace, YouTube, and the Future of American Politics* (Piscataway, NJ: Rutgers University Press, 2008).

20. *18 in '08.*

21. *Youth Voters in the 2010 Elections,* Center for Information and Research on Civic Learning and Engagement, Tufts University, Medford, MA, November 9, 2010, http://www.civicyouth.org/.

22. Kirk Johnson, "Fewer Young Voters See Themselves as Democrats," *New York Times,* September 2, 2010.

23. Susan Saulny, "Young in G.O.P. Erase the Lines on Social Issues," *New York Times,* August 8, 2012.

24. Ibid.

25. Ibid.

26. Kate Zernike, *Boiling Mad: Inside Tea Party America* (New York: MacMillan, 2010).

27. Ibid.

28. Kevin Brennan and Josh Lederman, "Tea Party Movement Alienating Young Voters," Associated Press, October 30, 2010.

29. "Tea Party Could Hurt GOP in Congressional Races, Quinnipiac University National Poll Finds; Dems Trail 2-Way Races, But Win If Tea Party Runs," news release, Quinnipiac University Polling Institute, March 24, 2010, http://www.quinnipiac.edu/institutes-and-centers/polling-institute; Kenneth P. Vogel, "Poll: Tea Partiers Like GOP," *Politico,* March 23, 2010, http://www.politico.com; Kate Zernike and Megan Thee-Brenan, "Poll Finds Tea Party Backers Wealthier and More Educated," *New York Times,* April 14, 2010; "National Survey of Tea Party Supporters," documents .nytimes.com, *New York Times,* April 5–12, 2010.

30. "Millennials Not Hopeful About the Future of Social Security," iOme Challenge, August 2011, http://iomechallenge.org/.

31. *Working Americans and Retirement Survey,* TD Ameritrade, December 20, 2011, http://www.amtd.com/.

32. "Romney Trails Among Young Adults," Center for Information and Research on Civic Learning and Engagement, Tufts University, Medford, MA, July 31, 2012, http://www.civicyouth.org/.

33. *Millennials & Politics: Occupy Wall Street, Activism, and Voting,* YPulse .com, October 13, 2011.

34. Anna Greenberg, *OMG! How Generation Y is Redefining Faith in the iPod Era,* Greenberg Quinlan Rosner Research, April 1, 2005, http://www.greenberg research.com/.

35. *Background on the Millennial Generation,* Center for Information and Research on Civic Learning and Engagement, Tufts University, Medford, MA, February 2007, http://www.civicyouth.org/.

36. Ibid.

37. *Democrats' Edge Among Millennials Slips: A Pro-Government, Socially Liberal Generation*, Pew Research Center, Washington, DC, February 18, 2010, http://pewresearch.org/.

38. "The Capitol's Age Pyramid: A Graying Congress," chart, *Wall Street Journal*, October 2010, http://online.wsj.com/.

39. Ben Smith, "Social Conservatism Fades in 'Generational Transition,'" *Politico*, December 10, 2010, http://www.politico.com.

40. Barack Obama interview with Robin Roberts, transcript, ABC News, May 9, 2012, http://abcnews.go.com/.

41. Peter Baker, "Same-Sex Marriage Support Shows Pace of Social Change Accelerating," *New York Times*, May 11, 2012.

42. Martha Irvine, "Young Voters: Obama's Race as an Asset, Non-Issue," *USA Today*, June 6, 2008.

43. Dana Goldstein, "Why Fewer Young American Jews Share Their Parents' View of Israel," *Time*, September 29, 2011.

SIX: Globalized

1. Wael Ghonim, speech at One Young World, Zurich, September 3, 2011.

2. *The Social Network*, Foreign Box Office Totals, *Box Office Mojo*, accessed March 20, 2011, http://boxofficemojo.com/.

3. Wael Eskandar, "Egyptian Revolution Takes 'The Social Network' to the Streets," *Ahram Online*, March 8, 2011, http://english.ahram.org.eg.

4. Michael Sheridan and Tracy Connor, "20-Year-Old Student, Marisol Valles Garcia, Made Police Chief of One of Mexico's Most Violent Towns," *New York Daily News*, October 20, 2010.

5. John Quinones, "Young Mexican Police Chief Flees to U.S.," ABC News.com, May 10, 2011.

6. Larry Elliot, "Gordon Brown to Warn against Global Youth Unemployment Epidemic," *Guardian* (UK), January 18, 2011.

7. "Young, Jobless and Looking for Trouble," *Economist*, February 3, 2011; Bonnie Kavoussi, "Youth Unemployment: One in Eight Global Youths Will Be Unemployed This Year, Report Says," *Huffington Post*, May 22, 2012.

8. Nicholas Kulish, "As Scorn for Vote Grows, Protests Surge Around Globe," *New York Times*, September 27, 2011.

9. Nick Clegg, speech to Liberal Democrat Spring Conference, Sheffield, UK, March 11, 2011, http://www.libdems.org.uk/.

10. Benjamin Wallace-Wells, "Inflamed," *New York Magazine*, August 14, 2011.

11. Nicholas Kristof, "America's 'Primal Scream,'" *New York Times*, October 15, 2011.

12. Brannon Cullum, "Oscar Morales and One Million Voices against FARC," n.d., Movements.org.

13. Preston Mendenhall, "Iranian Youth Hoping to Flex Muscle," MSNBC .com, June 17, 2005.

14. Krista Mahr, "Top 10 Heroes of 2009: No. 2, Neda Agha-Soltan," Time .com, December 8, 2009.

15. Brian Stelter and Mark Landler, "Washington Taps Into a Potent New Force in Diplomacy," *New York Times*, June 16, 2009.

16. "2009 World Population Data Sheet," Population Reference Bureau, August 12, 2009, http://www.prb.org/.

17. John Zogby, *The Way We'll Be: The Zogby Report on the Transformation of the American Dream* (New York: Random House, 2008).

18. Ibid.

19. Ibid.

20. Cryn Johannsen, "Unemployed, Educated and Indebted: More Millennials Seeking Work Outside U.S.," *USA Today College*, May 17, 2011.

21. Thomas Friedman, "A Theory of Everything (Sort Of)," *New York Times*, August 13, 2011.

22. "Nonfiction Review: Battle Hymn of the Tiger Mother," *Publishers Weekly*, November 15, 2010.

23. *Millennials: The Challenger Generation*, EuroRSCG.

24. Barbara Pollack, "CHINA: The Next Generation," *ArtNews*, October 6, 2011.

25. Elizabeth Weise, "As China Booms, So Does Mandarin in U.S. Schools." *USA Today*, November 20, 2007.

26. *This Digital Life*, *Prosumer Report* 13 (2012), EuroRSCG Worldwide, http://www.prosumer-report.com/.

27. Andrew Ho, "Philanthropy Heard 'Round the World," Socialcitizens .org, May 31, 2011.

28. Nicholas Kristof, "After Osama Bin Laden . . ." *New York Times*, May 2, 2011; Tony Karon, "Why Bin Laden's Death No Longer Really Matters," Time .com, May 1, 2011.

29. "Tony Blair Speaking to OneVoice Leaders in Jerusalem" and "Tony Blair Meets with OneVoice Palestinian and Israeli Youth Leaders," press releases, *OneVoice*, June 20, 2008, http://blog.onevoicemovement.org/.

30. Nicholas Kristof, "D.I.Y. Foreign-Aid Revolution," *New York Times Magazine*, October 20, 2010.

31. "Peace Corps Announces Eighteen Percent Increase in Applications," PeaceCorps.gov, October 22, 2009; "Peace Corps Reaches 40-Year High in Number of Volunteers," PeaceCorps.gov, October 28, 2010.

32. "American Students Studying Abroad at Record Levels: Up 8.5%," news release, Institute of International Education, November 12, 2007, http://www .iie.org/; "Study Abroad by U.S. Students Slowed in 2008/09 with More Students Going to Less Traditional Destinations," news release, Institute of International Education, November 15, 2010, http://www.iie.org/; "International Student Enrollments Rose Modestly in 2009/10, Led by Strong Increase in Students from China," news release, Institute of International Education, November 15, 2010, http://www.iie.org/.

33. "Japan Challenge," StudentsRebuild.org, http://studentsrebuild.org/japan

34. "NYU Abu Dhabi Announces Inaugural Class," New York University Abu Dhabi, June 21, 2010, http://nyuad.nyu.edu/.

EPILOGUE

1. "At Least 80 Electoral Votes Depended on Youth," Center for Information and Research on Civic Learning and Engagement, Tufts University, Medford, MA, November 7, 2012, http://www.civicyouth.org/.

2. *Survey of Young Americans' Attitudes towards Politics and Public Service*, 22nd ed., Harvard University Institute of Politics, Cambridge, MA, October 17, 2012, http://www.iop.harvard.edu/.

3. "Millennials Are on Par with Boomers in Voter Turnout," Center for Information and Research on Civic Learning and Engagement, Tufts University, Medford, MA, October 29, 2012, http://www.civicyouth.org/.

4. Kathryn Zickuhr et al., *Younger Americans' Reading and Library Habits*, Pew Research Center, Washington, DC, October 23, 2012.